Luton Six

Daily Mail

The History of the

WEMBLEY
FA CUP FINAL

Daily Mail

THE HISTORY OF THE
WEMBLEY
FA CUP FINAL

COMPILED BY ANDREW THRAVES

WEIDENFELD AND NICOLSON • LONDON

The publishers would like to thank Greg Hill, Andrew Thraves and Fiona Hunter for their invaluable work in compiling this book. The publishers are particularly grateful to Steven Torrington, Bob Dignum, Paul Rossiter, Brian Jackson, David Shepherd and their colleagues at the *Daily Mail* picture and reference library, without whose help this book would not have been possible.

The illustrations in this book are reproduced by courtesy of Associated Newspapers Ltd, except for the illustration of the FA Cup on page ii which is reproduced by courtesy of Bob Thomas Sports Photography and the illustration of Wembley Stadium on page viii which is reproduced by courtesy of Wembley Stadium Ltd.

The publishers acknowledge the rights of the copyright holders in the illustrations throughout this work.

First published in Great Britain in 1994
by Weidenfeld and Nicolson
The Orion Publishing Group Ltd
Orion House
5 Upper St Martin's Lane
London WC2H 9EA

ISBN 0 297 83407 X

A CIP catalogue record for this book is available from the British Library.

Photoset in Monophoto Century Schoolbook by
Selwood Systems, Midsomer Norton, Avon
Printed and bound in Great Britain by
Butler & Tanner Ltd, Frome and London

CONTENTS

PREFACE

Have you ever looked up the original White Horse Final of 1923? Or remember the David and Goliath struggle in 1992 between Second Division Sunderland and the favourites, Liverpool? How about 1988, when the Dons carried all before them . . .

You know the feeling. As summer approaches every year, Cup fever begins and the memories come flooding back. The draw for each round, the impossible strokes of luck (good, bad and downright incredible), the thrill of putting the ball into the back of the net against all the odds – you can't match the ups and downs on the road to Wembley in any other sport.

Football's crowning achievement draws the crowds like a magnet. Millions more around the world settle down at home for the highlight of the football year. And as someone who has been privileged to know the world of the Cup from the inside – when Manchester United beat Leicester City 3–1 in 1963 – I can state quite truthfully that the tension in the Wembley tunnel is far greater than anything you might experience as a spectator! But it's all part of the build-up to those magic ninety minutes. Win or lose, playing at Wembley is something you never forget. Each time I watch a Cup Final now, I experience that old thrill again.

This book provides a terrific insight into the Cup Final over the years. And like the best action replays, it gives you the chance to relive the highlights of each match. It's all here – the facts, the fans, the *Daily Mail*'s excellent photographs, and the chances in a million that made for those crucial goals.

Pure pleasure! I hope you enjoy reliving your Cup Final memories as much as I do.

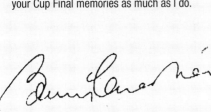

Bobby Charlton, CBE

THE ROAD TO WEMBLEY

The FA Cup is the oldest football competition in the world, and the Final has a place in the heart of millions. Not only is it avidly watched all over Britain, but it is also broadcast to countries all over the globe.

The first ever FA Cup Final was held in the 1871–72 season and was played at the Kennington Oval in London. The idea of a knock-out Cup Final was the brain-child of Charlie Alcock, then Secretary of the Football Association. He originally intended it to be for amateur clubs, and indeed the first winners were Alcock's own Team, The Wanderers, who beat The Royal Engineers 1–0. The goal was scored by Matthew Betts, and all of 2 000 people were there to see him make history as the first person ever to score in a Cup Final match.

Over the years, the Cup competition grew from an amateur knock-out to professional status and changed venue several times. It moved north for some years and then returned south to Crystal Palace in 1895. However, Crystal Palace was requisitioned as a service depot during the First World War, so Chelsea's Stamford Bridge was briefly used as a replacement ground. In 1922, Huddersfield Town beat Preston North End there by one goal to nil. It was obvious by this time that a much larger venue was required for the FA Cup, to accommodate the growing crowds.

Attention turned to Wembley Stadium, which had been built in just three hundred days at a cost of £750 000. An infantry battalion was used to test the strength of the terraces before the stadium was opened to the public. Wembley was bought in 1923 by Arthur Elvin, who assumed responsibility for the major sporting events, such as the FA Cup, which were to be held there. Elvin was later knighted for his efforts on behalf of war charities and his statue now stands outside Wembley Stadium.

On 28 April 1923, the Wembley turnstiles opened for the first time . . .

1923

BOLTON WANDERERS 2
WEST HAM UNITED 0

ATTENDANCE
(official) 127 000;
(unofficial) 210 000–250 000

REFEREE
D. H. Asson (West Bromwich)

GOALSCORERS
Jack, J. R. Smith

TEAMS
Bolton Wanderers	West Ham United
Pym	Hufton
Haworth	Henderson
Finney	Young
Nuttall	Bishop
Seddon	Kay
Jennings	Tresadern
Butler	Richards
Jack	Brown
J. R. Smith	Watson
J. Smith	Moore
Vizard	Ruffell

THE ROAD TO THE FINAL
Bolton Wanderers
2nd round
v Leeds United 3–1 (h)
3rd round
v Huddersfield Town 1–1 (a)
Replay 1–0 (h)
4th round
v Charlton Athletic 1–0 (a)
Semi-Final
v Sheffield United 1–0

West Ham United
2nd round
v Brighton 1–1 (a)
Replay
v Brighton 1–0 (h)
3rd round
v Plymouth Argyle 2–0 (h)
4th round
v Southampton 1–1 (a)
Replay 1–1 (h)
2nd replay 1–0 (a)
Semi-Final
v Derby County 5–2

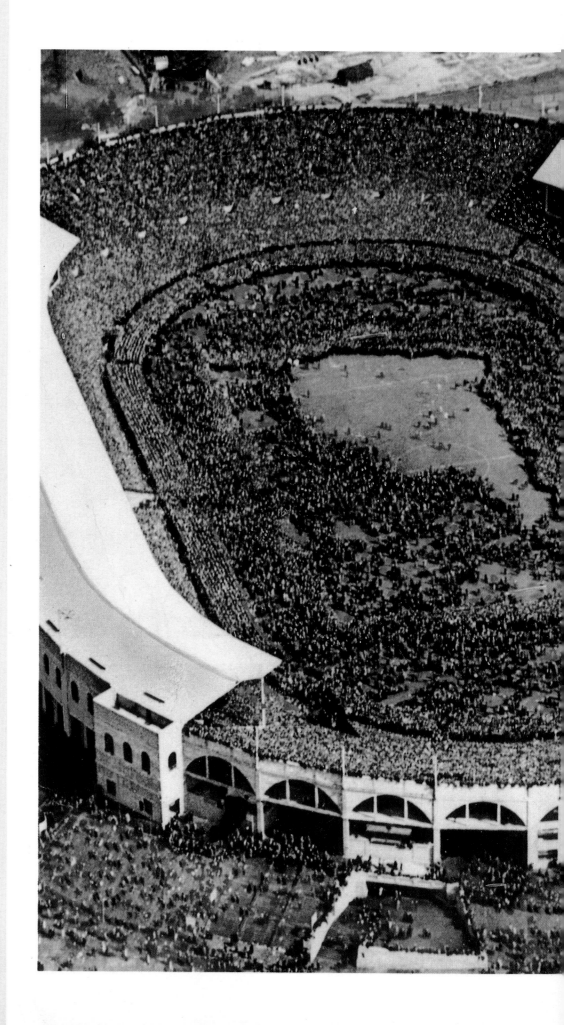

Wembley Kicks Off

Cup Day: Great Football Final – How to Reach the Ground

THE FINAL TIE of the Football Association Challenge Cup, to be played this afternoon on the Empire Stadium at Wembley between West Ham United and Bolton Wanderers, will probably attract one of the largest crowds ever seen at a football match in the United Kingdom. The King will be one of the most interested spectators.

The match will be the first to be played on the magnificently equipped arena at the British Empire Exhibition, which is likely to be the home of the match for many years to come. The Stadium, which has been constructed inside 12 months, on part of the old Wembley golf course, is the finest sports ground in the kingdom. There is seating under cover for 24 500 people, with seats round the track for another 10 000.

The total holding capacity is 125 000 and every spectator will have a good view of the game. There are dressing rooms, refreshment rooms, and offices on an elaborate scale. The total cost is estimated at £300 000.

The King

His Majesty King George V will arrive at about 2.45 p.m., and after the teams have been presented to him in the arena he will watch the match throughout from the Royal Box. At the end of the match he will present the Cup and medals to the victors.

The result of the match is very open and the football should be of better quality than in the Finals played since the War. The teams appear to be most evenly matched, but if West Ham play with the dash, skill and confidence they displayed in the semi-final they should bring the Cup to London.

The kick-off is fixed for 3 p.m. In the event of the scores being level at the end of the 90 minutes an extra half-hour will be played. If the match is not then definitely decided the teams will meet again next Wednesday on the same ground.

Five thousand people will come from Bolton to London, a 200-mile journey, to see the match, and are expected to be joined at Wembley by at least 115 000 enthusiasts from London and other parts of the country. The Stadium will accommodate 125 000 spectators. There are seats for 35 000.

Catering for so vast a multitude is a gigantic task. Among the supplies which will be served on the ground are 10 000 dozen bottles of beer, 8 000 dozen bottles of mineral waters, 500 gallons of tea and 200 000 sandwiches.

Although the kick-off is not until 3.00 p.m. the grounds will be opened at 11.30 a.m., and earlier if circumstances warrant it. It is expected that there will be queues outside from the earliest hours.

Most Amazing Football Final

THAT THIS FINAL was ever carried out must, for the purposes of football history, stand as a tribute to the calm, tolerant police of London, particularly those mounted men who so cleverly manoeuvred their horses against the human wall of men and women on the playing pitch without doing harm to a soul. People were hurt, but it was not due to the police.

The official organisation went like feathers in a wind. Stewards and officials seemed to know nothing. They were useless. The Press Box suffered in the general chaos. Dozens of people got into it who had no right to be there at all.

Brilliant Jack

Both teams were at full strength, West Ham playing the same 11 men as won such an astonishing victory (5–2) against Derby County in the semi-final.

Almost from the start one felt that it was going to be Bolton's day. Obviously the Wanderers had thought out their game to thwart those fast, fluent methods that have brought West Ham so much

King George V watching the remarkable crowd

fame this season. None of the Wanderers hesitated a second to dash in at a West Ham man when the latter got the ball. There was no ceremony about the Wanderers.

When pressed – it was only occasionally – the Wanderers swept into the five half-back formation. It told, for Pym in the Bolton goal had no more than one trying time during the whole course of the game.

West Ham's farewell to the Cup started just two minutes from the kick-off. Then Jack scored a beautiful goal for Bolton. He is the brilliant footballing son of Robert Jack, the present manager of Plymouth Argyle. Young Jack has simply 'pulled' the Wanderers to the Final. In four Cup matches he has been the only man on his side to score and on three occasions he has enabled his side to win. Jack's goal, so early, was a distinct blow to West Ham. They never became their real footballing selves. There was seldom a flash of the form that swamped Derby.

West Ham's Best Attempt

Eleven minutes from the kick-off, play was stopped. The crowd surged over the touch-line just in front of the Royal Box and once again we saw the mounted police, with almost a company of foot police, pressing back the young men and

Headwork by Bolton in front of their goal

in many cases their young women. Red Cross men reappeared and gave first aid to the injured on the playing pitch with the players looking on. Another amazing sight!

At last order was restored and play restarted, with the police riding up and down the touch-line to keep it clear for the linesman.

Soon afterwards came West Ham's final attempt at a goal. Brilliantly, Richards beat two Bolton men and then shot. The ball was going swiftly for goal and Pym dashed out to meet the shot. He did not actually stop it, but he broke the force of the shot and he got the ball away at the second attempt. Afterwards West Ham seldom threatened to score. The checking scheme of the Wanderers was always apparent.

Bolton led with Jack's goal at half-time. The players, owing to the congestion, did not leave the ground and restarted at once. Within a minute or two the Wanderers left no doubt as to where the Cup was going, for the only Scot in their players, J. R. Smith, centre forward, scored with a 'header', which struck the under-part of the crossbar, came down into the actual goal area, and ricocheted into play again. A curious goal, but still a goal in spite of West Ham's protest. This Smith has brought off a great 'double' – he already held a Scottish Cup medal and now he has an English Cup medal.

Little need be said of the play after Smith's goal. It simply frittered out and finished sadly.

Cup Crush Inquiry at Once

More than 900 persons were injured when tens of thousands of people tried to storm their way into Wembley Stadium during the FA Cup Final.

Wembley is one of the most accessible districts round London, and it was the biggest Cup-tie on record, much bigger than the authorities concerned had expected. More than 200 000 were in the Stadium, the estimated capacity of which is 127 000. The outer gates were closed shortly before 2.00 p.m., but tens of thousands of people who were refused admission forced their way over the barriers or through a narrow tunnel entrance. Police reinforcements were rushed to the Stadium from all parts of London, and shortly after the arrival of the King, whose presence had a steadying moral effect, order was restored.

In a statement, Lieut.-General Sir Travers Clarke, deputy chairman of the British Empire Exhibition Standing Administrative Committee, the body which controls the Stadium, said that an immediate inquiry will be held into the causes of the amazing scenes. Sir Travers Clarke, who was present at the match, also said, 'The whole trouble was that the tap of traffic had been turned full on, and nobody could turn it off.'

The scene of the first Wembley Final on 28 April 1923, as crowds swarm on to the pitch, delaying the start of the game by 40 minutes

The Wembley white horse, destined to become a legend for years afterwards. The horse, with its rider PC George Scorey, played a large part in keeping the crowd under control

3

1924

NEWCASTLE UNITED 2
ASTON VILLA 0

ATTENDANCE
91 695

REFEREE
W. E. Russell (Swindon)

GOALSCORERS
Harris, Seymour

TEAMS

Newcastle United	Aston Villa
Bradley	Jackson
Hampson	Smart
Hudspeth	Mort
Mooney	Moss
Spencer	Milne
Gibson	Blackburn
Low	York
Cowan	Kirton
Harris	Capewell
McDonald	Walker
Seymour	Dorrell

THE ROAD TO THE FINAL

Newcastle United
2nd round
v Derby County 2–2 (h)
Replay 2–2 (a)
2nd replay 2–2 (h)
3rd replay 5–3 (a)
3rd round
v Watford 1–0 (a)
4th round
v Liverpool 1–0 (h)
Semi-Final
v Manchester City 2–0

Aston Villa
2nd round
v Swansea Town 2–0 (a)
3rd round
v Leeds United 3–0 (h)
4th round
v West Bromwich Albion 2–0 (a)
Semi-Final
v Burnley 3–0

Football Cup Final – a Surprise of the Season

THE THOUSANDS AND thousands of folk who had seen the Villa before Saturday's sorrowful match had every reason to expect they would win. But the Villa in this Final were something like a shadow of their former selves. The Villa forwards, thinking, no doubt, of their wonderful achievements in scoring before this match, seemed to perform as though all that was necessary for them to do was *to walk the ball into the net*. They played as if that were their proper and sole function. What a mistake it was! It lost Villa the Cup!

Why Newcastle Won

Now, taking this by no means great Final as it was, it is possible to say that the Villa had, on the whole, more of the ball. But they failed to press home this advantage. The Newcastle men, on the other hand – particularly the forwards, when-

Seymour (far left) setting the seal on United's great Cup victory

No Repeat of Last Year

There need not be the slightest anxiety as to any recurrence of the 'scenes' which marred the Final for many last year. On this occasion it has been wisely ruled that there shall be no admission but by ticket. Besides, in the loudspeaker, science has newly given us a uniquely effective means of regulating great crowds for their own convenience and safety.

The Newcastle team acclaimed by exuberant supporters on their way to collect the trophy

ever they got away – always seemed the more dangerous. They were more enterprising with their shots. The Villa's forwards were chiefly to blame; there was no adventure in their shots.

And yet it is possible to say that both these teams, survivors of so many football ordeals this season, were very nervous and highly strung. Neither played with the same excellence as they have performed in League encounters this season! It sounds incredible, but it is a fact.

The keynote of Newcastle's success was Neil Harris, their centre forward. Constantly he was offside, and just as constantly he was pulled up, but he was always dangerous and always 'rattling' the Villa defence. His tactics had a great deal to do with the goals. In company with McDonald and Cowan, Harris started an assault as Spencer spun the ball forward in the last eight minutes of the second half. There was a beautiful exchange of the ball between the three forwards mentioned. Despite Smart and Mort trying valiantly to stop it, Harris was on the ball like a flash, and in another flash it was in goal.

Goal of the Match

Still, the goal of the match was Seymour's. This sturdy Newcastle outside left had not shown much of his skill until the game was near its finish. Suddenly he dashed inwards as the ball came over from his right, and as it fell at his feet he let fly. The next second we saw the ball crashing into the net from a glorious shot. This came a few minutes before the end, and by then the Villa were down and almost out.

Even so, the result of this game might have been very different. Within a minute of Harris's goal, the Villa attacked fiercely and the ball came over perfectly from the left wing. Kirton head-flicked the ball past the wrong side of the post. A few inches more and it would have been an equalising goal, and then what might have happened?

You cannot tell, but one can say this much: as things went, and developed in that second half, Newcastle thoroughly deserved to win the Cup.

The crowded scene on one of the roads near Wembley

The Clubs and their Records

The Final of the Football Association Challenge Cup between Aston Villa and Newcastle United will be played this afternoon at Wembley.

Both Aston Villa and Newcastle United have distinguished records in the history of the game. The Villa made a record when they won the Cup for the sixth time in 1920, and their League Championship successes also number six.

Newcastle United, a more modern organisation, have played in five Cup Finals since 1905, but have won the trophy on one occasion only. They have won the League Championship three times.

The match should produce one of the best Finals of recent years, for both teams can play fast and skilful football. The Villa will be favourites on the strength of their great record in the Final ties, and their fine performances this season. The Villa appear to have the sounder backs, and a more skilful line of half backs, and superior defence may turn the scale in their favour.

Moss Optimistic

Frank Moss, the Aston Villa captain, is quite optimistic. 'It will be a great Final,' he said, 'of that I am convinced. And we players of Aston Villa desire nothing but a good Final. We play our best football in big games; that is a tradition of the club, and tradition goes a long way.'

Hudspeth, the captain of the Newcastle team, was reserved but confident. 'All the boys are fit and happy,' he said. 'We have enjoyed our stay very well in Harrow, and we are ready for the big struggle.'

THE CUP FINAL. By TOM WEBSTER.

OUT OF A THOUSAND PLAYERS THAT TRIED TO GET INTO THE CUP FINAL 22 ONLY REMAIN. THEY BELONG TO ASTON VILLA AND NEWCASTLE UNITED AND WERE BOUGHT SPECIALLY FOR THE PURPOSE. IN ORDER TO HELP THE CROWD RECOGNISE THE PLAYERS WE WILL GIVE ENLARGED PHOTOGRAPHS OF THE TWO TEAMS.

READING FROM LEFT TO RIGHT FULL FACE VIEW OF THE ASTON VILLA SIDE.

READING · VERY CAREFULLY. FROM LEFT TO RIGHT FULL FACE VIEW OF THE NEWCASTLE TEAM.

INSET. SUPPORTER OF ONE OF THE SIDES SHOWING CONSIDERABLE ASTONISHMENT AT ANYBODY GETTING INTO THE CUP FINAL.

READING FROM RIGHT TO LEFT SIDE VIEW OF THE ASTON VILLA ELEVEN.

READING THE BEST WAY POSSIBLE SIDE VIEW OF NEWCASTLE UNITED. NOTE. THE MAN MARKED WITH A CROSS IS NOT LOOKING HIS BEST.

DESPITE WHAT RIVAL SUPPORTERS SAY. IT IS ALMOST IMPOSSIBLE TO TELL WHICH TEAM WILL WIN.

NIL DESPERADO IS OUR MOTTO. WE SHALL NEVER CEASE KICKING THE BALL UNTIL WE HAVE WON.

WE ARE A MUCH FINER COLLECTION THAN ASTON VILLA AND WE DO NOT PROPOSE TO LOSE THIS MATCH.

IT IS FAR EASIER FOR A CAMEL TO LEAP GAILY THROUGH THE EYE OF A NEEDLE THAN FIND THE WINNER OF THIS MATCH BUT PERSONALLY

WE HAVE WON

I'M AFRAID YOU HAVE

I SHOULD LIKE MY PIECES OF EIGHT ON THE TEAM THAT SCORES THE FIRST GOAL.

ABOVE WE GIVE INTERVIEWS WITH THE RIVAL CAPTAINS.

1925

SHEFFIELD UNITED 1
CARDIFF CITY 0

ATTENDANCE
91 763

REFEREE
G. N. Watson (Nottingham)

GOALSCORER
Tunstall

TEAMS

Sheffield United	Cardiff City
Sutcliffe	Farquharson
Cook	Nelson
Mitton	Blair
Pantling	Wake
King	Keenor
Green	Hardy
Mercer	W. Davies
Boyle	Gill
Johnson	Nicholson
Gillespie	Beadles
Tunstall	J. Evans

THE ROAD TO THE FINAL

Sheffield United
2nd round
v Sheffield Wednesday 3–2 (h)
3rd round
v Everton 1–0 (h)
4th round
v West Bromwich Albion 2–0 (h)
Semi-Final
v Southampton 2–0

Cardiff City
2nd round
v Fulham 1–0 (h)
3rd round
v Notts County 2–0 (a)
4th round
v Leicester City 2–1 (h)
Semi-Final
v Blackburn Rovers 3–1

Sheffield United win by the Only Goal

Sheffield make a raid on the Cardiff goal

– Victors Always Cooler and Quicker

AT KENNINGTON OVAL in 1872 Sheffield United won the FA Challenge Cup for the first time by a solitary goal. At Wembley on Saturday they won the trophy for the fourth time – again by a single goal.

From an early hour, special after special, packed to capacity with living freight, had arrived from the north and west. And long before the kick-off the

---

Today's Cup-Tie Match

Thousands are pouring into London for the Cup Final tie match, which is played today at Wembley between Cardiff City and Sheffield United. For the welfare of the 95 000 people who are expected to be present, everyone will hope that the weather this afternoon will be on its best behaviour.

There are critics who gloomily complain of the passion for watching games. The complaints seem overdone, so long as work is not neglected for pure amusement. The ideal is to work hard and play hard; but no reasonable person would declare that recreation in the open air, taken in the form of watching a Final, is in itself evil.

The severest censor of modern manners must admit that, as a popular amusement, Association football is far better than the ancient diversions of cock-fighting or bull-baiting, both of which were essentially cruel sports.

The real defect of Finals in the Cup-tie contest is that the players on each side are usually so nervous that they fail to show their full skill; and the game is largely dependent for that reason upon chance. But the event is always a great open-air holiday, and its popularity seems to increase with each year.

great arena was gay with the vivid red of Sheffield and the royal blue of Cardiff. Then the noise! Nearly every one of the spectators seemed to regard it as his mission in life to cheer; and many had brought rattles and bells and gongs with them to supplement their brazen lungs.

Sheffield Superiority

Sheffield did not play great football, but they played about as well as they generally play. They were far steadier than Cardiff, they were quicker both mentally and physically. They controlled the ball and passed and manoeuvred without weaving fancy patterns.

But although the United were so clearly the better side, excitement ran high until the last. You never can tell in football – there is always the chance of a snap goal. So with Sheffield leading by only the narrowest possible of margins, the Welshmen went on hoping and cheering – till the whistle sounded for the last time.

The match had lasted 32 minutes when Tunstall scored the goal which was destined to win the game. The ball was swung across from the right to Tunstall at outside left. He was fully 20 yards from goal when he trapped it, and Wake, the Cardiff right half back, looked in a perfect position to defend and tackle. But Wake hesitated; he seemed like a man in a dream, and Tunstall with the ball at his feet was not wasting time. He was on and round the vacillating half in seconds and was able to kick the ball into the net well wide of Farquharson.

It was all over more quickly than the incident takes to describe, and while the Sheffield fans fairly shrieked with joy, the Welshmen looked bewildered. 'What on earth was Wake thinking about?' was the mildest remark applied to the poor half back.

The Mastermind

Fleet, nimble Tunstall did many good things in the match besides scoring that goal, but the mastermind of the forwards was Gillespie, the captain, at inside left. He took to himself a roving commission, and Keenor, the Welsh centre half, did not seem to know where to find him. He was always bobbing up in such unexpected places.

King, Sheffield's clever centre half, was the pivot of the side. On the whole there was not seen much passing between the half backs and the forwards. The middle line on both sides was purely a defensive

Cup Final Money – How it is Divided

The Football Association takes one-third of the net receipts, the remainder being equally divided between the two clubs. The exhibition authorities receive an agreed sum for the use of the Stadium. The Football Association's share in 1923 was £9 452, and last year, when the attendance was lower, £6 449.

A fine clearance by the Sheffield goalie

factor. But King was an exception to his fellows. He did feed, with well-modulated strength, the men in front of him – and

especially he fed Gillespie. In brief, it was because Sheffield had such a left wing as Tunstall and Gillespie, so clever an

The Duke of York – the future King George VI – presenting the Cup to Sheffield's captain Gillespie. To the left are the Duchess of York – now HRH the Queen Mother – and Ramsay MacDonald

outside right as Mercer, and so resourceful a centre half as King, that the Cup was taken to Yorkshire.

Cardiff were frankly disappointing. The mistake of Wake could be forgiven; such mistakes are common in football. But quite as disastrous to the side were the errors of the forwards when close to goal – their lack of steadiness, their ill-judged kicking, their want of accuracy.

Cardiff's defence was better than the attack. Except when he was up against Gillespie, Keenor did good work, and Hardy was difficult to pass, but Wake, probably upset by his blunder in the first half, was generally shaky. Nelson and Blake at back were sound and nothing more, and Farquharson made one or two moderately good saves.

There have been far better Cup Finals – and there have been far worse. There were some fouls; there were cases of misplaced energy; but the game did not degenerate into a scramble of unscientific vigour.

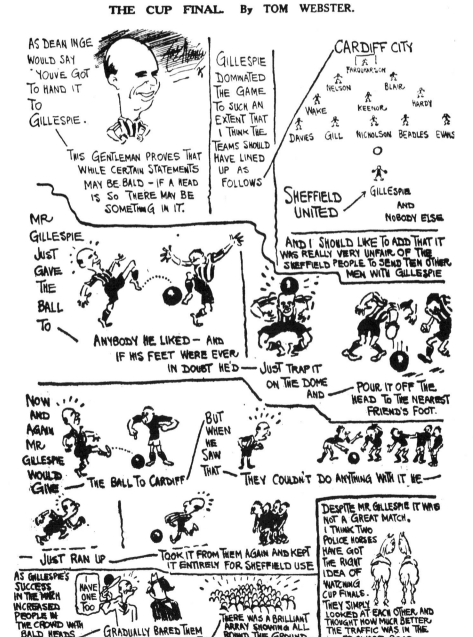

THE CUP FINAL. By TOM WEBSTER.

Man with 300 Tickets cannot Get Rid of Them

There is a man in London who is in despair because he has not so far been able to get rid of nearly 300 Cup Final tickets. He is Mr F. W. Knight of Jersey. The tickets he holds are those paid for by a number of Jersey residents who since November last have been subscribing towards an excursion steamboat to take them to England for the match. The steamer is not being run, as the number of excursionists has not reached the stipulated 500.

ATTENDANCE
91 447

REFEREE
I. Baker (Crewe)

GOALSCORER
Jack

TEAMS

Bolton Wanderers	Manchester City
Pym	Goodchild
Haworth	Cookson
Greenhalgh	McCloy
Nuttall	Pringle
Seddon	Cowan
Jennings	McMullan
Butler	Austin
Jack	Browell
J. R. Smith	Roberts
J. Smith	Johnson
Vizard	Hicks

THE ROAD TO THE FINAL

Bolton Wanderers
4th round
v Bournemouth 2–2 (a)
Replay
v Bournemouth 6–2 (h)
5th round
v South Shields 3–0 (h)
6th round
v Nottingham Forest 2–2 (a)
Replay
v Nottingham Forest 0–0 (h)
2nd replay
v Nottingham Forest 1–0 (a)
Semi-Final
v Swansea Town 3–0

Manchester City
4th round
v Huddersfield Town 4–0 (h)
5th round
v Crystal Palace 11–4 (h)
6th round
v Clapton Orient 6–1 (a)
Semi-Final
v Manchester United 3–0

The Triumph of Bolton

Jack, down on one knee, sees his shot hit the net

THERE WERE MANY remarkable and memorable features about Saturday's Football Cup Final at Wembley. Three deserve especial emphasis because they are likely to remain in the recollections of nearly 100 000 people for very many years.

One of the features that stood out was the all-round excellence of the play. Saturday's game was so good, and so often thrilling, that it kept the crowd on tenterhooks from beginning to end.

Touts Routed

The second feature that calls for mention was the rout suffered by the ticket touts who, long before the play started, prepared themselves for the gathering in of a rich harvest.

They were completely beaten. There were rumbles of the coming storm in the early morning, when men with pocketfuls of tickets took up their positions and offered them at double and treble their value. The tempest did not break, however, until the game was almost due to begin. By then, 2s tickets were being hawked at 15s and £1, while £10 was unblushingly demanded for a seat in the stands.

That was more than the ticketless could endure. As though at a command, they descended on the speculators and in many cases chased them out of the ground. For nearly an hour the approaches to the field were the scenes of noisy free-fights, and it was the intervention of the police that saved some of the touts from serious injury.

Splendid Football

The third feature was the most stirring. This was a demonstration of enthusiasm and affection for the King that was as striking as it was heart-filling. Never, not even previously at Wembley, had the National Anthem been sung with such fervour, with such grandeur, with such noble, breath-catching feeling. There was in the singing of this great gathering a quality that made it magnificent.

The football this year was altogether splendid, but it was that unrehearsed singing of the Anthem at the end that turned it into an unforgettable occasion.

Bolton were thoroughly entitled to their victory. In most departments of the game they were steadier than their opponents and also more skilled. In the early stages it was evident that among the Manchester men were some whose nerves were twanging like banjo strings.

Roberts, the centre forward, was one of these. There has, perhaps, never been an afternoon when he was so completely subdued. For three parts of the game he was scarcely in the picture at all, but it was not his nervous system so much as Seddon, the big Bolton centre half, that blotted him out. Roberts played only as well as Seddon permitted him to play. He was dispossessed and defeated almost every time he touched the ball, and it is but bare truth to say that of the three men who did the finest work, Seddon was the one who earned the most praise.

The others were Pym, the Bolton goal-keeper, and McMullan, the Manchester half back. Pym was the equivalent of a stone wall. He executed many brilliant saves, but the biggest thing he did was to stop a 'header' from Johnson in the second half. This effort of the Manchester forward would have shot the ball into the

Bolton win Lucky No. 11 room

The 'lucky' No. 11 dressing room is to be occupied by the Bolton Wanderers. It is stated that all the teams which have won the Cup Final at Wembley have occupied this room. In view of this superstition a coin was tossed to determine which team had No. 1, the other dressing room. The luck of the toss, which took place before two witnesses, fell to the Wanderers.

Bolton Wanderers: the heroes of the day

net on nine occasions out of ten but Pym, with a jump and a quick out-throw of the hands, deflected the ball over the line in a fashion that can only be described as miraculous.

McMullan was the greatest-hearted man of the 22. He was half back, full back and forward, all combined in one. His attack was as good as his defence, and it was certainly not his fault that his team were beaten.

The Only Goal

Bolton's goal came when almost everyone was settling down for a period of extra play. It was quite unexpected and it did not seem to have been consciously worked for. The play was at midfield when the ball was suddenly kicked out to Butler on the right wing.

On the instant, with McCloy in close attendance, he darted down the touchline, but just when it seemed certain that the ball would go out of play he swerved swiftly on his heels and cross-kicked a long pass to Vizard on the opposite wing.

The Welshman had plenty of time to sum up the opposition. There was no defender very near him, and David Jack was standing absolutely unmarked in front of the Manchester goalmouth. It was to Jack, therefore, that he flicked over one of his accurate centres. The goal was made from that tick of the clock. All that Jack had to do was bang the ball into the net. He did so with the greatest ease, for Goodchild, the Manchester goalkeeper, never had a chance of touching it.

Business As Usual

The Vizard–Joe Smith partnership was not so conspicuous as usual, but it was nevertheless very efficient. Smith, the Bolton centre forward, was too well shadowed to do much, but Jack and Butler were always prominent.

As a team, Manchester were not so well together as Bolton on the day, the latter once again proving that the side that only scrapes through the preliminary games of the Cup competition usually carries it home with them when the Final has gone down into history.

For Bolton Wanderers, it was business as usual yesterday when they left Euston station by the 1.25 p.m. train for Birmingham, ready for their next League Cup match, against Aston Villa. They will return to Bolton tomorrow.

Cup Tie food – 25 000 Ham Rolls!

Preparations for the football Cup Final have been completed.

Provisions for the 91 000 spectators include:

50 000 bottles of beer – to be conveyed in 20 lorries; 1 500 bottles of whisky; 30 tons of minerals; 700 lb of tea; 25 000 ham rolls; 12 000 packets of biscuits; 120 000 packets of cigarettes; 10 000 boxes of matches; 2 000 lb of cake; 2 vanloads of chocolates.

300 gallons of draught beer are being delivered on the day. There is a catering staff of 400, who will be divided between 10 buffets and the restaurants, which seat 1 000.

CARDIFF CITY 1
ARSENAL 0

ATTENDANCE
91 206

REFEREE
W. F. Bunnell (Preston)

GOALSCORER
Ferguson

TEAMS

Cardiff City	Arsenal
Farquharson	Lewis
Nelson	Parker
Watson	Kennedy
Keenor	Baker
Sloan	Butler
Hardy	John
Curtis	Hulme
Irving	Buchan
Ferguson	Brain
Davies	Blythe
McLachan	Hoar

THE ROAD TO THE FINAL

Cardiff City
4th round
v Darlington 2–0 (a)
5th round
v Bolton Wanderers 2–0 (a)
6th round
v Chelsea 0–0 (a)
Replay 3–2 (h)
Semi-Final
v Reading 3–0

Arsenal
4th round
v Port Vale 2–2 (a)
Replay 1–0 (h)
5th round
v Liverpool 2–0 (h)
6th round
v Wolverhampton Wanderers 2–1 (h)
Semi-Final
v Southampton 2–1

The 'Ifs' of the Cup Final

A tense moment in front of the Cardiff goal

– Arsenal Beaten by Curious Goal

ALTHOUGH THE 'IFS' that are so common in Cup Final football were in their most impish mood at Wembley on Saturday, I am convinced that Cardiff would not have won the Cup had it not been for the fact that Lewis, the Welsh-born Arsenal goalkeeper, was for a few palpitating seconds rendered helpless by a 'football-solar-plexus-blow', dealt him by the ball.

The boxing solar-plexus punch, as is well known, rids a man of the use of his limbs but not of his senses. When Lewis collapsed after he had caught the hard drive from Ferguson, the Cardiff centre forward, his fall was so pronounced that his forehead, as well as his knees, struck the turf. There was a brief interval before he began to right himself and I felt, as he scrambled about, that his excited efforts to get up were not caused so much by the nearness of Len Davies, the Cardiff inside left, as by the fact that his limbs were not obeying his commands.

Turned the Wrong Way

All might have been well even then, however, if he had turned to his right instead of his left. The closest player on his right was one of his own backs, but on his left there was nothing save the yawning goalmouth.

Lewis was still practically on all fours, when his left arm seemed to shoot out,

Special *Daily Mail* photographs of the players, with Cardiff City on the left and Arsenal on the right

and the next thing the astonished spectators saw was the ball trickling away from him. As it moved (the goal having, by this time, been scored), Lewis made one last despairing effort to regain control of it, but without success.

There could have been only one unhappy Welshman in the world on Saturday. That was Lewis, who in a manner that I think must be unique had presented a team from his own land with the sort of extraordinary gift-goal that may never be repeated in our time.

Cardiff Lucky

To say that Cardiff were lucky to win is simply stressing what must have been said by the vast majority of the great crowd that saw the game. In the first half, they were so far below their customary form as to make one wonder how on earth it came about that they managed to keep the Arsenal out.

Their half-back line was steady enough, but the backs were flustered, while the forwards floundered about to such an extent as to convey the impression that

the one thing they had neglected to do was to map out a plan of campaign.

The football played during this period was crude and bad and disappointing, and yet the Arsenal were so superior to Cardiff that they should have placed the result beyond doubt. They had many excellent chances of scoring, but there was not one so bright as when Buchan ran clear through the opposition by adopting the old strategy of pretending to kick hard. He covered nearly half the length of the ground – with the defence tangled into a knot – before he sent a perfect little pass to Hoar, on the left wing, but the latter very surprisingly muffed the glorious opportunity by shooting both weakly and inaccurately.

The Arsenal have every reason to believe that the fates were being unkind to them, but they have themselves to blame for not making better use of that part of the play when things went very much their way.

Uninteresting Play

If Cardiff and the Arsenal had been

'I Knew Who Won'

Sir,
I knew the result of the Football Association cup match without reading or hearing of it.

I was driving along the Bath road towards London late on Saturday afternoon when a motorcoach load full of passengers wearing the Arsenal colours came by. Their faces showed clearly enough that Arsenal had not won. A few minutes later a coachload of Welsh supporters passed, all beaming.

The news was confirmed.

J. M.,
Baker Street,
London W1

meeting in an ordinary match on Saturday we might have seen a spectacle worth remembering, but as it was the only section of the game deserving of a memory was that which followed the scoring of the winning goal.

Before that – right up to the instant when McLachan swung across the pass that Len Davies skidded on to Ferguson – the play was not only indifferent, but almost entirely uninteresting. It lacked method and was completely devoid of thrills. The teams were too well matched for sensations, but it was rather astonishing to find that not even Buchan, master strategist and veteran schemer, was inclined to wander away from the well-beaten paths. Every movement was so deliberate and so bereft of risk that it savoured of the over-rehearsed kind and it was probably this constant clinging to established tactics that robbed the game of the incidents and episodes that are the fabric of first-class football.

For all the excitement that was created, except for the 15 minutes at the close, the affair might have been an unimportant struggle between two boys' teams in a park. But that is becoming usual in Cup Finals. It must be the 'atmosphere' and not the play that the great crowds go to see.

Lewis fails to retrieve the goal that sent the Cup to Wales

Puzzled Goalkeeper's Own Story

Arsenal's goalkeeper Daniel Lewis cannot recall enough of his embarrassing moment to explain how the ball went in:

'Ferguson sent in a stinging shot and it appeared to be diverted by Parker. Still low, it shot towards the goal and I got down to it and stopped it. I can usually pick up the ball with one hand, but as I was lying over the ball, I had to use both hands to pick it up, and already a Cardiff forward was rushing down on me.

'The ball was very greasy. When it touched Parker it had evidently acquired a tremendous spin, and for a second it must have been spinning beneath me. At my first touch it shot away over my arm. I sent my hand after it and touched it. I may have sent it quicker over the goal line with this touch, but I think it would have reached in any case.

'When I was leaving the ground one of the spectators accused me of deliberately letting the Welsh team win because I am Welsh. It was a terribly cruel thing to say.'

The Captains' Views

Keenor, the Cardiff City captain, interviewed immediately after the match, said: 'I think we were very lucky to win, because, to be candid, I think the Arsenal deserved to do so. Wales will be delighted. I hope that although we are taking the Cup out of the country we shall return to Wales with the good wishes of all English sportsmen. I should like to say that the Arsenal played a clean, hard, sporting game.'

Buchan, the Arsenal captain, when asked to say a few words on the result, replied: 'My congratulations to Cardiff City on being the first club in history to take the Cup out of England. We did our very utmost to prevent them doing so, but we did not succeed. There is no one who more heartily congratulates Cardiff than the captain of the losers. Cardiff played an honest, clean game, each member of the team obviously striving to do his utmost. Good luck to the City and good luck to Wales and its Association Football now that they have the Cup.'

1928

BLACKBURN ROVERS 3
HUDDERSFIELD TOWN 1

ATTENDANCE
92 041

REFEREE
T. G. Bryan (Willenhall)

GOALSCORERS
Roscamp (2), McLean
Jackson

TEAMS

Blackburn Rovers	Huddersfield Town
Crawford	Mercer
Hutton	Barkas
Jones	Goodall
Healless	Steele
Rankin	Wilson
Campbell	Redfern
Thornewell	Smith
Puddefoot	Stephenson
Roscamp	Brown
McLean	Kelly
Rigby	Jackson

THE ROAD TO THE FINAL

Blackburn Rovers
4th round
v Exeter City 2–2 (a)
Replay 3–1 (h)
5th round
v Port Vale 2–1 (h)
6th round
v Manchester United 2–0 (h)
Semi-Final
v Arsenal 1–0

Huddersfield Town
4th round
v West Ham United 2–1 (h)
5th round
v Middlesbrough 4–0 (h)
6th round
v Tottenham Hotspur 6–1 (h)
Semi-Final
v Sheffield United 2–2
Replay 0–0
2nd replay 1–0

Blackburn's Convincing Cup Success

McLean scores Blackburn's second goal

– Huddersfield Outplayed by All-Round Strength

BLACKBURN ROVERS' SUCCESS over Huddersfield Town in the FA Cup Final was so clean-cut and decisive that the beaten side were left without that grinning skeleton of an excuse – the hollow mockery of the might-have-been.

I am convinced that the Lancashire side were 30 per cent better than their opponents, man for man and as a combination. They were well equipped with those essential qualities of pluck, determination, dash and confidence.

An Effective Leader

The Rovers' forwards showed an understanding, a virility, and a keenness of anticipation that were almost totally lacking in the semi-final. They were most effectively led by Roscamp, who was fearless, thrustful, and splendidly alert. He responded intelligently – as did the rest of the line – to the clever schemings of Puddefoot, and many times during the game we saw the Huddersfield defence doing the wrong thing, because it was planned that they should.

It was as if the first quick goal had been a shrewdly planted blow to the jaw which paralysed the Huddersfield brain, although the limbs moved automatically. Blackburn's declared policy of not allowing the other side to settle on to the ball was carried out with energy and spirit, and with rare exceptions, scrupulous fairness.

Blackburn were a well-balanced side, particularly strong at half back. Rarely did Healless, Campbell or Rankin make a mistake. Jackson never had any room in which to work, and presently we saw Campbell's destructive work converted into positive action. He was not only beating Jackson for possession, but coming through with the ball and placing it to advantage.

The Right Policy

Almost from the beginning, Blackburn avoided a purely negative policy. Hutton played one of his best games and Jones, fast-moving and resourceful, was just as sound.

In my opinion Huddersfield made a fatal error in tactics – in a game where speed was bound to be a determining factor – in clinging to the W-shaped forward formation. It is not as if Stephenson and Kelly had the legs of young men. Their policy of lying back with their own half backs left the attack to three men, and Jackson, Brown and Smith are

Prelude to Rovers' first goal: Roscamp dashes into Mercer, Huddersfield's goalie

not capable of smashing up a rock-like defence such as Blackburn possess.

In reality, with Jackson subdued and Smith in a cautious mood, Brown was left to plough a lone furrow, an impossible task. Crawford had few clear shots to cause him anxiety. It was fortunate for him that Kelly was kicked just before he shot from a 12-yard range, and consequently lofted the ball. At that time the score was 2–0 in Blackburn's favour.

Women's Cup Tie Fever

A feature of recent football Cup ties is the large number of women spectators. A great number occupy stand seats, but the majority brave the discomforts of long queues and the crushes to see the games.

Women are often among the earliest arrivals, waiting as long as six hours to see 90 minutes' play.

One woman who asked why her sex are becoming so interested in professional football said: 'More women play games themselves, and they take a more intelligent interest than they used to!'

Blackburn Rovers show off the Cup to supporters

Kelly was carried off the field and returned at outside right. It was while Jackson was in an inside position that he scored Huddersfield's only goal, 12 minutes from the interval.

The Tragic Goal

The first-minute goal came about in this way. Thornewell lobbed the ball to Puddefoot, who hooked it into the goalmouth. It appeared to be a perfectly harmless situation, but Mercer made an error of judgement. He caught the ball, was too leisurely in getting rid of it, and Roscamp bundled him over the line.

McLean's goal, 23 minutes from the start, was so well worked for that either Rigby, McLean, or Roscamp could have scored. But at the time Goodall was off the field injured, and the Huddersfield right flank was bared for a shrewd thrust. Mercer got one hand to the ball; if he had gone down with both hands he might have stopped it, although this is problematical.

Roscamp's second goal, five minutes from the end, was a beautiful effort. It came hot on the heels of a Huddersfield attack. A long pass up the field gave Roscamp possession, and when challenged he passed out to Thornewell. The outside right swept on, gave the ball to Roscamp at the right moment and in the right position, and the pace and direction of the shot were so well judged that Mercer made no move to stop it.

Previously Puddefoot had got the ball into the net, but was rightly given offside.

When the King handed the Cup to Healless and said 'Your team have played well', he was echoing the thoughts of the 92 000 spectators.

Thrills and Fears of a Cup Final

Robert Kelly, Huddersfield Town's brilliant international forward, describes the emotions of the players in the Cup Final:

'The great majority of the spectators at Wembley tomorrow will feel no excitement due to partisan feeling, for it is one of the anomalies of the Cup Final that only a fraction of the enthusiasts most keenly interested can hope to enter the gates of Wembley. Huddersfield probably has 20 000 inhabitants desirous of following us to London, but as the official quota for the club is only 2 750 tickets, the majority who wish to see the game might just as well try to get into the London Zoo on Sunday.

'Thanks to the march of science, however, the disappointed ones will not be so badly placed as their prototypes of a few years back. I am told that listening to a broadcast account of a match is quite a thrilling pastime. The scene at Wembley is one that grips the imagination and thrills.

'The psychological aspect of the contest is all-important. For days before the great event the players find themselves enveloped in a haze of emotions – elation, fear of failure, over-anxiety to do their best, and so on. They fear that they will not play so well as usual.

'Then comes the day of the great event, and the finalist is waiting in the dressing room. This is the worst hour of all. If there is any general gaiety, it is of the forced variety, and there is genuine relief at the captain's 'Ready, boys?' Once the game has commenced, the average man realises that he will best serve his side if he is not discouraged by the prospect of defeat nor elated at the prospect of victory.'

Mercer Explains: It was a Mistake

The question most people were asking on Saturday night was: 'What happened to Mercer during the seconds when he held the ball to his chest and looked straight at the Rovers' centre forward, Roscamp?'

Mercer explained: 'It was a terrible experience, and the most disappointing of my career. The whole thing happened in seconds. I was not in the least nervous. Roscamp's shot was a dropping one and I thought that it was a 'catching' ball.

'Ordinarily it is the golden rule of goalkeeping never to hold the ball if it can safely be got rid of by being punched away. In a flash I saw two white shirts – my own defenders, Goodall and Wilson – and I concluded that they would protect me from attack. I had no sooner touched the ball – or so it seemed to me – than Roscamp dashed straight into me. His head struck me in the mouth and broke part of a tooth, cracked the upper denture, and cut my lip. I was knocked over, and the ball went over the line.

'It was a mistake, the sort of mistake that is difficult to get over, but I thought, and still think, that it should not have been possible that I was charged. I don't blame anybody, of course. During my whole career I have not experienced another goal in such circumstances or so soon after the start. It is all in the luck of the game!'

BLACKBURN'S MASCOT. By TOM WEBSTER.

1929

BOLTON WANDERERS 2
PORTSMOUTH 0

ATTENDANCE
92 576

REFEREE
A. Josephs (South Shields)

GOALSCORERS
Butler, Blackmore

TEAMS

Bolton Wanderers	Portsmouth
Pym	Gilfillan
Haworth	Mackie
Finney	Bell
Kean	Nichol
Seddon	McIlwaine
Nuttall	Thackeray
Butler	Forward
McLelland	Smith
Blackmore	Weddle
Gibson	Watson
W. Cook	F. Cook

THE ROAD TO THE FINAL

Bolton Wanderers
4th round
v Liverpool 0–0 (a)
Replay 5–2 (h)
5th round
v Leicester City 2–1 (a)
6th round
v Blackburn Rovers 1–1 (a)
Replay 2–1 (h)
Semi-Final
v Huddersfield Town 3–1

Portsmouth
4th round
v Bradford City 2–0 (h)
5th round
v Chelsea 1–1 (a)
Replay 1–0 (h)
6th round
v West Ham United 3–2 (h)
Semi-Final
v Aston Villa 1–0

Bolton's Superb Record: Tactics that Brought a Great Triumph

The rival captains at the kick-off

Pym, the Wanderers' goalkeeper, deflecting a shot from Weddle, the Portsmouth forward

Seddon's Tribute

James Seddon, captain of Bolton Wanderers, said after the match:

'Portsmouth put up a great fight, particularly in the first half. But we succeeded in wearing them down after the interval, and I think that our better staying power was one of the big factors in our success. The game was an unusually good one for a Final. Neither side showed any trace of nerves and, in fact, Portsmouth, who were making their first appearance at Wembley, settled down even more quickly than we did. Portsmouth are a fine sporting side, and the game was a pleasure to play in.'

Note: Five Bolton players – Seddon, Pym, Nuttall, Haworth and Butler – have now won three Cup medals each.

BY SCORING 2 goals in the last 13 minutes in the FA Cup Final at Wembley on Saturday, Bolton Wanderers definitely set the seal on their superiority over Portsmouth.

They have now taken the Cup to Lancashire 17 times in its 54 years' history. It is a splendid record, achieved by sound and workmanlike, rather than brilliant, methods.

Portsmouth played hard, dogged football. They were unfortunate in being compelled to rearrange their left flank after an injury to Bell, their left back. But they were clearly worn down and almost overcome before Bell's second injury. He had been knocked out in the first half and had recovered. Twenty minutes from the end of the game he missed the ball and fell heavily in a twisted fashion that foreshadowed the worst. On returning to his position, his suffering was apparent and he was immediately sent to outside left.

Machinery ran Down

This change meant the dropping back of Thackeray, placing Watson in Thackeray's position and bringing Cook to inside forward. Then the wheels of the Portsmouth machinery, which had begun to run more slowly as time passed, almost ceased to function.

Thirteen minutes from time saw the first goal scored. Butler was well placed to take a pass from Nuttall. He ran in, rounded Thackeray, who seemed not to have realised that he was now a back, and sent a hard shot flashing across the goal-line. Gilfillan could not get to it; it sped past his left hand and had almost reached the far post when Mackie dashed in. The ball appeared to strike his right leg, hit the farther post and glance from it into the net. Had the ball hit Mackie on the other leg, it would have been deflected out of and not into goal. Mackie was entirely blameless. The Bolton forwards later said they were amazed that he reached the ball at all. They strongly believed that Butler's shot would have been fatal to Portsmouth anyhow.

Fortunately it was not the decisive goal.

A fine save by Gilfillan

Two minutes from time Butler engineered another. Thackeray and he dashed for the ball, which appeared to be winning the race for the line – so much so that Butler half-hesitated as though to give up the chase. Thackeray did give up – and Butler, the quick-witted, dashed past him, hooked the ball with his right foot in the nick of time and gave Blackmore a beautiful opening from the penalty spot.

Blackmore's left foot drive would have beaten any goalkeeper. Gilfillan was left defenceless with his backs spreadeagled. To Butler belongs the honour of forcing the issue. But to Seddon and his colleagues in defence lies the credit of playing coolly under great stress, of being content to bide their time without being flurried. They exerted their determined pressure when Portsmouth had become tired men beating in vain against a defence of granite.

Willing to Shoot

The Bolton attack had its deficiencies, but the desire and ability to shoot when the chance came were not among them. Gilfillan was a superman in dealing with shots from Blackmore and McClelland before he was finally beaten. The whole team were grim courage personified.

The spirit of the game was in keeping with the great occasion. The Prince of Wales presented the Cup to the winners and medals to both teams.

Cup Winners at the Theatre

The Bolton Wanderers team, the winners of the Cup Final, visited the National Sunday League concert at the London Palladium last night. They took the Cup with them and occupied a complete row of stalls.

There was an outburst of cheering when the team was observed by the audience, who demanded to see the Cup. Seddon, the captain, with the trophy, went on to the stage and made a short speech of thanks.

The Lord Mayor of Portsmouth, Councillor J. E. Smith, entertained the Portsmouth football team and club officials to dinner at the Portsmouth Guildhall in honour of having reached the Final.

Canon Draws a Lesson from the Cup Final: 'It's Worth 10 Sermons'

'A visit to the Cup Final on Saturday was as good as 10 sermons,' said Canon Ellis N. Gowing at a special service for the Southend, Westcliff and District Chamber of Trade at St Mary's Church yesterday.

'The wonderful spirit of sportsmanship on the part of the thousands of spectators, and the manly way in which the Portsmouth team and their supporters bore their defeat, was a lesson for all'.

1930

ARSENAL 2
HUDDERSFIELD TOWN 0

--- ATTENDANCE ---
92 488

--- REFEREE ---
T. Crewe (Leicester)

--- GOALSCORERS ---
James, Lambert

--- TEAMS ---

Arsenal	Huddersfield Town
Preedy	Turner
Parker	Goodall
Hapgood	Spence
Baker	Naylor
Seddon	Wilson
John	Campbell
Hulme	Jackson
Jack	Kelly
Lambert	Davies
James	Raw
Bastin	Smith

--- THE ROAD TO THE FINAL ---

Arsenal
4th round
v Birmingham 2–2 (h)
Replay 1–0 (a)
5th round
v Middlesbrough 2–0 (a)
6th round
v West Ham United 3–0 (a)
Semi-Final
v Hull City 2–2
Replay 1–0

Huddersfield Town
4th round
v Sheffield United 2–1 (h)
5th round
v Bradford City 2–1 (h)
6th round
v Aston Villa 2–1 (a)
Semi-Final
v Sheffield Wednesday 2–1

Where Huddersfield Failed: Only Two Real Forwards

The airship Graf Zeppelin passing over Wembley while the match is in progress

THE DEFEAT OF Huddersfield by Arsenal in the FA Cup Final at Wembley was accomplished in a manner which left no doubt even in the minds of the beaten team. Parker, the Arsenal captain and right back, is a man of unbounded energy and enthusiasm, and he gave his last ounce in their bid for victory.

But, personally, I preferred the cool, unhurried work of Goodall, the Hud-

Preedy of Arsenal hurt in a goalmouth scramble

dersfield right back, whose kicking was deliberate and whose positional play was rarely mistaken.

Work Well Done

Huddersfield's Goodall found his task made more difficult because of the presence of Naylor in place of the injured Fogg at right half back. I do not wish to suggest that Naylor was a weak link. I thought he came out of the match with distinct credit. But Goodall's mental outlook must have been disturbed and his feet led him to strange places in an attempt to see that the enforced change did not mean a breach in the defensive chain. Then there was Campbell, Huddersfield's left half, who leaves another splendid memory of work well done.

As for Smith, he retains his power of changing direction with effortless ease, and his centres are as precisely accurate as if the field were marked with chessboard squares. And the irony of it! It was Smith's genius that exposed the long-suspected limitations of the Huddersfield attack. It was as if the commander of a

flotilla of destroyers had turned a search-light on his own boats and revealed them to be cardboard.

Just Spluttered

Especially in the second half, which opened so promisingly and spluttered out like damp squibs, Huddersfield's inside forwards were incapable of driving home any of these repeated attacks. The horns of the attack, Smith and Jackson, were there, but the spearhead was missing.

Quite early in the game – before the Arsenal's first goal – Jackson, as is his wont, appeared out of the blue, timing his arrival to the fraction of a second, to take Smith's cross pass on his head. The ball flashed past Preedy, just wide of the post. That was one of the few occasions on which Jackson eluded John.

The goal, when it came, in the 16th minute, was worthy of a Cup Final in the presence of the King. A free kick for a technical foul on James was taken promptly by that player. He pushed the ball out to Bastin and signalled to him to return it. Bastin first tricked Goodall into thinking he was going down the touchline and then cut in. When he passed squarely to James neither Turner nor Spence gave the Arsenal forward much 'daylight', and I cannot conceive any other forward doing what James did so swiftly and neatly. He hit the ball with the outside of his right foot, and it had the same effect as a golfer's sliced drive. The ball passed Spence and eluded Turner as if an invisible hand had turned it in the air.

Clapped his Hands

In past Cup ties, the worth of Jack has been proved over and over again. At Wembley, with the Arsenal left wing so

Arsenal Mobbed
– Cup Enthusiasm at Civic Reception

30 000 Londoners are wondering how the Arsenal football team, winners of Saturday's Cup Final, escaped unnoticed from Islington Town Hall yesterday afternoon.

For nearly two hours people had packed the street and stood on roofs waiting to see the players leave after their reception by the Mayor, Alderman W. E. Manchester, councillors and officials of the borough.

They cheered when they saw the motor coach in which the team had arrived back up to the doors of the Hall, but it was not the players who emerged. It was the Mayor, holding the Cup on high.

The team, unable to undergo a repetition of the enthusiastic handling they had endured on arrival, had left by a side door. On their arrival, men and women dashed through the police cordons, all traffic was stopped, and scores of admirers clambered into the players' motor coach. Some people were knocked down, a number being slightly hurt.

As Parker, the Arsenal captain, holding the Cup, and the other players stepped down from the coach they were swallowed up by the crowd and mounted police had to go to their aid and carry them to the Hall.

supremely able and confident, Jack was well content with less of the limelight, and he went through an afternoon of calmly efficient work without coming into great prominence. But it was because each of the Arsenal's five forwards was a potential match winner that the Huddersfield defence could never afford to concentrate on one particular spot.

Arsenal's second goal was an illustration. James held the ball long enough to make halves and backs uncertain of his intentions. Then he pushed it straight down the middle, to Lambert, who let the ball roll past him, waited until Turner was compelled to leave his goal and placed it so gently to his right that it almost seemed like a mockery.

Then Lambert turned and clapped his hands, clapped them at James, the arch-schemer, who had found the way, seven minutes from time, to make Arsenal's position unassailable.

Tom Parker, one of Arsenal's backs, with the Cup

The Spirit of Good Sportsmanship

I hope we shall never again go back to the old Cup Final conditions where the winners went away to celebrate their triumph and the losers stole off to some secluded place to reflect on their failure. I was in the Arsenal dressing room shortly after the match and it was crowded with Huddersfield players congratulating Arsenal.

On the field the teams had fought each other with magnificent spirit and intensity, but now it was all over, they laughed away the thought of defeat together. Then the teams drove away together, danced together, and sang together.

The right note had been struck before the game, when it was arranged that the teams should go on to the ground as friends. For the first time in the history of football we saw the two captains walk out together, and if they had linked arms the gesture could not have been more complete.

WEST BROMWICH ALBION 2
BIRMINGHAM CITY 1

ATTENDANCE
92 406

REFEREE
A. H. Kingscott (Long Eaton)

GOALSCORERS
W. G. Richardson (2)
Bradford

TEAMS

West Bromwich Albion	Birmingham City
Pearson	Hibbs
Shaw	Liddell
Trentham	Barkas
Magee	Cringan
W. Richardson	Morrall
Edwards	Leslie
Glidden	Briggs
Carter	Crosbie
W. G. Richardson	Bradford
Sandford	Gregg
Wood	Curtis

THE ROAD TO THE FINAL

West Bromwich Albion
4th round
v Tottenham Hotspur 1–0 (h)
5th round
v Portsmouth 1–0 (a)
6th round
v Wolverhampton Wanderers 1–1 (h)
Replay 2–1 (a)
Semi-Final
v Everton 1–0

Birmingham City
4th round
v Port Vale 2–0 (h)
5th round
v Watford 3–0 (h)
6th round
v Chelsea 2–2 (h)
Replay 3–0 (a)
Semi-Final
v Sunderland 2–0

Albion's Faith in Themselves Carries the Day

BIRMINGHAM WERE BEATEN so convincingly by West Bromwich Albion in the Cup Final that the referee's mistake in disallowing them a perfectly good goal within seven minutes of the start can be effaced from the memory.

That the referee made a mistake in ruling Gregg offside I am certain; Mr Kingscott made an entirely correct decision *from what he saw.*

In this instance, some of us were better placed than the referee.

This was the position. Towards the centre of the field and facing Cringan as he took a free kick near the touchline was the referee. Fifteen yards behind him, and slightly nearer the West Bromwich goal, was Gregg, Birmingham's inside left. Directly the ball left Cringan's foot, Gregg started to run. By the time Mr Kingscott had turned, Gregg had passed Shaw. He took the ball beautifully on his head and Pearson was beaten.

Thus unkind chance robbed Birmingham of a goal that Wembley history tells us means so much. But the subsequent play was a complete vindication of the Albion's all-round superiority.

Whatever had happened in the seventh minute, I think West Bromwich would have triumphed eventually.

Real Confidence

The supreme confidence of this team of youths was magnificent. Their best friends spoke bold words with quaking hearts. The spectre of stage-fright stalked heavily in their midst.

Gregg scores the Birmingham goal which was disallowed for being offside

But the reality? No Cup Final played at Wembley has seen more dashing, fearless tactics, such unwavering confidence, such implicit team faith.

Before the captains had tossed I noticed Bradford pulling at the bandages on his left knee. It was a significant gesture. Not once during the game did the Birmingham leader trust his left leg; he pivoted on his right, he used his right foot to pass the ball, he scored a glorious goal – the like of which we cannot hope to see again – with his right boot.

Birmingham's Handicap

Thus partly by chance, and to an even greater extent by design, Birmingham's tactics had their strict limitations.

With Bradford playing at half speed I would have used all my available men in a persistent effort to attack. An immediate retirement to the second-line trenches was a complete exposure of weakness. When time became a precious feature, I saw Barkas converting himself into a sort of forward-half back. It was a supreme realisation that the other policy had failed.

The First Goal

This happened when Glidden, challenged by Leslie, fell and the ball came back to Magee. He pushed it forward to Carter, who took it almost to the dead line – and away from the goal – before turning and passing inwards to the penalty spot.

Here was Richardson (W. G.). I think Hibbs could have cleared but for the intervention of Barkas. But when Richardson shot and fell the fumbling effort of the back placed the ball once more at the feet of the Albion centre forward, and before

WBA's Pearson dashes out to meet a shot

Hibbs had a chance Richardson had recovered and scored.

The second goal, which came so hot on the heels of Bradford's equalising shot that the vast crowd had not ceased to cheer Birmingham's success before Hibbs was beaten again, was due to another mistake in the Birmingham defence.

The Albion inside forwards went ahead straight from the kick-off. A pass back to Magee by Carter saw the ball sent ahead again beyond Richardson (W. G.).

Cringan took it and endeavoured to answer Hibbs' call for a pass back. But he sliced his kick, the ball came out to Richardson, and the centre forward had scored in a twinkling.

Birmingham's Heroes

There may be heartburnings in the Birmingham camp today. There always are when you have lost a Cup Final. But I am sure that the City men can look back and recall things that might have been better done. In a clean, sporting, honest and often thrilling game – in many respects, a great game – City were overwhelmed by a side in which skill and youth made a striking and incomparable blend.

Gleddon, the captain, carries the Cup on
WBA's lap of honour

An Ugly Pot

What is this Cup, that so monopolises
the interest of hundreds of thousands?
Is it a magnificent piece of art? Is it
worth a king's ransom?

No, it is just a plain silver Cup,
described by artists as 'ugly' – the kind
of which it has been the tradition to
give at sports meetings in Britain for
generations.

How many of the enthusiasts who
will cheer their teams today would care
if they were told that the gleaming
trophy perched up in front of the vast
Wembley stands is worth about ten
pounds?

It cost more, indeed, when it was
made in 1910, but now that silver has
fallen to the low level of 1s $1\frac{1}{2}$d per
troy ounce, its intrinsic value is rapidly
dwindling.

But, of course, mere monetary value
means nothing to the sportsmen who
play for it and those who watch it
played for. The team that wins the ten
pound Cup this afternoon will have
attained the highest football honour
there is possible to attain anywhere in
the world.

1932

NEWCASTLE UNITED 2
ARSENAL 1

ATTENDANCE
92 298

REFEREE
W. P. Harper (Stourbridge)

GOALSCORERS
Allen (2)
John

TEAMS

Newcastle United	Arsenal
McInroy	Moss
Nelson	Parker
Fairhurst	Hapgood
McKenzie	Jones
Davidson	Roberts
Weaver	Male
Boyd	Hulme
Richardson	Jack
Allen	Lambert
McMenemy	Bastin
Lang	John

THE ROAD TO THE FINAL

Newcastle United
4th round
v Southport 1–1 (h)
Replay 1–1 (a)
2nd replay 9–0 (h)
5th round
v Leicester City 3–1 (h)
6th round
v Watford 5–0 (h)
Semi-Final
v Chelsea 2–1

Arsenal
4th round
v Plymouth Argyle 4–2 (h)
5th round
v Portsmouth 2–0 (a)
6th round
v Huddersfield Town 1–0 (a)
Semi-Final
v Manchester City 1–0

Newcastle Worthy Cup Winners – though One Goal *Was Lucky*

Arsenal on the offensive. Left to right: McInroy and Nelson, Lambert and Jack, and a lone Newcastle defender

NEWCASTLE UNITED ARE holders of the FA Cup on their merits. That one of the goals by which they beat Arsenal should be a legitimate subject of controversy is regrettable.

When, in the 42nd minute of the game, Boyd, the Newcastle outside right, centred for Allen to score a goal that equalised the goal headed by Arsenal's John 15 minutes from the start, I had no doubt that the ball had crossed the dead line before Boyd kicked it.

But the referee did not see this, and as he did not he was absolutely right to defend his decision. The referee is the sole arbiter on questions of fact, and no power on earth can now affect the issue. If all the members of the FA Council thought he was wrong, it could not make any difference.

I am glad that, for the sake of the Newcastle team as a whole, the goal that won the match was so beautifully complete in its conception and execution.

Flash of Inspiration

Richardson sent the ball down the middle to Allen. The centre forward brushed past the centre half, and then, in a flash of inspiration, did a surprising thing. Instead of going straight through, he veered suddenly to the left, putting Hapgood immediately out of position. He ran along the 25 yard line, parallel to the goal, until he neared Parker. Then he turned sharply and with his left foot, shot low and swiftly between the backs towards the far corner of the goal. Moss's headlong dive and outflung hands could not stop the ball, which hit the inside of the post and turned inwards.

A gem of a goal, scored in the 29th

minute of the second half, when Newcastle's superiority was clearly evident.

Workmanlike

Arsenal's goal was sound and workmanlike, if not brilliant. Hulme received an accurate pass from Bastin, side-stepped Fairhurst, ran on and centred perfectly. McInroy tried to intercept but failed, and temporarily knocked out Nelson. John had come in, anticipating Hulme's move, and headed into an empty goal.

Late in the second half there was a reshuffling of the Arsenal forwards. Jack went to the centre, Bastin to inside right, and Lambert to inside left. The move came within an ace of success. In the last five minutes John headed to the feet of Jack, who attempted to place a shot wide of both McInroy and Nelson, obstructing him. It went just outside the post.

More Convincing

Always Newcastle played the more convincingly. Boyd and Lang made a mess of a number of centres in the early part of the game, but later they were more dangerous, and the general team work was splendid. There was nippiness and accuracy in the work of the halves. The backs, particularly Nelson, were rarely at a loss. The Arsenal goal, scored by a move that spreadeagled the defence in the first quarter of an hour, could not be repeated.

Jack of Arsenal gets his head to the ball in front of the Newcastle goal, but McInroy is ready to save the shot

Cup Final 'Nerves' – by a Former Finalist

In my first Cup Final I was a bundle of nerves, hardly knowing where I was for the first 15 minutes. The second time, a good many years after, there was a peculiar feeling inside that I call excitement, for want of a better word. I have talked to many players who have played in the Final. They have all felt this excitement.

During the week of training there is no concern; no one worries about the game until the last night. It is easy to say: 'Go to bed early and have a good night's sleep.' I doubt if I had five hours' sleep before either of my Cup Final experiences. My mind kept turning to what might happen. What I must not do, what I must do. Mentally I played against my particular opponents time and time again.

There is an idea that the players are kept in bed late on the day of the match. That did not happen to us, for the simple reason that our trainer knew every man would be awake, and what his thoughts would be. Distraction, that was wanted, and we had it. We were taken out in motor cars, allowed a break to walk and prevent stiffness, and then we had lunch at 12 o'clock. You might be interested in that lunch. It was boiled mutton, dry toast and tea. That is all. Then we rested, not formally, for anything formal might bring on ultra nervousness.

Good football is not common in Cup Finals. That does not surprise me; on the contrary, I marvel that one ever does anything right. I was a defender – not for anything would I be a forward who has to score. Even now, when I think of the Final, that something called 'excitement' is there inside me.

Cup Final Goal Dispute – Referee has No Doubts, but Film Suggests a Mistake

The Cup Final of 1932 will go down in history as the 'disputed goal Final'. There has never been so much argument over a goal as the one with which Newcastle United equalised against The Arsenal in Saturday's Final at Wembley, and yesterday the possibility of an appeal to The Football Association against the referee's ruling was being freely discussed.

This, however, is the last thing that can happen, in spite of the fact that many people in the ground thought that Mr W. P. Harper, the referee, blundered when he permitted Allan's shot to count.

The referee in any football match is the sole judge of fact, and any decision that he may make is final; and although members of the FA Council, who received the King and Queen at the match, all expressed opinions that the goal was legitimate, these were purely private. No action can or will be taken in the matter. In the opinion of Mr James H. Freeman, the Daily Mail's expert at the game, and also of Mr Frank M. Carruthers, the ball was clearly over the goal-line before Boyd, the Newcastle outside right, screwed it back to Allen, who scored.

But in the absence of any flag by the linesman, Mr Harper, being satisfied in his own mind that a goal had been fairly scored, pointed to the centre spot.

The Arsenal players were dumbfounded and appealed strongly to the referee to consult the linesman. This Mr Harper, having acted on what he saw, declined to do.

But a film of the game shows clearly that Boyd took the ball over the line before he centred it for Allan to score.

'I gave my decision according to the rules,' declared Mr Harper after the match. 'I was certain the goal had been fairly scored; otherwise, I should not have given it. I stand by my decision, whether there is an inquiry or not.'

Arsenal players and officials alike declined to discuss the question.

Mr Andy Cunningham, manager of the Newcastle United team, said last night that Boyd never touched the ball.

'The player who centred the ball,' he said, 'was Richardson. I was near the touch-line and in a perfect position.

'The referee also was in a good position, and was obviously convinced that the ball was in play.'

Allan said: 'Richards had sent the ball over to me. From my position, however, I could not see whether it had gone out of play or not. The referee is the best judge.'

The game was one of best Finals ever seen at Wembley, and Newcastle broke a record of 22 years when they won after being a goal down.

Jolly Old Pals   By TOM WEBSTER

[Daily Mail Copyright.]

1933

EVERTON 3
MANCHESTER CITY 0

ATTENDANCE
92 950

REFEREE
E. Wood (Sheffield)

GOALSCORERS
Stein, Dean, Dunn

TEAMS

Everton	Manchester City
Sagar	Langford
Cook	Cann
Cresswell	Dale
Britton	Busby
White	Cowan
Thomson	Bray
Geldard	Toseland
Dunn	Marshall
Dean	Herd
Johnson	McMullen
Stein	Brook

THE ROAD TO THE FINAL

Everton
4th round
v Bury 3–1 (h)
5th round
v Leeds United 2–0 (h)
6th round
v Luton Town 6–0 (h)
Semi-Final
v West Ham United 2–1

Manchester City
4th round
v Walsall 2–0 (h)
5th round
v Bolton Wanderers 4–2 (a)
6th round
v Burnley 1–0 (a)
Semi-Final
v Derby County 3–2

Wembley Nerves Spoil Another Cup Final

A friendly handshake at the start of the match

– Dean and the Occasion too much for Manchester City

ONE PICTURE OF the Football Association Cup Final on Saturday will linger in my memory long after many of the details of play have been blurred by the passage of time.

As Dean triumphantly held the Cup aloft for all to see, a little knot of men moved slowly, almost disconsolately, across the turf not 50 yards away from the celebrations. They were the Manchester players.

Not for them the cheers and the fêtings and a line writ large in the record books. Only the torturing thoughts of the Might-Have-Been.

Watching them, it was impossible to avoid asking two questions:

What was the cause of Manchester's complete inability to reproduce more than a shadow of the form that had earned them the right to play at Wembley? When are we to see *real* football in a Cup Final?

Panic Defence

The answer to the first question is Nerves. Wembley gripped and shook Manchester City – as it has done other teams – and reduced them to impotence.

Only when – and if – these Cup Final Nerves can be eradicated can there be a hope of playing real football at Wembley.

The light beats very fiercely on a goal-keeper in a Cup Final match, and it dazzled Langford in this game. He was not happy in his fielding of a high ball across the goalmouth; he did not seem comfortable at all when corner kicks were taken. He made two mistakes which cost goals, but did one good thing in the second half which prevented the total reaching four goals for Everton.

With Dean racing towards him, clear of all pursuit, he came out, flung himself on the ball and got it away.

Manchester City's backs were in no better state than Langford. Cann's efforts were of a negative kind, his kicking a matter of wild conjecture. Dale was more timely in his tackles, but he and his partner had no understanding, and their work was flurried and hesitating.

Too Ambitious

Busby made a man's job of it at right half. Cowan was too ambitious and attempted too much. He was torn between a determination not to leave Dean and a desire to help his forwards. He broke down between the two. Toseland clung to the idea of following the touch-line and the cool and calculating Cresswell was never at a loss in dealing with him. Brook strove in spasms – very good work in making ground, unaccountable lapses in finishing.

Geldard Weak

Despite being the better team in many ways, Everton's forward line was out of balance, and it was Geldard who failed to even the scales. Not until the last ten minutes did he approach his club standard. Johnson and Stein were a success, however, and it was Dean who assisted so largely in making them so.

The highlights of the game were the three goals and a few bad misses. Eighteen minutes went by before Everton made one scoring shot, and it came too high for Dean's foot. Three corner kicks to Everton showed up defensive weaknesses of the men in red. Cowan made a mistake which let Dean through, but Langford

Dean falls into the net after scoring Everton's second goal

made one of his best saves of the match from Stein. Brooks might have scored first for Manchester if he had made full use of a pass from Herd, but gradually it became

Cup Final Change: All the Players to Wear Numbers

For the first time in the history of the FA Cup Final, all the players will be numbered when Manchester City and Everton meet at Wembley. This innovation, which has long been advocated by many people, was agreed upon yesterday, and it will prove of the greatest help to the 93 000 spectators in identifying the men during the game.

Everton will wear the numbers 1 to 11 in black on white shirts, and Manchester City 12 to 22 in white on scarlet shirts.

In making the preparations for the refreshment of the crowd, the authorities have had to reverse two items of the menu.

People in the south of England favour sandwiches, but those from the north prefer meat pies. As the north will predominate at Wembley, the number of meat pies ordered has been increased from 14 000 to 17 000 and the order for sandwiches reduced in proportion.

Dixie Dean leaving the Royal Stand with a prized possession

apparent that Everton were going to be permanent masters of the situation.

Langford's Lapse

When Dean failed to score from a centre by Stein after 40 minutes, it was due to over-anxiety to place the ball. He missed it completely.

Almost at once, however, a goal came. A long centre from Britton should have been held by Langford. He tried to keep one eye on Dean and the other on the ball. He came out a step too far, the ball just flicked his outstretched hands and dropped at Stein's foot – an easy goal.

Seven minutes after the interval Britton lobbed across another centre which again caught Langford in two minds. He hesitated a split second before coming out, then his hands shot up just that little bit too late to prevent Dean's head getting there first.

The forward work of Manchester in the Everton goal area was too slapdash to cause much anxiety and Everton's third success, eight minutes from time, only emphasised their superiority. Geldard placed a corner kick well. Up bobbed Dunn's head and the ball was in the net for a spectacular goal.

If Wembley were Twice as Big – How Public Interest has Grown

Although the official record gate for football was that at the last England v Scotland match at Hampden Park, Glasgow, when 134 000 paid for admission, there is no doubt that the FA Cup Final is the greatest event of the season, and if Wembley Stadium had adequate accommodation, the attendance would be more than doubled.

The first year the match was played at the Stadium, the gates were rushed, thousands of people entered the ground without paying, and it was estimated that 150 000 people were present.

The popularity of the Cup competition has grown amazingly during the past ten years. This is shown by the increase which has taken place in the attendance and receipts. For three years previous to the Final being staged at Wembley it was played at Stamford Bridge, and the most attractive match there was that between Tottenham Hotspur and Wolverhampton Wanderers in 1921. Then the attendance was 72 805 and the receipts £13 414.

The increase in interest is even more marked when a comparison is made with the Finals which were played at the Crystal Palace before 1914. Of the matches at Sydenham, only three attracted over 100 000 people.

Today the Final at Wembley produces about £25 000. Of this, one third goes to the Football Association, and one third to each of the competing clubs.

1934

MANCHESTER CITY 2
PORTSMOUTH 1

ATTENDANCE
93 258

REFEREE
S. F. Rous (Herts)

GOALSCORERS
Tilson (2),
Rutherford

TEAMS

Manchester City	Portsmouth
Swift	Gilfillan
Barnett	Mackie
Dale	W. Smith
Busby	Nichol
Cowan	Allen
Bray	Thackeray
Toseland	Worrall
Marshall	J. W. Smith
Tilson	Weddle
Herd	Easson
Brook	Rutherford

THE ROAD TO THE FINAL

Manchester City
4th round
v Hull City 2–2 (a)
Replay 4–1 (h)
5th round
v Sheffield Wednesday 2–2 (a)
Replay 2–0 (h)
6th round
v Stoke City 1–0 (h)
Semi-Final
v Aston Villa 6–1

Portsmouth
4th round
v Grimsby Town 2–0 (h)
5th round
v Swansea Town 1–0 (a)
6th round
v Bolton Wanderers 3–0 (a)
Semi-Final
v Leicester City 4–1

Masterly Cup Final Goals

Swift, the Manchester goalkeeper, clears from a corner kick

Manchester Deserved Success – But Allen's Injury Helped

MANCHESTER CITY RECEIVED the FA Cup from the hands of the King at Wembley on Saturday after one of the most dramatic and thrilling Finals in the history of the competition.

Portsmouth, by clever and resourceful play, had scored in the 27th minute through Rutherford. That goal was stamped with the hallmark of genius in strategy, and the opportunism of the young outside left was equalised only by his coolness at the critical moment.

Portsmouth clung to the lead until only 17 minutes remained for play. Then Allen, their tall centre half, crashed into an opponent and fell unconscious in the Portsmouth penalty area. Following the custom to which he had adhered strictly throughout the match, the referee did not stop play until the ball was dead. Allen was carried to the touch-line near the Portsmouth goal, and while he was being restored, Tilson equalised for Manchester.

Allen returned looking as if he were dazed – as indeed he was – and four minutes from time Tilson scored again.

How much of this victory was due to Allen's mishap cannot be properly gauged. But it is definitely beyond dispute that, on the play as it went, Manchester City merited their success.

Splendid Goals

The goals were really splendid, and I would give them all equal merit. When Rutherford scored for Portsmouth, the chance was given to him by Weddle. The centre forward had worked to the penalty line and lobbed the ball over Cowan's head to the outside left. Rutherford closed in, reached a point 15 yards from goal and almost opposite the penalty spot, saw Dale running across, changed the ball from his left foot to his right, and banged it home. Swift, the 19-year-old goalkeeper, dived for the ball a fraction too late.

Good as this was, Tilson's first goal was even better. Brook was the inspiration – Brook, who had been running all over the field, even to the extent of being on the right wing for a throw-in by Busby.

Brilliant Move

He was given a pass on the touch-line, worked the ball swiftly halfway across the front of Portsmouth's massed defence, and then, when everyone expected him to pass out to Toseland, he swung round and flicked the ball to Tilson, who had run forward and to the left.

It was a brilliant move. Mackie sensed the danger and closed on the Manchester centre forward. But as the two men came into contact and Tilson was falling over, he shot with his left foot.

The third goal of the match was equally

Cup Final Secrets – avoiding Wembley nerves

Some of the greatest secrets of the week are: how will the Football Association Cup Final teams – Manchester City and Portsmouth – travel to London for the match at Wembley Stadium on Saturday?

And: when will they arrive, and where will they stay until the kick-off at 3 p.m.?

These secrets are closely guarded by the managements of the teams, for there must be no chance of enthusiasts, or anyone else, worrying the players.

It is certain that only one real problem is before those who have to train and watch over these 22 men. Everything is being done to keep their minds off the game, and keep away that dread bogey 'Wembley nerves'.

The critical time will be the last half-hour before the kick-off, which will be at 3 o'clock.

There are likely to be royal spectators at what is regarded as one of the greatest sporting events of the year.

Although more than 92 000 people will watch the game, there is no possibility of any scrambling to get into the Stadium, for all the tickets have been allotted, and the receipts are considerably more than £20 000.

Each spectator will stroll up to an entrance, go through a turnstile, and then to the place marked on his ticket. Everybody will be able to see all there is to see.

And all the experts are agreed that – 'It should be a great game'.

good, though less spectacular. Toseland, whose second-half game was infinitely superior to his pre-interval tactics of trying to round Smith on the outside, put over a centre which was quickly transferred to Tilson. He was so well placed that Gilfillan had no chance.

Portsmouth's bad Luck

The first half was so clearly Portsmouth's that the Manchester defence was constantly in difficulties. In this half J. W. Smith was at his best; he and Easson worked with smoothness and skill and their distribution of the ball was excellent. But the Manchester City half backs, the mainstay of the team all through, were rarely at fault. Busby was brilliant. He looks so innocuous with that curious bent-body run of his when he has the ball at his feet, but his passes are a delight, and he seldom fails to draw the defence first. It is a fact that Tilson did not have one shot at goal before Allen was off the field – that is, nearly 75 minutes' play.

Taken by itself, the fact suggests Portsmouth were really unlucky. But there are other phases of the game to be considered, and Manchester City undoubtedly won on their merits.

Manchester City on the attack

King George V presenting the Cup to Cowan, Manchester City's captain

Touching the Cup – for Luck

What happens after the Cup Final? There is jubilation – champagne has been seen being drunk from the Cup. Players have been seen dancing and singing round the Cup, but these are natural things. Some of the others are more surprising.

The winners are surrounded by a crowd of their supporters. The losers come out almost unnoticed. One team has been known, in fact, to go out another way – and the crowd's disappointment was very intense.

Autographs are wanted from the heroes. The winning captain carries the Cup high so everybody can see it.

Through the crowd the winners' motor coach moves slowly. For at least two miles progress is at walking pace, and never for one second are the running boards clear of excited people.

They clamber on at the risk of serious injury, and the cry is always the same: 'Let me see the Cup, please may I touch it for luck?'

Is it superstition that to touch the Cup is lucky? Mounted policemen have been seen riding alongside, pushing their heads through the coach window to make the same request.

Women who can set foot on the vehicle will not get off until they have been allowed to touch the trophy.

Whoever wins the Cup: thousands of people will want to touch it – for luck.

SHEFFIELD WEDNESDAY 4

WEST BROMWICH ALBION 2

ATTENDANCE
93 204

REFEREE
A. E. Fogg (Bolton)

GOALSCORERS
Palethorpe, Hooper, Rimmer (2);
Boyes, Sandford

TEAMS

Sheffield Wednesday	West Bromwich Albion
Brown	Pearson
Nibloe	Shaw
Catlin	Trentham
Sharp	Murphy
Millership	W. Richardson
Burrows	Edwards
Hooper	Glidden
Surtees	Carter
Palethorpe	W. G. Richardson
Starling	Sandford
Rimmer	Boyes

THE ROAD TO THE FINAL

Sheffield Wednesday
4th round
v Wolverhampton Wanderers 2–1 (a)
5th round
v Norwich City 1–0 (a)
6th round
v Arsenal 2–1 (h)
Semi-Final
v Burnley 3–0

West Bromwich Albion
4th round
v Sheffield United 7–1 (h)
5th round
v Stockport County 5–0 (a)
6th round
v Preston North End 1–0 (h)
Semi-Final
v Bolton Wanderers 1–1
Replay 2–0

Wednesday's Half-Time Talk Paves the Way to Victory

West Brom's Boyes driving the ball high into the net to make the score 1–1

– Rimmer's Two Vital Goals After Unhappy Beginning

SHEFFIELD WEDNESDAY BEAT West Bromwich Albion fairly and squarely in the thirteenth Cup Final at Wembley.

In the drama of its changing fortunes, in the breathtaking incidents which it provided, in the number of goals scored – in fact, in nearly everything that the public desire on the day of football's greatest pageant – this game was almost supercharged.

The huge assembly had barely settled in their seats after cheering the Prince of Wales on his return from receiving the players when Wednesday scored, within two minutes of the opening. From the kick-off, a harmless-looking movement on the Albion left wing saw Catlin come over to Nibloe's place and receive a hastily kicked ball in the stomach.

He fell to the ground writhing, and while he lay there, with Mr A. E. Fogg running up towards the Albion goal to follow the play, the ball spun out to Hooper on the Wednesday right. The little winger returned it promptly. There was Palethorpe, in the centre of the penalty line.

He was almost leisurely in his movements. He stopped the ball with his left foot, half turned, and placed it along the carpet of green just inside the post. Pearson had no chance.

The Perfect Goal

Twenty-two minutes from the start came Albion's first goal. It was Shaw who started the movement. A punt up the field, a forage by Starling, and a pass to the centre, where eventually Carter came into possession. A beautiful cross from Carter to the left wing was the result. Boyes took the ball in his stride; it was too far beyond

Millership for the centre half to count; too much to the left of Nibloe for the back to move in time.

Boyes went forward, and a left foot shot was driven high into the net out of Brown's reach. This proved to be the nearest approach to the perfect goal that the game produced.

At half-time the teams were on an equality, and justly so. West Bromwich were speedily off the mark again, and a curling shot from Glidden was completely missed by Brown. It went outside the post. Starling, with his deceptive leg-flutter, came down to the Wednesday left wing and centred to Palethorpe, who fumbled the chance in his eagerness. But a moment later came one of the real thrills.

Great Save

Palethorpe, dribbling strongly, swung out to the right. There he passed inside to Surtees, who lobbed the ball over and Starling headed it in. Pearson had come out of goal, and the ball was running into an empty net, when out of the blue came Murphy. He hooked the ball out with his right foot for a corner and did not finish

Sheffield Wednesday come home with the Cup

The Prince of Wales – the future King Edward VIII – is introduced to the Wednesday team

Human Side of the Cup Final

Strange how the little human incidents of a great match stick in one's mind! There were plenty of them at the Cup Final, but none matched the little drama near the end played by the Optimist and the Pessimist in the West Brom team.

The chief figure in it was goalkeeper Pearson. Beaten for the fourth time, almost tearful from vexation, inconsolable, he fished the ball out of the net and vented his feelings upon it.

Again and again he kicked it into his own net – and looked like doing so indefinitely until Richardson, centre forward and one-time omnibus inspector, came dashing up. Richardson, by frantic arm waving and shouting, commanded that the ball be returned to the centre for the restart.

Though the score was 4–2 and only a minute remained for play, Richardson, a super-optimist, thought there was still a chance to save the game! Stout fellow!

his own desperate dash until the back net pulled him up.

In a few minutes Starling was moved to outside right, but back again he came to the left wing. From this position he got rid of an Albion defensive block by passing inside to Hooper.

Hooper shot – but not very cleverly. Yet it sufficed. The ball hit the inside of the post and trickled over the line without enough pace to carry it into the net. So, for a second time, Albion had to wipe out a lead, and they did it in 5 minutes – in the 27th minute of the second half.

Deflected

A quick throw-in from the touch-line by Boyes found Sandford. The inside left hooked the ball with his left foot and, though Brown might have saved it had it come to him direct, Millership's head was struck in passing and the ball was lofted over Brown's arms. Two-two – and the remainder of the game packed with thrills! W. G. Richardson put outside in a storming Albion attack with only Brown to beat; back they came again, and Boyes headed in only to see the ball returned by the post, and not the goalkeeper.

But tragedy waited on the Albion. Carter, who had developed a limp, could not therefore accept a chance that came his way, and a forward kick by Sharp eventually reached Rimmer in the goal area. Pearson came out, and Rimmer headed over his arms into the yawning goal.

Once more Pearson was beaten – within a minute of the end. Hooper shot in, Pearson pushed the ball out, and Rimmer was given another chance to add to his remarkable Cup-tie record of scoring in every round.

BRITISH BIRDS

bottled by Worthington

BAILEY.

The CUPFINCH or WEMBLER

(Stadium deliriosa)

During the winter months usually found in 'pools.' A gentle twitterer when alone, this bird in coveys or "associations" becomes dangerous and bloodthirsty. Migrates in Spring to an open space near London where combats take place between selected males.

Plumage : Drab, but for bright-coloured flecks that appear suddenly on Saturdays.

Song : Mostly derisive.

Food : This bird's resistance to climate and other hardships is held to be due to regular refreshment with Worthington — both before and after flocking.

Cup Final Team's Secret Out
– where Wednesday are Hiding

'Early to bed' was a general order for both the West Bromwich Albion and the Sheffield Wednesday football teams when they arrived in London last evening for the Cup Final at Wembley tomorrow.

So anxious were the Wednesday team to avoid the attention of football enthusiasts that they left Sheffield by motor car and joined a London train at a station further down the line.

They had planned to keep their temporary headquarters in London secret – to go into hiding until tomorrow – but soon after their arrival were located at Bushey, Hertfordshire.

The Albion, however, do not care who knows where they are – and for a very good reason. They are staying at the same hotel in Harrow, Middlesex, at which they stayed in 1931, when they won the Cup!

On their way from Paddington to Harrow, they visited the Cenotaph and placed a wreath there.

Tonight they will come out of their seclusion at Harrow when they attend the first performance at the Palladium. The second show would be *much* too late!

1936

ARSENAL 1
SHEFFIELD UNITED 0

ATTENDANCE
93 384

REFEREE
H. Nattrass (New Seaham)

GOALSCORER
Drake

TEAMS

Arsenal	Sheffield United
Wilson	Smith
Male	Hooper
Hapgood	Wilkinson
Crayston	Jackson
Roberts	Johnson
Copping	McPherson
Hulme	Barton
Bowden	Barclay
Drake	Dodds
James	Pickering
Bastin	Williams

THE ROAD TO THE FINAL

Arsenal
4th round
v Liverpool 2–0 (a)
5th round
v Newcastle United 3–3 (a)
Replay 3–0 (h)
6th round
v Barnsley 4–1 (h)
Semi-Final
v Grimsby Town 1–0

Sheffield United
4th round
v Preston North End 0–0 (a)
Replay 2–0 (h)
5th round
v Leeds United 3–1 (h)
6th round
v Tottenham Hotspur 3–1 (h)
Semi-Final
v Fulham 2–1

One Touch of the Real Drake won the Cup for Arsenal

Smith, the Sheffield goalkeeper, saving his charge as Bastin dashes in

DRAKE, ARSENAL'S CENTRE forward, ex-invalid, and only a shadow of his usual devil-may-care, dashing self, scored the goal that mattered in the 29th minute of the second half of the Cup Final at Wembley.

It goes without saying that it was the best thing he did in the game. It was very nearly the only thing.

There were two reasons for this. 1) Thomas Johnson, Sheffield United's dour, omnipresent centre half. 2) Behind the

A hectic scene at the Sheffield goalmouth – Smith turns the ball round the post

There was one incident, in the 17th minute of the second half, which appeared to make Dodds guilty of culpable negligence. Williams swung a very fast ball from the Sheffield left wing across the Arsenal goal area. Pickering, Dodds and Barclay were in line. Pickering left it to Dodds, Dodds kicked and missed, and Barclay had no time to do anything.

Afterwards I heard that Dodds's foot was a yard away from the ball, that he made a better effort than most people could imagine to reach it, and that the apparent simple miss was an illusion due to the angle of vision.

There was no illusion about a blazing shot from Pickering that went just over the Arsenal bar during Sheffield's frantic efforts to get on terms.

Wilson's Slip

Cup Finals usually produce one mistake that is fatal. Arsenal's goalkeeper Wilson was guilty of an error in the first few minutes that made 93 000 people hold their breath.

Sheffield attacked strongly; their passing movements were crisp and incisive; the Arsenal defence was running hither and thither, and Sheffield were keeping the ball. Over it came, from the right wing, swish went Pickering's foot. Wilson tried to field the shot, fumbled it; it ran over his forearms and hit the ground.

mind of Drake, so it seemed, was the haunting anxiety, would that left leg, the subject of his recent cartilage operation, stand the strain?

Injury Handicap?

Yet it was the left foot that scored the goal that put gallant, hard-playing, never-say-die Sheffield United into the position of runners-up.

What influence a first-half injury to Jackson, Sheffield's right half back, played in the result will never be known. I believe, however, that but for a pronounced second-half limp, the ball that James put to Bastin when the second half was two-thirds gone would not have reached him.

Bastin got it anyhow, and put Hooper out of the running when he feinted and cut inside him. Then he passed to Drake.

Drake was confronted by Johnson. He moved to the right, and still Johnson blocked his view. Then the Arsenal centre pivoted, seemed to stumble, swung his left leg and – the ball crashed into the net.

That was a touch of the old Drake – unexpected, thrustful, with the kick of a horse.

An Escape

It came at a period when, with the wind behind them and the forwards playing with something like the old Arsenal system again, Arsenal always looked to be on the verge of winning.

Yet no sooner had they taken the lead than blind chance only prevented Sheffield from scoring.

A furious attack on the Sheffield right wing saw the ball come over from Barton to Dodds. For once Robert's head was nowhere near, and Dodds, six yards from goal, headed away from Wilson. The ball hit the junction of bar and post with Wilson isolated.

But if the United followers could scarcely conceal their chagrin, dismay was writ largely on the faces of Arsenal fans when Bowden, eight yards from a yawning goal, foozled a shot completely. And substitute Bastin, usually so sure, hit a pass skywards when the back of the net looked so inviting.

Crayston Excels

Crayston was a better half back than any of the other five. Though his splendid work made Male's task the easier, it did not lessen my admiration of the most polished and effective specimen of full back play that I can remember seeing for a long time. Male was superb.

Smith was much the better of the two goalkeepers; he did not make a mistake; his work was cool, clean and accurate.

If the match were played over again, I still think Arsenal would win – narrowly. The suggestion in some quarters that they scored a second goal is rubbish. When an Arsenal player (Bowden or Drake, I think) headed the ball from a scrimmage and Smith fielded it, his body was partly over the line. But the ball, in his outstretched hands, was well inside the field of play.

Mr H. Nattrass, the very efficient referee, was right on top of this incident. He justified his ability all through to be up with the play, and proved to the hilt the wisdom of the FA's choice.

Policeman Begs to touch Cup – Triumphant Drive on Roof

Arsenal footballers – and the FA Cup, which they won on Saturday by beating Sheffield United – were driven in triumph for two miles through London's streets yesterday while thousands of people cheered.

Players and club officials went by motor coach to a civic reception in Islington Town Hall.

The roof of the coach was opened and Alex James, the Arsenal captain, stood with his head through it, holding the Cup.

But that was not enough for the crowd. They shouted for James and for Drake, the man who scored the goal that won the Final at Wembley.

In the end these two had to climb on to a covered part of the roof and exhibit the Cup between them.

One mounted policeman galloped alongside the coach and asked to touch the Cup. Before the party started from the Arsenal stadium, another mounted officer asked that the trophy should be brought to the back of the coach, so that some children could see it. He made the same request of Alex James – and the children were twice lucky.

1937

SUNDERLAND 3
PRESTON NORTH END 1

ATTENDANCE
93 495

REFEREE
R. G. Rudd (Kenton)

GOALSCORERS
Gurney, Carter, Burbanks
F. O'Donnell

TEAMS

Sunderland	Preston North End
Mapson	Burns
Gorman	Gallimore
Hall	Beattie
Thomson	Shankly
Johnson	Tremelling
McNab	Milne
Duns	Dougal
Carter	Beresford
Gurney	F. O'Donnell
Gallacher	Fagan
Burbanks	H. O'Donnell

THE ROAD TO THE FINAL

Sunderland
4th round
v Luton Town 2–2 (h)
Replay 3–1 (a)
5th round
v Swansea Town 3–0 (h)
6th round
v Wolverhampton Wanderers 1–1 (a)
Replay 2–2 (h)
2nd replay 4–0 (a)
Semi-Final
v Millwall 2–1

Preston North End
4th round
v Stoke City 5–1 (h)
5th round
v Exeter City 5–3 (h)
6th round
v Tottenham Hotspur 3–1 (a)
Semi-Final
v West Bromwich Albion 4–1

Sunderland Get First Cup

Preston's centre forward F. O'Donnell receives attention after an injury

– Decisive Form in Second Half

SUNDERLAND, A GOAL down 38 minutes from the start, became holders of the FA Cup for the first time by as decisive a second-half victory over Preston North End as Wembley has ever witnessed.

Preston scored in an opening half that had little distinction apart from this goal and a miss by Gurney, the Sunderland centre forward, from a position so simple that here, we thought, was tragedy.

Gurney was not more than eight yards

from goal when Carter slipped the ball across to him, scarcely knee high and at an easy pace. Gurney was alone and unchallenged, but he hooked the ball hurriedly with his left foot high up in the blue sky over Burns's head.

It was an instance of the high nervous tension all the players were having at this period and it was a lone blot – an understandable error.

The tension was less evident in Dougal, Preston's outside right, who was largely responsible for Preston's goal. He sensed an opening, ran inside and was in the position of inside left when he received the ball. He passed it swiftly to O'Donnell, for the moment at inside right. O'Donnell's raking shot was always travelling away from Mapson, whose position was hopeless.

Doubtful Free Kick

There had been doubts in my mind whether the free kick which ultimately gave rise to this goal-scoring movement was rightly awarded to Preston.

O'Donnell, in going for the ball with Gorman, had jumped high and appeared to foul the back. But the referee, Mr R. G. Rudd, who never hesitated in any decision he gave throughout the match, judged that Gorman had committed a foul in his attempts to tackle O'Donnell.

There couldn't have been more than a fraction of a second between the two offences. But the referee was better placed to see than I was, anyhow.

One reason for the comparatively dis-appointing character of the first-half play was traceable to the over-keenness and nervousness of the two teams. Of 26 free kicks, mainly for technical offences, Preston were awarded 15 and Sunderland 11.

The run of the play had steadily favoured Preston, for whom Fagan had come near to scoring twice – though not dangerously so – and the hard-working Beresford had shot behind following a free kick.

Fault-Free Goal

I could find no fault with the goal that Gurney scored seven minutes after the interval, which marked the definite turn of the tide in Sunderland's favour.

A corner kick had been taken by Bur-

Cup Finalists
Won't be Numbered

In the hope that it would assist spectators to identify individual players at Wembley on Saturday, the Football Association invited the two clubs to agree to the men bearing numbers on their backs.

But both clubs refused yesterday, and so the Association has had to abandon the plan. I understand that neither team offered any reason.

The rules do not provide for the num-bering of players, but the experiment was made in the Final between Everton and Manchester City four years ago and was successful. It was also adopted in this season's Burnley international.

The majority of clubs, however, have declined to accept the system, the only reason given being that the game is so easy to follow owing to the standardised positions of players that it is unnecessary.

Plenty of Toast
for Sunderland

Preston will not be 'petted'! They leave Preston tomorrow afternoon for Northwood, Middlesex. They will stay at an hotel, but there will be no late dinners, special breakfasts or luncheon menus. The teams have disdained all diets save those supplied by their wives or landladies.

Trainer Bill Scott told me, when I mentioned diet, 'There is no petting of players at Preston. You say Sunderland are having a lot of toast – well, I hope it does them good.'

Carter, immediately behind the Preston goalkeeper on the ground, scores Sunderland's second goal

banks, and for a few seconds the ball hovered in the Preston goalmouth. Then it came to Carter, confronted by Gallimore, with Gurney behind the back, and only a few yards from goal. Carter headed the ball forward, just brushing past Gallimore, for a decisive goal by Gurney.

From then to the end Sunderland played with a freedom and power that made this half a most pleasant memory.

The play of their wing halves, Thomson and McNab (particularly the latter) was inspiring in the extreme, and the linking-up work of Carter and Gallacher was unerringly accurate and tactically sound. Burbanks was brought into the game time after time, and he repeatedly beat Gallimore by sheer speed.

Burbanks had a part in the second goal. He put the ball across to Gurney, from whose head it went to Carter, impeccably sure of his shot at goal.

Double Sure

Fourteen minutes from the end Sunderland made doubly sure with a goal by Burbanks. The pass that Gallacher gave him was a gem, and the left-foot shot made in Burbanks' stride unstoppable.

In their efforts to pull together an attack that had become ragged, Preston switched Dougal to inside left and Fagan to outside right. But their wings were never so effective as those of Sunderland, and their teamwork did not approach the form that had got them into the Final.

Gurney, in stripes, scores Sunderland's equaliser

Cup Winners' Rousing Homecoming

Eleven shy supermen came home to Sunderland tonight to turn a town upside down in a delirium of hero-worship.

With their captain, Horatio Carter, still the bashful bridegroom (on the eve of his postponed honeymoon) holding the glittering trophy aloft, the victorious FA Cup Final team returned from Wembley to be swept off their feet with adulation.

With a scream to prepare the street crowds for the team's arrival, their train drew into the station, every possible fitting bearing the red and white colours of the club.

Carter, torn apart from his wife by the back-slappings of his admirers, was swept out of his carriage on to the platform, and the Cup was rescued from his hands by a less lionised friend as he slipped into the ticket collector's office to broadcast a little speech.

Of a full strength of 200, some 144 police, hand in hand and mounted, were placed all along the route to the Roker Park ground to keep the crowds from the street and pave a way for the procession.

Unforgettable Scenes

The teams saw sights they will never forget. They saw people perched precariously on narrow window ledges to give them a cheer; as they rode over Wearmouth Bridge they heard sirens of welcoming ships and saw dare-devil boys climbing like flies about the elevated girders. Even cinema performances were stopped while the operators stood on the roof and joined in the cheering, and every window bulged with families on this, the happiest night in Sunderland's sporting history.

At the town hall civic reception, happy little speeches were broadcast to the crowd. The mayor expressed Sunderland's pride in a team of 'clean, good-living lads', and the sportsmanlike game that had placed the club on the international map of sport.

Carter listened for a few moments to the speeches in the boardroom, and then slipped away to join his wife for their honeymoon.

1938

PRESTON NORTH END 1
HUDDERSFIELD TOWN 0

ATTENDANCE
93 357

REFEREE
A. J. Jewell (London)

GOALSCORER
Mutch (penalty)

TEAMS

Preston North End	Huddersfield Town
Holdcroft	Hesford
Gallimore	Craig
A. Beattie	Mountford
Shankley	Willingham
Smith	Young
Batey	Boot
Watmough	Hulme
Mutch	Isaac
Maxwell	MacFadyen
R. Beattie	Barclay
O'Donnell	Beasley

THE ROAD TO THE FINAL

Preston North End
4th round
v Leicester City 2–0 (h)
5th round
v Arsenal 1–0 (a)
6th round
v Brentford 3–0 (a)
Semi-Final
v Aston Villa 2–1

Huddersfield Town
4th round
v Notts County 1–0 (h)
5th round
v Liverpool 1–0 (a)
6th round
v York City 0–0 (a)
Replay 2–1 (h)
Semi-Final
v Sunderland 3–1

Dramatic Cup Final Ending

Preston's Holdcroft makes an agile save

– Mutch Dared Not Watch Penalty Shoot

THE STARK DRAMA of Preston North End's penalty goal victory over Huddersfield Town in the last 20 seconds of extra time lives in the memory to the exclusion of everything else in the 1938 Cup Final.

I can see now, hours after the game, Mutch lying flat on his face, with his feet a yard inside the penalty area. I can see Young's despairing gesture as if he would disclaim all intention of a wilful foul, and the referee's inexorable finger. The hushed silence could be felt.

Mutch rose slowly, helped by colleagues. There was a noticeable pause of a few seconds. Who would take the kick? The ball was on the spot. Mutch shook his head as if partly dazed.

Then the Preston inside right turned, took a six-yards run, and the ball hit the roof of the net as Hesford flung up his arms.

A foot higher and the shot would have gone over the bar. It wasn't a workmanlike shot – but it served, and Preston won the Cup with only 15 seconds to spare to save 22 tired men the agonies of a replay.

Mutch danced up and down; five Preston players hung on his arms and round his neck. Holdcroft, the green-jerseyed Preston goalkeeper, ran three-quarters of the length of the field to shake Mutch by the hand.

Hesford's reluctant hands picked the ball out of the net, threw it upfield, MacFadyen kicked off once more, and the final whistle went. It was as near as that.

From the Records

Let it first be placed on record that this was the first case of extra time at Wembley, where the Final has been played from 1923 onwards.

The pity of it was that Alfred Young, Huddersfield's outstanding captain and dominating figure of the game, was concerned in the penalty.

As Mutch received the ball, he was outside the penalty area and almost square with Barclay, Huddersfield's inside left, who was lying well back.

Preston's perseverance pays off – captain Smith with the Cup

Mutch ran in, swerved to put Boot out of position, and was a foot or so inside the penalty line when Young, tackling him from the front, thrust out his left leg. Mutch fell as if a steam-hammer had hit him in the back. But his recovery from the physical shock was swift. I was told afterwards that his shake of the head before he took the penalty kick indicated his disagreement with a sympathetic suggestion that he wasn't quite fit!

Other Penalties?

Sitting up in the eyrie allotted to the Press, I would have said that there were two other occasions – and a possible third – when a penalty kick might have been given, one to either side.

The first concerned Hulme, Huddersfield's very capable outside right, who got over his first five minutes' reluctance to come inside when occasion offered and, as I saw it, played as well as any forward on the field.

Hulme and Isaac had combined in one movement in the first half which left Hulme with the ball, running inwards at an angle from which he had scored many goals in his Arsenal days.

I thought he delayed his shot a second and when he did attempt to kick, his legs

were knocked together and he fell inside the penalty area.

Then Watmough, in the first quarter of an hour of extra time, was brought down heavily in a collision with Mountford.

On both these occasions Mr A. J. Jewell, the very excellent referee, saw what happened at close range and did not think the incident justified a penalty kick.

The other 'possible' penalty also came during extra time. Young, with arms full out, threw himself forward to intercept a centre from the left wing and appeared to strike the ball with his fists. In this case, I do not think Mr Jewell could see what happened.

Nerves and a blustering cross-wind played their part in this Final. I should say one record was established – the number of times the ball was out of play. Even Andrew Beattie, Scotland's left back, cool, calculating and methodical, fluffed some of his clearances. And Holdcroft, in the Preston goal, gave his supporters a heart attack every time the ball crossed his front. He failed badly in his timing – or did the wind give the ball an unexpected swerve?

Four Real Shots

Two of the only four shots worth the name

The King meets the Huddersfield team

in the match – except the penalty goal – came from Huddersfield's outside left, Beasley. He took one cross from Hulme, ran in, and hit a fast, deceptive shot to Holdcroft's left, which the goalkeeper just reached with his extended left hand. Beasley's other scoring effort was in the last quarter of an hour in extra time, as it was tipped over the bar by Holdcroft.

It was a game primarily of defences. Actually the first shot to trouble a goalkeeper came in the 36th minute, a left-foot hook shot by Isaac, Huddersfield's quite capable inside right.

But the drama of the finish made up for much that was drab and colourless in the preceding two hours' play.

Preston in their last-chance conference before the start of extra time

Cup Final Hymn

Sir,
The hymn *Abide With Me* has no doubt brought solace to thousands in times of trouble, but I am sure I am not alone in thinking it unsuitable for such an occasion as the Cup Final.

The passages 'fast falls the Eventide' and 'change and decay in all around I see' cast a note of gloom on this sporting event.

S.W.K.
Cobham, Kent

Unforgettable Moment

Sir,
It is impossible to understand why your 'religiously minded' correspondent objects to the singing of *Abide With Me* at the Cup Final. Many who have joined in this hymn at Wembley have assured me it was one of the great and unforgettable moments of their lives.

The good influence on those who sing and hear such hymns 'even at a football match' can never be fully estimated.

E. T. Airey,
Lytham, Lancs

PORTSMOUTH 4
WOLVERHAMPTON WANDERERS 1

ATTENDANCE
99 370

REFEREE
T. Thompson (Lemington-on-Tyne)

GOALSCORERS
Barlow (2), Anderson, Parker, Dorsett

TEAMS

Portsmouth	Wolverhampton Wanderers
Walker	Scott
Morgan	Morris
Rochford	Taylor
Guthrie	Galley
Rowe	Cullis
Wharton	Gardiner
Worrall	Burton
McAlinden	McIntosh
Anderson	Westcott
Barlow	Dorsett
Parker	Maguire

THE ROAD TO THE FINAL

Portsmouth
4th round
v West Bromwich Albion 2–0 (h)
5th round
v West Ham United 2–0 (h)
6th round
v Preston North End 1–0 (h)
Semi-Final
v Huddersfield Town 2–1

Wolverhampton Wanderers
4th round
v Leicester City 5–1 (h)
5th round
v Liverpool 4–1 (h)
6th round
v Everton 2–0 (h)
Semi-Final
v Grimsby Town 5–0

New Standard of Cup Football by Portsmouth

Walker, Portsmouth's goalkeeper, under pressure from the Wanderers' attack

PORTSMOUTH SET UP a new standard of Cup Final football in defeating – overwhelming is a more complete word – Wolverhampton Wanderers at Wembley before the King and Queen on Saturday. Their calm, unhurried style, their precise methods, their accuracy and, above all, their teamwork were magnificent.

Wolverhampton struck me as being either stale or nervy – or both. But the comparative failure of this wonder team of 1938–39 should not take one tittle from the splendour and completeness of Portsmouth's triumph.

The fourth goal to Portsmouth and the last of the match came in the 23rd minute of the second half. If the winners had not taken matters in more leisurely style after this I believe they could have set up a Wembley goal record that would have taken some beating.

Picture of Game

The only period in which Wolverhampton made a semblance of the fight which their supporters expected of them was in the first ten minutes of the second half, when they were three goals down. That Portsmouth lost the initiative just for this brief space gives a cameo picture of the game as a whole. It may be significant that in their previous Cup ties Wolverhampton had never been behind.

The writing was on the wall when Barlow – a Wolverhampton player until this year – scored Portsmouth's first goal in the 31st minute. It became plainly visible when Anderson put through the second less than two minutes before the interval.

Barlow's goal was beautifully clear cut. Guthrie, Portsmouth's captain and a keen, swift-tackling half back if occasionally a little over-vigorous, pushed the ball forward to Anderson, who veered to the right, drew Cullis and Taylor away from the goalmouth, and then passed cleverly to Barlow. The inside left placed a rising ball with pace and accuracy beyond Scott's reach.

Misunderstanding

Anderson's success had no such sharp outline. Whether there was a mis-understanding between Cullis and the other defenders I cannot say, but when Worrall, a prince among right wing men, put over a fairly high ball, Cullis seemed to time his interception wrongly. Anyhow, he was beaten by the bounce, and Ander-son had the ball on his foot, knee-high from the ground, when Scott lunged for

Guthrie, Portsmouth's captain, is chaired off the field with the cup

it, missed, and the ball went into goal.

The third goal, 30 seconds after the interval, was the sequel to a combination of Wolverhampton mistakes. Galley back-heeled the ball near the half-way line, but Morris could not reach it, and Parker (a brilliant opportunist on this day of days) nipped in and passed squarely to Barlow. The inside left shot without punch – and nobody favouring Wolverhampton saw any cause for anxiety.

But Scott failed to get his body in line with the ball. He shot out his right hand, fumbled it, fell, and grabbed the ball again as it reached the white line. There ball and goalkeeper remained for an appreci-able second. Then up dashed Parker and kicked the ball into the back of the net from under Scott's hand.

Dorsett Scores

Wolverhampton's one and only rally fol-lowed this. With nothing to lose that was not already lost, Cullis tried to infuse life into his forward line by coming through with the ball. It was a Cullis pass that sent the ball into the Portsmouth penalty area and a cross from the right that came to the feet of sharp-shooting Dorsett. A very good shot indeed beat Walker, who,

Young Portsmouth supporters in merry mood

in this game, was as confident and cool and competent as the rest of his team-mates.

Portsmouth's final goal was the best of the bunch. The admirable Worrall sent

That Cup Final feeling . . .

'Plane Engine Failed over Cup Crowd

A woman pilot was cruising above the 100 000 crowd which watched the Cup Final at Wembley on Saturday when her 'plane developed engine trouble. It began to lose height – however, she managed to make a safe landing on Sudbury Golf Course.

over a centre of such accuracy that Parker, near the far post, ran in and completed the movement with his head and with such perfect timing that the Wolverhampton defence might have been foot-tied.

Altogether a new and strange but completely admirable Portsmouth, who played football that won them the high esteem of an ungrudging crowd. Mr T. Thompson's control of the game was a fine example of the manner in which a first-class referee gets into the best position to give a prompt and unassailable decision.

Wife will Break Her Vow and See Cup Final

A young wife, who vowed a year ago never to watch another football match, has changed her mind. She will travel from Lemington-on-Tyne to Wembley to see her husband, Mr Thomas Thompson, referee the Cup Final.

A year ago she saw her husband knocked unconscious when struck by the ball during a Cup tie. It was then she determined never again to enter a football ground. But now – well, it's the Cup Final, and her husband is refereeing it.

'I couldn't miss that match, whatever happened,' she said. 'Usually when Tommy goes to London I travel with him and spend the day looking at the shops, but this time I shall be watching him.'

Mr Thompson was chosen as Cup Final referee on his 36th birthday. He is chief clerk to an insurance firm in Newcastle upon Tyne. He will choose a medal instead of a fee for his services at Wembley.

'I think a successful referee is made in the home,' he said. 'Each week when I come back from a match I leave my black bag in the hall. The next Friday it is there again, in the same position, with everything ready for me. My wife sees that I start off in a good temper, and that probably has a lot to do with it.'

1940 TO 1946

The War Years

An overall view of play during the Chelsea v Millwall match. Note the absence of photographers!

AFTER HOSTILITIES WERE declared in 1939, it proved very difficult to continue the FA Cup in its usual form, a state of affairs that continued throughout the war years. Many of the players had been called up to serve overseas, while those remaining in the UK were often not near enough to their home grounds either to train or to play. Furthermore, petrol shortages and public transport difficulties made the idea of travelling right across the country to play away games less than practical.

Wembley Stadium itself was not in a position to be used as a Cup Final venue. Troops were often billeted in the area around the stadium, and it was considered unwise – indeed, dangerous – to assemble a large crowd of spectators while London was still open to attack by air.

Some so-called 'Cup Final' matches were played during the war, but they were designated unofficial and so no records appear in the official football archives for these years. Portsmouth, the last team officially to have won the Cup Final before the war, was therefore able to hold on to the title for six years.

Instead, 'Victory Matches', as they were known, were occasionally held between teams such as the Metropolitan Police and Civil Defence groups, and fund-raising matches were sometimes played to raise money for the war effort.

Many clubs did not participate in the Football League for much of the war, and so were not available to take part in FA Cup-type tournaments. Aston Villa, for example, did not play from 1939/40 to 1941/42; Sunderland did not play in 1939/40 or 1940/41, and Wolverhampton Wanderers did not play in the 1940–1 season.

Interestingly, however, the teams which did gain honours in the war years were very often those which had been at the top before the outbreak of hostilities, despite

Bartram, the Millwall keeper, leaps out to save the ball

scratch practice and the 'guest player' system, which allowed players to play for a team near their wartime base. Talent will out?

The dangers of wartime Britain – bombs and doodlebugs – did not prevent either the Royal Family or VIPs from attending football finals where possible. In 1944, the Supreme Allied Commander, General Eisenhower, was guest of honour at the League South Cup Final. And as the match took place just before D-Day, there were plenty of American servicemen in the crowd that afternoon. The following year, King George VI, the Queen and Princess Elizabeth all attended the League South Cup Final, which Chelsea won.

The pictures on these pages are all from the 1945 League South Cup Final, in which Chelsea beat Millwall 2–0.

A mighty punch for Chelsea's goalkeeper

1947

CHARLTON ATHLETIC 1
BURNLEY 0
(after extra time)

'I Heard the Winner Whizzing past Me'

Bartram, Charlton's goalkeeper, punches the ball clear from a Burnley attack

LONG AFTER THE other memories of the 1947 Cup Final have faded, I shall remember two men in the moment of their triumph.

The one who sat alone among the 99 000 people; the other, standing motionless, unbelieving, his hands raised high, while the Wembley Roar told the world that Charlton had won the Cup.

The man who directed the triumph, Jimmy Seed, spent the match sitting alone on a chair by the touch-line. He never gave a sign of the terrific nerve-strain of watching his team battling for victory in the greatest of all soccer occasions until the goal was scored.

Then he stood up, clapped his hands once, and quickly sat down as if slightly ashamed of displaying his emotion!

The man whose right foot brought the victory, little Chris Duffy, provided an unforgettable picture.

For what seemed seconds after he had crashed in a picture goal he made no move. Then, as the roar of the crowd seemed to pierce his dazed bewilderment, Duffy wheeled in a full circle and ran 40 yards straight into the arms of Shreeve, with the rest of the Charlton team streaming after him. For a few seconds they clutched each other in the excitement of the moment, while the rest of the team patted and pummelled their appreciation.

How Goal Came

Let Don Welsh, the Charlton skipper, complete the story of the goal which brought the Cup back to London after 11 years, and has given Charlton the trophy for the first time ever: 'Centre forward Billy Robinson veered out to the right and crossed the ball hard,' said Welsh. 'I went up and my head diverted it to the left. Before I could turn round I heard the ball whizz past me into the net.'

With only six minutes left for play in extra time, Duffy had volleyed in a superb goal.

Were Charlton lucky? Maybe. Yet they did get the ball into the net. Burnley could have made sure early on, but the nearest they got to scoring was a terrific drive from Potts which struck the cross-bar.

The goal-line clearance for Charlton by 'new boy' Whittaker was evened up when Mather, at the other end, kicked away a Dawson header with his goalkeeper beaten.

Superb Defence

It wasn't a great match, yet the thrills came in plenty. As I figured, it developed into a battle of defences, with the Charlton rear-guard standing supreme. The Charlton forwards had fewer chances, but they always looked slightly more dangerous than the Burnley line.

Wembley nerves beat Morris and Harrison; they failed with gilt-edged chances, which would have been taken in a League match. A different story might have been written had they forgotten the place and the setting.

The Charlton defence, which carried the side through to the Final, I cannot fault. Phipps, Croker and Johnson were

Good Morning! A Comment from the Editor

The Cup Final today will be the first of these great contests between a London and a Lancashire club since the original Wembley Final of 1923.

It will be the first really normal Cup Final since all the boys came marching home from the wars.

At least 10 000 fans will come from Burnley to see it; probably an even greater number from the north in general. We welcome these determined pilgrims to our city, wish them fine weather, and a grand match.

We think it splendid that, in spite of hard times, hard taxes and hard transport troubles, they have made the journey to 'follow their favourites', and see the greatest game in the United Kingdom.

If the fine Charlton team win, we in London shall be proud.

But if the famous Burnley team take the honours, we here will be equally pleased to hail them.

Five steps to triumph ...

WELSH HEADS ...

DUFFY'S THERE ...

... HE SHOOTS

"IT'S A GOAL!"

perhaps outstanding; Bartram made two typical saves; Shreeve was never flurried, while young Billy Whittaker, after being nursed for the first half-hour, did a grand job.

Croker was Master

An extra word for Croker. He not only

Charlton's captain, Welsh, holds the Cup aloft

played England left winger Peter Kippax out of the game, but showed the class that stamps him as a coming international. He was never in trouble, and his positional play rendered ineffective the speed of his immediate opponent.

Duffy was the best Charlton forward. His wriggling, crab-like runs always spelled danger. Billy Robinson gave Alan Brown an unsettling match, and the surprise was the number of times he beat Brown in the air.

It was this which often shook the hith-

erto almost impregnable Burnley defence. The fair-haired Woodruff played a sound game, while Attwell gave Welsh very little room. The energetic Harrison was good, except for his finishing.

Morris supplied one of the best flashes of football in the game when body-swerving his way into the Charlton penalty area past two men, but then he spoiled what would have been a picture goal by passing tamely.

That really sums up the Burnley forwards. They knew what they had to do, but very rarely did it.

The Wembley Ball

Ask any one of the 99 000 spectators at today's Wembley Cup Final 'What is the most important thing in the function?' ... and then fill up a large notebook with the variety of answers received.

Here are a few lines of thought ... the players, the pitch, the referee, the presence of royalty, the police control of traffic, the speed with which the Stadium is cleared after the game, and so on.

First Thrilling Kick

My vote goes to a small detail which ensures the match being played – the piece of animated cowhide known as the ball!

Bright yellow, standing out clearly on the vivid green Cumberland turf which is Wembley's pride, it waits for the first kick at 3 o'clock this afternoon which will start the 1947 FA Cup Final.

The ball is one of a number submitted by manufacturers for selection. Like its fellows, there is no mark to distinguish it from the next. After inspection at the FA offices at Lancaster Gate, a number are taken to Wembley, and then the referee takes over. Today it is Mr J. M. Wiltshire of Sherborne, Dorset.

In his dressing-room under the giant west banking, the referee, after first examining the pitch and cocking an eye at the weather conditions, will make his choice from the number of footballs he has been given.

That is the ball which gains for the manufacturer the coveted stamp of 'Used in the 1947 Cup Final'. His representative is not told until after the game – but the expert knows whether it is his ball the moment it appears under the arm of the referee as he

emerges from the gloom of the tunnel to the roar of the giant crowd.

Item 2 in the FA laws of the game gives this definition of the football used in first-class matches:

'The ball shall be spherical; the outer casing shall be leather, and no material shall be used in its construction which might prove dangerous to the players. The circumference of the ball shall not be more than 28 ins, nor less than 27 ins. The weight of the ball at the start of the game shall not be more than 16 ounces, nor less than 14 ounces.'

Million-to-One Burst

Incidentally, the referee makes his choice (assisted by his two linesmen) entirely by his hands, from the bounce and feel of the ball.

A few hours before last season's Cup Final the chosen referee, in a broadcast, declared it was 1 000 000 to 1 against a ball bursting in the Cup Final. The huge odds were defeated, for the ball used in the Derby County v Charlton match burst 30 seconds from full time!

An impression of the scene when Duffy, scorer of the winning goal, 'ran away' from congratulations

MANCHESTER UNITED 4
BLACKPOOL 2

ATTENDANCE
99 000

REFEREE
C. J. Barrick (Northampton)

GOALSCORERS
Rowley (2), Pearson, Anderson
Shimwell, Mortensen

TEAMS

Manchester United	Blackpool
Crompton	Robinson
Carey	Shimwell
Aston	Crosland
Anderson	Johnston
Chilton	Hayward
Cockburn	Kelly
Delaney	Matthews
Morris	Munro
Rowley	Mortensen
Pearson	Dick
Mitten	Rickett

THE ROAD TO THE FINAL

Manchester United
4th round
v Liverpool 3–0 (h)
5th round
v Charlton Athletic 2–0 (h)
6th round
v Preston North End 4–1 (h)
Semi-Final
v Derby County 3–1

Blackpool
4th round
v Chester 4–0 (h)
5th round
v Colchester 5–0 (h)
6th round
v Fulham 2–0 (a)
Semi-Final
v Tottenham Hotspur 3–1

Cup was Won by a Save at the Other End

Shimwell gets the first blood for Blackpool

IT IS MIDNIGHT. The Blackpool team's Cup Final dinner at a London hotel is near its end. The losers have been congratulated; the players have forgotten their first sharp disappointment. Stanley Mortensen, whose dynamic display did so much towards nearly winning the Cup for Blackpool, turned to me suddenly and said: 'If I had shot the ball into the crowd instead of to the goalkeeper, the score would still have been 2–2 – and we might not have lost!'

Mortensen was recalling the dramatic moment when, with only 11 minutes to go, he impudently stole the ball from Chilton, streaked on, and crashed a shot wide to the right of Crompton. A magnificent save by the United goalkeeper, a quick clearance to Anderson, a short pass to Pearson, and United had won the Cup.

It all happened so quickly that when Pearson's shot entered the Blackpool net Mortensen was still walking out of the United penalty area!

Secret of Delaney

That was the turning point of one of the finest football matches I have ever seen. And the reason for this magnificence? Both teams went on to the Wembley turf with the same instructions: 'Play football, take your chances, but if you lose, then lose by playing football.' How well the men obeyed will long remain in the memories of the 99 000 privileged to watch this soccer feast.

So much happened in this Final that it is difficult to set down all the highlights. Perhaps the drama of the goals made it outstanding, so here is the story of them, told by the central figures:

1. (12 minutes). The referee unhesitatingly whistled for a penalty as Mortensen was brought down by Chilton. Said the official: 'I was behind the play, but was certain

The first of United's four goals on its way to the net

that Mortensen was in the area when he was tackled. I did not consult my linesman, but looked to him for confirmation. His flag pointed to the spot.' **Shimwell** scored. Blackpool led 1–0.

2. (28 minutes). Blackpool's centre half, Hayward, describing it: 'Delaney's lob floated over my head as my goalkeeper Robinson called "Right". I felt **Rowley** flash past me. He hooked the ball out of Robinson's hands, and dribbled into the empty net.' Score 1–1.

3. (35 minutes). Kelly's version: 'I headed forward Matthews' quickly-taken free kick. **Mortensen**, like a flash, picked up the pass, turned in his stride and hit the ball to the opposite corner.' Blackpool ahead 2–1.

Wearing Hats

Sir,
A gentle hint might be given to spectators not to wear trilby hats at the Cup Final. For the not-so-tall man who has to stand behind, two-thirds of the pitch is blotted out. I've heard it said that in Scotland the offending hats would be forcibly removed. Alas, we poor English!

S. Lyon
Manchester

MANCHESTER UNITED WEMBLEY

v. CHARLTON → v. PRESTON → v. DERBY →

4. (69 minutes). **Rowley**, scorer of a great goal, said this: 'I saw Morris's free kick soaring between two Blackpool defenders, thought "this is it" and dived forward to head the ball into the net by the far post.' Score 2–2.

5. (79 minutes). **Pearson**, the scorer: 'Anderson's through pass was a beauty. All I had to do was run on and score, but I placed the ball so far away from the goalkeeper that for a second I thought it was going outside. But it hit the inside of the post and rolled across to the opposite corner of the goal.' Manchester in front for the first time, 3–2.

6. (83 minutes). Blackpool skipper Johnston saw the last goal like this: '**Anderson's** 30-yard lob appeared to be covered by our goalkeeper, but the ball struck Kelly's head and was deflected away from the goalkeeper.' Result, 4–2.

Blackpool must consider themselves unlucky after leading twice. After a breathless first half, during which the ball flashed backwards and forwards in table tennis fashion, Blackpool were definitely the better side for the first 20 minutes of the second half.

It was a match without a failure. None played below normal club form. Several rose above it. A special word for Crosland, who, playing out of position in his first Cup-tie, did so well that he is obviously one of the season's discoveries. He played Delaney cleanly and coolly, and gave no indication of Wembley nerves. His only worry, he told me, was that he might let the rest of the team down. He didn't.

Rowley equalises for Manchester in the 28th minute

Two Guinea Cup Seats – £16 and Nylons

The Cup Final crowds from the north were pouring into London in the early hours today, beribboned and wearing their teams' colours in rosettes of all sizes. First of the special trains from Lancashire arrived at Euston shortly after midnight, and the fans began the usual search for refreshments.

Everyone was cheery. It was certain that the Cup would go north.

Two guinea tickets for the Final were fetching up to £16 last night, as frenzied bids jumped the price of the black market route to Wembley. Lower price tickets changed hands at ten times their value.

In the towns of the finalists – Manchester United and Blackpool – spivs had one of their best days.

A man from Belfast offered a pair of nylons in addition to the over the odds price for every Wembley ticket offered to him. Ticket touts worked the stations as the first of 31 special trains left for London.

Hundred of coaches were Wembley-bound before midnight. For this all-Lancashire Final there will be more than 40 000 visitors from the north among the 100 000 crowd.

Happiest Blackpool supporter yesterday was Miss Peggy Hargreaves, who stepped aboard the London train with Mrs Stanley Matthews, wife of the Blackpool right winger.

Peggy had only just heard that her boyfriend, Johnny Crosland, 25, former Fleet Air Arm pilot, who won his DSC against the Japs, is to play in the Final.

Crosland, who was unable to train with the team regularly because he is studying for his finals as an accountant, is replacing the injured Stuart at left back.

How they got there – the *Daily Mail's* view

1949

WOLVERHAMPTON WANDERERS 3
LEICESTER CITY 1

ATTENDANCE
99 500

REFEREE
R. A. Mortimer (Huddersfield)

GOALSCORERS
Pye (2), Smyth
Griffiths

TEAMS

Wolverhampton Wanderers	Leicester City
Williams	Bradley
Pritchard	Jelly
Springthorpe	Scott
Crook	W. Harrison
Shorthouse	Plummer
Wright	King
Hancocks	Griffiths
Smyth	Lee
Pye	J. Harrison
Dunn	Chisholm
Mullen	Adam

THE ROAD TO THE FINAL

Wolverhampton Wanderers
4th round
v Sheffield United 3–0 (h)
5th round
v Liverpool 3–1 (h)
6th round
v West Bromwich Albion 1–0 (h)
Semi-Final
v Manchester United 1–1
Replay 1–0

Leicester City
4th round
v Preston North End 2–0 (h)
5th round
v Luton Town 5–5 (h)
Replay 5–3 (a)
6th round
v Brentford 2–0 (h)
Semi-Final
v Portsmouth 3–1

Men in the Middle Tell Cup Crisis Story

Bradley punches out this Hancocks corner kick, but a second later Pye had slipped the ball into the net

LEICESTER CITY LOST the chance of possible Cup victory by a yard. That was the distance Ken Chisholm was offside when he scored what would have been an equalising goal against Wolverhampton Wanderers in the 22nd minute of the second half at Wembley. Leicester, two down at half time, and apparently well beaten, pulled a goal back immediately after the restart and not only regained a firm grip on the game everybody thought was all over, but got on top.

The determination and fire restored by Griffiths' goal shook Wolves out of their calm, cool demolition of the City defence.

Offside ... but Only Just

Then, with the Wolves defence completely entangled – Williams was out of his goal, and even Billy Wright was caught out of position – Leicester right winger Griffiths lifted a beautiful ball over the head of a Wolves defender.

Victorious – Billy Wright, Wolves' captain

Billy Wright meets the Duke of Edinburgh before the match

Chisholm was there, and on the instant, smacked the ball from an acute angle across and into the net to raise the biggest cheer of the day. The Leicester players excitedly pounded their congratulations on Chisholm's broad back. But they could not see the drama being enacted behind them.

The referee, who was bang up with the play, was pointing not for a goal but for an offside kick to the Wolves.

It was the correct, and instantly made, decision. Chisholm was offside . . . but only just.

Realise the meaning of this hair-line decision. If the burly young Scot had been

one stride farther away from the Wolves goal, Leicester would have been level, and with every chance of winning.

Terribly Disappointed

The usually smiling Chisholm was terribly disappointed when I spoke to him afterwards. 'You can imagine how I felt,' he said. 'Naturally, I accepted the referee's decision, but I feel that when Mal hooked the ball to me it must have been slightly deflected when a Wolves player tried to head it, because as I saw the ball coming, I shaped to "kill" it with my left foot. Instead, it changed direction slightly and I had to drag it forward with my right foot before I could shoot.'

Upset though the Leicester players were, there was no protest to the referee – striking commentary on the magnificent sportsmanship of both sides throughout the match.

Bewildered by Congratulations

The final blow to Leicester came a minute later, when the flame-haired Irishman Sammy Smyth wove his way through to score perhaps the finest goal ever seen at Wembley. This made the score 3–1, and finished the game as a contest.

Picking up the ball after it had been partially cleared, Smyth coolly dribbled 50 yards upfield, evaded three tackles, touched the ball only three times, and leisurely cracked it into the net past the oncoming Bradley.

Still a little bewildered by the many congratulations he had received when I spoke to him later, Smyth confessed: 'I just went on and on, and the Leicester defenders fell away from me.'

Leicester battled pluckily on, but most of their regained punch and confidence had been knocked out of them. Indeed, Wolves nearly scored another when Pye hooked over a great cross from Hancocks.

Wolves Fix Age Limit

Wolverhampton Wanderers will sell Cup Final tickets on Monday only to people over 18 years old.

Reason: 'The youngsters have more time to see future matches,' say Club officials.

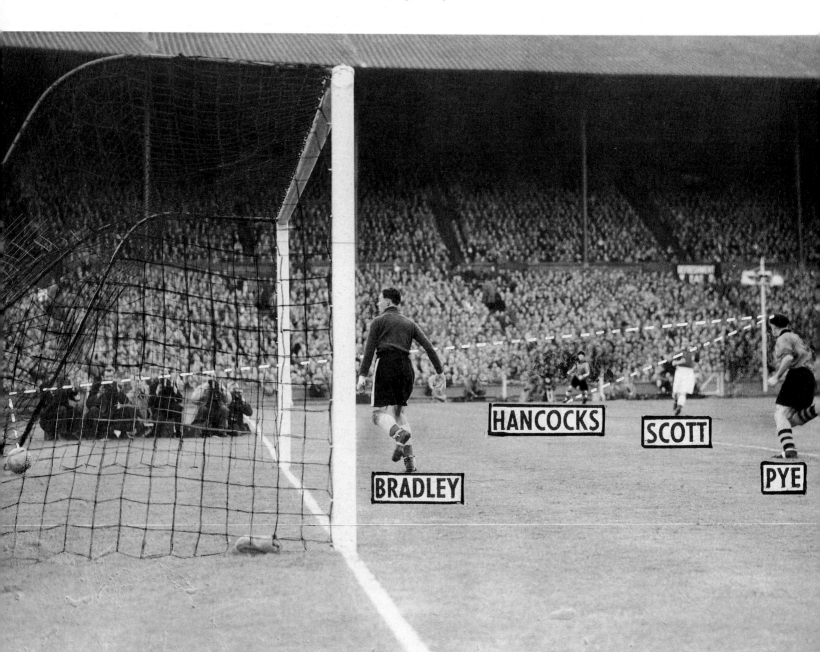

The route to Wolves' first goal

1950

ARSENAL 2
LIVERPOOL 0

ATTENDANCE
100 000

REFEREE
H. Pearce (Luton)

GOALSCORER
Lewis (2)

TEAMS

Arsenal	Liverpool
Swindin	Sidlow
Scott	Lambert
Barnes	Spicer
Forbes	Taylor
L. Compton	Hughes
Mercer	Jones
Cox	Payne
Logie	Barron
Goring	Stubbins
Lewis	Fagan
D. Compton	Liddell

THE ROAD TO THE FINAL

Arsenal
4th round
v Swansea 2–1 (h)
5th round
v Burnley 2–0 (h)
6th round
v Leeds United 1–0 (h)
Semi-Final
v Chelsea 2–2
Replay 1–0

Liverpool
4th round
v Exeter 3–1 (h)
5th round
v Stockport County 2–1 (a)
6th round
v Blackpool 2–1 (h)
Semi-Final
v Everton 2–0

A Wembley Classic

Swindin makes a save on the goal-line from a shot by Payne

THAT IRON CURTAIN defence slipped once or twice, but I always had the feeling that, if Liverpool did score, Arsenal would always score one more.

Both their goals, to which Liverpool could make no reply, were brilliantly taken, with the first, all-important effort ranking among the Wembley classics. Here's the flashback to that electric moment when the ice-cool Reg Lewis wrote Arsenal's name on the trophy:

Eighteen minutes had gone, Liverpool having had the bulk of play, but with Arsenal showing signs of settling down to a steady rhythm. Hughes cleared upfield – a long, inconsequential kick which Leslie Compton's head effortlessly flicked sideways to Barnes, as Stubbins came boring in. The back neatly placed the ball upfield to Logie, then occupying the inside left position. As the wee man diddled the ball between his feet to kill the spin, Goring moved away from the middle, taking Hughes with him. Then, like a flash, the ball sped through the defence, at the instant Lewis strode forward. Taking the perfect pass, and two more strides, Lewis slipped the ball smoothly past the helpless

Sidlow's left hand and wheeled away on the other side.

The goal bore all the hallmarks of being schemed in the Highbury back room. Moves earnestly planned and carried out, plus fighting team spirit, won the Cup.

Beaten Back

What went wrong with Liverpool? The unexpected speed of the Arsenal forwards and their accuracy in passing; the ability of every Arsenal player to make the ball do the work; the magnificent covering by an often overrun Arsenal defence; a sterling half back line in which Alex Forbes played a starring role – it was all too much for Liverpool.

Their inside forwards at times played so far back that their partners needed binoculars to spot them.

Laurie Hughes, under review as England's newly elected centre half, created a favourable impression against the vastly improved, intelligent and quick-moving Goring. The youngster played a great game and ranked high, with Logie, behind Alex Forbes – the first perpetual motion machine I have seen with red hair.

Joe Mercer chaired by his Arsenal team-mates

50 000 Cheer Cup Losers

Thirty people – mostly women – were hurt last night when a cheering crowd of 50 000 broke the police cordon outside Liverpool Town Hall, during a civic reception for the city's beaten Cup team.

The council chamber was used as a first aid station. Tea and sandwiches, intended for the reception, were given to the casualties.

A word to Swindin for his magnificent courage and anticipation, to Barnes, Scott, and Leslie Compton for rarely losing their positions; to Cox and Denis Compton for their contribution to the general triumph.

To Reg Lewis deservedly went the honour of scoring both goals. Each was taken coolly and well, and Sidlow had no possible chance. The second, 27 minutes from time, followed a long oblique pass by Goring, out on the left wing.

Cox, with his back to goal, flicked the

Henry Pearce, the 43-year-old Luton referee in charge

FACES IN THE WEMBLEY PICTURE—by ROSS

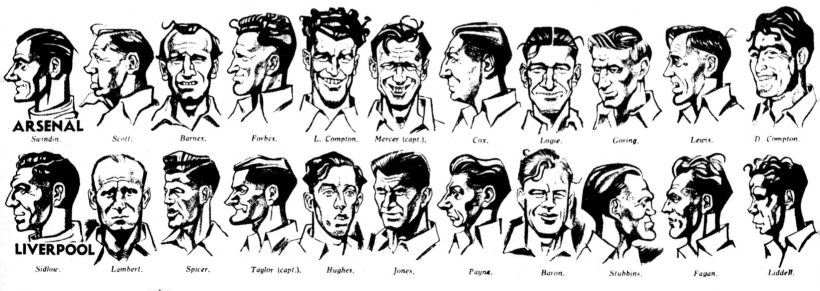

ARSENAL

Swindin.   Scott.   Barnes.   Forbes.   L. Compton.   Mercer (capt.).   Cox.   Logie.   Goring.   Lewis.   D. Compton.

LIVERPOOL

Sidlow.   Lambert.   Spicer.   Taylor (capt.).   Hughes.   Jones.   Payne.   Baron.   Stubbins.   Fagan.   Liddell.

ball past Spicer, and Lewis, shooting from the right of the penalty spot and about the same distance out, cracked low and hard into the near corner.

Taylor's Pluck

Second to Hughes on the Liverpool side I made skipper Phil Taylor, who throughout the match played the polished, cultured football we expected from him. And what a magnificent gesture when he returned to the field ten minutes from time, after being completely knocked out! Still clutching a sponge to dab away the blood from his battered nose, Taylor refused the signalled suggestion of a colleague that he should go on to the wing to recover.

Instead, he led his troops forward in one of those desperate sorties on the Arsenal goal which supplied such a thrilling close to Arsenal's third Cup triumph at Wembley.

Arsenal Firsts

Arsenal are the first club to reach Wembley without playing out of their own city, and the first to allow their players to spend the night before the Final at home.

Denis had His Final Fling – and It was Memorable

Arsenal, holding a 1–0 interval lead, are filing out of the dressing room at Wembley to resume the battle with Liverpool. Manager Tom Whittaker pulls aside the last player, Denis Compton, and says: 'You've probably got only 45 minutes left in first-class football. Give all you've got, even if it means falling flat on your face at the end.'

Away went Denis for his swansong in the April showers, to play in the second half as well as he has ever played in his life, after being comparatively unnoticed in the first.

All being well he will be on the cricket tour of Australia next winter – and he will be 32 this month.

Wife's Tears of Joy

It was sad that the person Denis most wanted as spectator at Wembley, his wife Doris, could not be there. She stayed at home with their eight-year-old son Brian, who had been suddenly taken ill with influenza. Together they listened to the match broadcast.

Mrs Compton told me that only when she heard the commentator say that the Arsenal players were hoisting skipper Joe Mercer on to their shoulders, did she realise that her husband's team had won the Cup. The tears started to roll down her face.

Young Brian said: 'Mummy, why are you crying?' Doris said: 'I always cry when I'm happy.'

The closing memory of Denis's 'last game' – he may play against Portsmouth at Highbury on Wednesday – is a peep at the brotherly comradeship existing between him and his elder brother Leslie (38 next September). As the Arsenal players moved into position to go to receive the trophy and medals from the Royal Family, Leslie pushed Denis forward, leaving himself last in line.

'Did your brother say anything?' I asked. And Denis replied: 'No, he was there behind me, as he has been all my life!' What a tribute each paid the other.

The Cup comes home to North London. Note the floral tribute on the coachfront!

1951

NEWCASTLE UNITED 2
BLACKPOOL 0

ATTENDANCE
100 000

REFEREE
W. Ling (Cambridge)

GOALSCORER
Milburn (2)

TEAMS

Newcastle United	Blackpool
Fairbrother	Farm
Cowell	Shimwell
Corbett	Garrett
Harvey	Johnston
Brennan	Hayward
Crowe	Kelly
Walker	Matthews
Taylor	Mudie
Milburn	Mortensen
Robledo	Slater
Mitchell	Perry

THE ROAD TO THE FINAL

Newcastle United
4th round
v Bolton Wanderers 3–2 (h)
5th round
v Stoke City 4–2 (a)
6th round
v Bristol Rovers 0–0 (h)
Replay 3–1 (a)
Semi-Final
v Wolverhampton Wanderers 0–0
Replay 2–1

Blackpool
4th round
v Stockport County 2–1 (h)
5th round
v Mansfield Town 2–0 (h)
6th round
v Fulham 1–0 (h)
Semi-Final
v Birmingham City 0–0
Replay 2–1

Milburn Goals that won Cup

Farm dashes out to save from Robledo, Newcastle's inside left

– England To Recall Him For Wembley Cap?

WHAT A DAY was Saturday for Jackie Milburn, Ashington Flyer and Newcastle United centre forward. He more or less framed The Order Of The Day by which Blackpool were beaten 2–0; he scored both the goals; and afterwards at the Cup banquet, he got a broad hint from Mr Arthur Drewry, England's chief selector, that he will be chosen to lead the England forwards against the Argentine on 9 May.

At the Newcastle team conference before the Final, every point for and against both sides had been discussed when up spake Jackie: 'Let's kick the ball about for the first ten minutes to get used to the turf and get rid of the butterflies. Keep the middle blocked to Mortensen, play football – and we are home.'

That is roughly how the game went, with Milburn's two goals in four minutes repeating for the fourth time this season in a Cup-tie, the paralysing, match-winning burst of this great Newcastle team.

Milburn, who has been in the international wilderness since last November, looked every inch the England leader. And it may be that alongside his 6-foot frame against the Argentine will be the 5 foot 4 in of his club-mate, ex-submariner Ernie Taylor.

Ernie looked so small when he was drinking the victory champagne from the

Cup that somebody held his legs, ostensibly to prevent him falling in!

Marksman Matthews

The match was an enthralling duel between two evenly matched sides in the

first half when, often, the players appeared to be moving faster than the ball.

The Newcastle plan of forcing Matthews inside and neutralising the rest of the Blackpool forwards paid handsomely.

Matthews suddenly blossomed as a marksman because his colleagues could not, or would not, get in a shot.

Blackpool kept in the game precariously by their offside tactics, with Newcastle's defence getting tighter and tighter and Milburn always threatening.

Within three minutes of the start of the second half the score could have been 2–2, but was still 0–0. Two minutes later Newcastle were ahead. Blackpool had been caught in their own offside trap. Robledo fought for a ball ten yards inside

Cup Final Contrasts

The *Daily Mail* suggests that the most fateful man-to-man contest at Wembley may be that of Matthews (Blackpool) and Corbett (Newcastle). Magic v Mettle could be the title for this winger v full back duel.

Stanley Matthews, outside right, will offer a defender the choice of at least three different tackles and, while the defender is deciding, will speed away to make a centre or a dreaded dash to the nearest goalpost. At 36, with over 50 England games behind him, this soccer idol is as fast and elusive as ever. Spent 17 seasons with Stoke before joining Blackpool 4 years ago. Runs a hotel and owns the racehorse Parbleu.

Bobby Corbett, left back, may be left wondering by Matthews, but will not be left standing. His speed in recovery makes him a persistent challenger. Cheery Corbett, a former miner, has touched England class this season, after eight years with Newcastle. Surprised himself by two good games as left wing deputy for Mitchell. A pigeon fancier, he travels ten miles a day to feed and exercise his birds.

The King shakes hands with Stanley Matthews before the match

the Blackpool half, pushed it through off Hayward's foot, and Milburn went racing off.

A hundred thousand voices were hushed by the sight of a smoothly travelling Milburn, fastest runner in football, rapidly closing the 50 yard gap with the help of outcoming goalkeeper Farm.

Milburn glanced left to note the running linesman waving him on, and slid the ball past Farm with the sureness of a true-hit putt.

Great Goal

Four minutes later came the goal of the century. Right winger Walker regained on the line a ball he seemed to have lost, tore downfield, and then cut in. A short pass to Taylor, about 25 yards out ... but let the wee Taylor carry on the story: 'Out of the corner of my eye I saw a black and white shirt. I knew it must be Jackie's, so I back-heeled the ball. The next instant I heard the thud of his boot and saw the ball flash past me into the net. What a smasher. I've never seen a shot like it.'

Almost off balance, Milburn had leaned to his right and hooked a tremendous left-foot shot past a helpless goalkeeper. Were Milburn's parents prophetic when they gave him the initials J. E. T.?

Farm, the Blackpool goalkeeper, is floored during an effort to save

Cup Team Defies FA Cloth Cap Ban

Sir Stanley Rouse, Secretary of the Football Association, yesterday wrote to the Cup finalists, Newcastle United and Blackpool, suggesting that cloth caps, the goalkeepers' usual headgear, should not be worn at Wembley.

The FA, he says, would like to see them in white cloth, baseball-type caps with long peaks, and green anti-glare facing. Newcastle object. 'A comic opera touch,' they say, but Blackpool accept. 'Our goalkeeper, George Farm, will definitely wear one,' said Mr Joe Smith, their manager, yesterday.

Jack Fairbrother, Newcastle's goalkeeper, said: 'I could not possibly wear the cap. The long peak blocks out my view of high balls and I believe it would be dangerous to other players.'

His is supported by Mr Stan Seymour, director and acting manager of the club. 'We do not want to go out for football's biggest occasion looking like something out of a comic opera,' he said.

'We have no objection to Fairbrother wearing the cap for the presentation before the game, but whatever the FA say, he will take his ordinary cloth cap out to wear should he need it.'

Newcastle are also asked to wear black stockings instead of black with white tops, to avoid clashing with Blackpool's black with tangerine tops.

Says Mr Seymour: 'We don't want to go into mourning *before* the game.'

1952

NEWCASTLE UNITED 1
ARSENAL 0

ATTENDANCE
100 000

REFEREE
A. E. Ellis (Halifax)

GOALSCORER
G. Robledo

TEAMS

Newcastle United	Arsenal
Simpson	Swindin
Cowell	Barnes
McMichael	Smith
Harvey	Forbes
Brennan	Daniel
E. Robledo	Mercer
Walker	Cox
Foulkes	Logie
Milburn	Holton
G. Robledo	Lishman
Mitchell	Roper

THE ROAD TO THE FINAL

Newcastle United
4th round
v Tottenham Hotspur 3–0 (a)
5th round
v Swansea Town 1–0 (a)
6th round
v Portsmouth 4–2 (a)
Semi-Final
v Blackburn Rovers 0–0
Replay 2–1

Arsenal
4th round
v Barnsley 4–0 (h)
5th round
v Leyton Orient 3–0 (a)
6th round
v Luton Town 3–2 (a)
Semi-Final
v Chelsea 1–1
Replay 1–0

Arsenal Missed Cup by Two Inches

Lishman, the Arsenal centre forward, hooks a shot at goal

ELEVEN MINUTES TO go at Wembley, no score, and ten desperately tired Arsenal players are achieving the impossible – holding the FA Cup holders, Newcastle United, in the Final.

Newcastle centre half Brennan concedes a corner, and every Arsenal player but goalkeeper Swindin, deputy right back Roper and centre half Daniel crowds into the Newcastle penalty area.

Corner kick expert Cox moves across to the left wing to take the kick and sends the ball soaring to the head of unmarked Lishman, who is playing the greatest game of his career. The 100 000 crowd rises as they see what seems momentarily to be an Arsenal goal. But . . .

Newcastle goalkeeper Simpson tells what happened next: 'The ball, hard hit, whistled over my head. I felt tremendous relief as I saw it strike the top edge of the bar and rocket over. Another two inches and it would have been a goal.'

The luck which had been so cruel to Arsenal in the pre-Final period remained perverse for when, five minutes later, the ball struck a post at the other end, it glanced into the net for the only goal of the match. And so Newcastle became the first team to win the Cup in successive years since Blackburn Rovers did it in 1890 and 1891.

The FA have given United permission to take the trophy out of Britain for the first time when they fly next week to tour South Africa.

Off Form

On Saturday's display, in which only their defence, with Cowell and McMichael outstanding, reached normal form, I thought Newcastle slightly lucky to have won. Although against an Arsenal team who lost right back Wally Barnes with torn knee ligaments in the 33rd minute, Newcastle had the more scoring chances, they never looked so well together as the losers, even when the Arsenal were short-handed.

Skipper Harvey said in his banquet speech: 'We did it for the Geordies, the bob-enders who pay our wages.'

The game was scrappy, with the Newcastle forwards never finding their bobbydazzling form, but wondering how long Arsenal's ten men could hold out kept a

Arsenal attempt a shot at goal but Simpson is ready to save

Cup Final not for TV

The Football Association last night decided, finally, that the Newcastle United v Arsenal Cup Final at Wembley today will **not** be televised.

The BBC were also told that, though they would be allowed to take television newsreel pictures of the match, these pictures must not be transmitted until at least 48 hours after the game. Arrangements to have the film specially processed for broadcast tonight have been scrapped.

Forged Tickets

A special force of security officers will mingle with the crowds today, on the lookout for hundreds of forged tickets which the Wembley authorities know to be in circulation. Anyone in possession of one of these tickets stands little chance of being admitted.

A Stadium official said yesterday: 'Every ticket presented will be examined. A forged ticket can be positively identified under scrutiny.

'The police can also take action against anyone selling tickets within a certain distance of the Stadium, and will deal with spivs who attempt to do last minute business.'

thrilling current running through it.

Off the Stage

Perhaps it was as well that the goal came when it did, for Arsenal must have folded up during extra time. Logie and Roper, who moved from outside left to right back, were near collapse at the finish.

But this Arsenal did not walk or limp from the ground. They ran – to the order of Joe Mercer, a skipper who had 'played himself into the ground'.

He said to his players: 'Let's show them we can still stand up – and leave the stage to Newcastle. It's their Cup, and they've earned it.'

Off-Stage

Let me tell you some of the off-stage drama repeated to me: Of Billy Milne, sitting all

Arsenal goalkeeper Swindin saves from a centre; Milburn and Robledo are lurking nearby

Bobby Mitchell: 'I carried on into the penalty area and saw George Robledo perfectly placed beyond the far post.'

George Robledo: 'I shaped to head across to the left-hand side of the goal, but Lionel Smith went up with me so I headed down to the near post.'

Swindlin: 'I had no chance. The ball struck just inside the post low down, and so into the net.'

through the second half in the dressing-room to keep Barnes company. Milne has not seen the end of a game since Easter – Arsenal have always had someone hurt.

Of that great-hearted little gentleman Jimmy Logie, telling me in the dressing-room: 'I'm giving my medal to my pal Tommy Gosling the jockey because, like us today, he was runner-up' (in the 2000 guineas race).

Of Barnes saying: 'Jackie Milburn didn't kick me when he missed his back-heel. I caught my studs in the turf and twisted my leg.'

Of an Arsenal player, telling me: 'None of us blames The Boss for including Logie and Daniel, whose fitness was in doubt. We are glad they played, nobody could have done better.'

Of Mr Whittaker's revelation at the Arsenal banquet: 'Last weekend Stan Mortensen (who was injured in the collision when Ray Daniel broke his wrist) phoned me from Blackpool to say "Don't say anything, but if Ray doesn't play at Wembley he can have one of my two runners-up medals."'

Off a Post

Finally, let's leave the players to tell the story of the goal which was Newcastle's 113th of the season and George Robledo's 39th:

Ted Robledo: 'I picked up the loose ball when Roper collapsed after clearing and slid it to Mitchell ...'

Their Football Trails Lead from Woolongong to Wembley

On to the Wembley turf today will walk two men, leading their teams into the FA Cup Final. Both can claim to be Tynesiders – one by birth, the other by adoption.

Both are former professional footballers who have risen to control two of the greatest clubs in the long history of the sport. And, but for the chance remark of one, the other might not now be in football.

The men are Mr Thomas J. Whittaker, secretary-manager of Arsenal, and Mr Stanley Seymour, vice-chairman and manager of Newcastle United.

Magic Hands

They were once colleagues in the England team which toured Australia in 1925. In a match at Woolongong, New South Wales, Whittaker received an injury which ended his playing days. Useless as a player for the rest of the tour, he assisted the trainer. While massaging Seymour before a game, the Newcastle player remarked, 'What terrific strength you have in your hands, Tom. You ought to take up massage work seriously.'

This stuck in Whittaker's mind. When he was finally given a negative verdict by the doctor he began serious study to fit himself as a trainer. He later came to be known as 'The Man with the Magic Hands'. Five years ago he was appointed manager at Highbury.

The two managers are an interesting study. Seymour, bullet-headed, volatile, who talks with a Geordie's machine-gun delivery; who drives his team on by the sheer force of his personality; who has covered almost every inch of the British Isles, ever seeking to improve the Newcastle team.

Whittaker, although Aldershot born, spent his school and teenage years in Newcastle. He is quieter; a free speaker, but not loquacious; idol of the players, who pull out just that little extra for 'Old Tom'; a top-class photographer; winner of the MBE for secret work as an RAF squadron leader in connection with the D-Day landings.

The two poker-faced friends have spent all week planning the downfall of the other's team. But whoever wins today, you can be certain that the losing manager will be first in the other's dressing-room to offer his congratulations.

--- ATTENDANCE ---
100 000

--- REFEREE ---
B. M. Griffiths (Newport)

--- GOALSCORERS ---
Mortensen (3), Perry
Lofthouse, Moir, Bell

--- TEAMS ---

Blackpool	Bolton Wanderers
Farm	Hanson
Shimwell	Ball
Garrett	Banks
Fenton	Wheeler
Johnston	Barrass
Robinson	Bell
Matthews	Holden
Taylor	Moir
Mortensen	Lofthouse
Mudie	Hassall
Perry	Langton

--- THE ROAD TO THE FINAL ---

Blackpool
4th round
v Huddersfield Town 1–0 (h)
5th round
v Southampton 1–1 (h)
Replay 2–1 (a)
6th round
v Arsenal 2–1 (a)
Semi-Final
v Tottenham Hotspur 2–1

Bolton Wanderers
4th round
v Notts County 1–1 (h)
Replay 2–2 (a)
2nd replay 1–0 (h)
5th round
v Luton Town 1–0 (a)
6th round
v Gateshead 1–0 (a)
Semi-Final
v Everton 4–3

FA Honour Stanley Matthews with Tour Offer

Blackpool's goalkeeper, Farm, clearly not expecting a goal after 90 seconds of play

A TRIBUTE TO one of the finest individual displays ever given by a player will go out this morning to Stanley Matthews from the Football Association. It will take the form of an official invitation to join the touring party who on Thursday leave for South America.

This will follow up the preliminary request made during Blackpool's victory celebrations in London after their dramatic last-minute 4–3 triumph over Bolton Wanderers in the most thrilling Cup Final Wembley has ever staged.

The Final, which looked like going down as the game of 'mystery' goals starting with a sensational Lofthouse goal in 90 seconds, faded and flared and then became 'Matthews' match'.

This was the way of it. In the 23rd minute of the second half Blackpool were 1–3 down to gallant, but slowly fading, Bolton, whose strength was sapped by having to cover up for an injured player. Then Matthews streaked into the Bolton penalty area and crossed the ball which put his team on the way to victory.

His spinning centre to the far post was a few tantalising inches too high for goalkeeper Hanson. He groped and eventually dropped the ball, and Stanley's faithful henchman Mortensen flicked it into the net as he crashed into a goalpost.

From then on, the cards were stacked against Bolton, forced to play a limping cripple, left half Eric Bell, at outside left from the 18th minute.

With left back Banks doubled up with cramp through chasing Matthews and the one-time left wing of Hassall and Langton trying to fill the gap in front of him, the Bolton flank disintegrated against the pressure as the glorious Matthews was sent away time and again by Taylor.

Bolton managed to hold out until two seconds from the end of what, but for constant injury stoppages, would have been full time.

Then yet another Matthews' centre found Mudie, and the whistle shrilled as the inside left was 'sandwiched', eight yards outside the penalty area. Shimwell

One Half Cup Final on Radio

Television will show the whole of today's Cup Final at Wembley – attended by the Queen and the Duke of Edinburgh. But only the second half, beginning at about 3.55 p.m., will be broadcast on sound radio.

In the hope that the FA might allow the preliminaries in the first half to be broadcast also, the BBC kept the period on the Light Programme open until the FA had made their decision.

Blackpool on the attack

started a lumbering run to take the free kick, but switched into the goalmouth at a signal from Mortensen. As he did, Mortensen's free kick blasted into the net through the disorganised defence and it was 3–3, with only injury time to play.

Matthews Magic

Everything Blackpool did in that tremendous spell was touched with the Matthews magic, and once again it worked. From Fenton to Taylor, the ball went, inevitably, to Matthews.

The 'magician' fooled Banks, rolled the ball past Barrass, and Perry crashed it home. As the giant Stadium thundered its tribute, those two great sportsmen from Bolton, Lofthouse and Barrass, stood and applauded the man whose efforts had robbed them of a Cup-winners' medal.

Lofthouse had started the game as though he was going to win it on his own. Ninety seconds after the start, he, in his own words, 'hit the ball from about 20 yards. It swerved, stood up a bit, hit Farm's shoulder ... and was I glad to see it in the net!'

In the 19th minute Lofthouse again roared through and fired in the best shot of the match. The ball crashed against an upright; Shimwell blocked Langton's rebound shot, and then one of six Blackpool feet forced the ball over the goal-line for a corner. Mortensen's version of his 36 minute equaliser: 'I aimed for the far post, and thought the ball might have gone in. But Hassall ran into the line of flight and diverted it into the near corner.'

In the 40th minute Holden beat Fenton and Mudie and passed to Langton. His accurate cross was knocked away from Farm's hands by Moir, and that was No. 2. At half-time Bolton led 2–1.

Safe Custody

Blackpool's allocation of 12 000 Cup Final tickets, sent by train from London, were taken by a patrol car to the police station last night, and kept in a cell.

After ten minutes in the second half came more clever work by Holden, and a beautiful centre. Lofthouse began his take-off, but checked as the injured Bell screamed '*Leave it*, Nat,' and his was the head that sent the ball into the net. So it was 3–1 for Bolton – until the Matthews witchcraft.

Two-Town Freeman Picks Bolton, Piques Blackpool

Piqued because Field Marshal Viscount Montgomery, Freeman of both Bolton and Blackpool, has announced his support of Bolton Wanderers for the FA Cup, Blackpool yesterday invited Mr Churchill to shout for them at the Wembley Final.

Field Marshal Montgomery, now visiting the United States, wrote from the *Queen Mary* when he heard that Bolton Wanderers were in the Final, asking Mr James Entwhistle, the Club Chairman, to tell the players he was looking forward to seeing the Cup in Bolton on his next visit.

Blackpool's Town Clerk, Mr Trevor Jones, cabled him yesterday asking if he had forgotten he was a Freeman of Blackpool.

The Mayor of Blackpool, Councillor Peter Fairhurst, followed up with a telegram to Mr Churchill at 10 Downing Street: 'Understand Field Marshal Montgomery, who is honorary Freeman of Blackpool and Bolton, has promised to support Bolton Wanderers at Cup Final. May we expect you, as Blackpool's most distinguished Freeman, to be shouting for Blackpool?'

Mr Churchill is Blackpool's senior Freeman. Field Marshal Montgomery is Bolton's only surviving Freeman.

This cable was sent to the Field Marshal from the Mayor of Blackpool: 'Understand you have promised support of Bolton Wanderers at Cup Final. May I express the hope that, as an honorary Freeman of Blackpool, we can have your undivided loyalty to both clubs if you are present?'

Mile after mile of cheers as Blackpool bring home the trophy

Blackpool Cup Roar Makes the Tower Shake

The roar that welcomed Blackpool, the Cup winners, home here tonight was enough to make the Tower shake.

An estimated crowd of 200 000 had lined the roads to see the team – and Stanley Matthews – bring back the English Cup.

In Preston, thousands of people – whose team just missed winning the League Championship – also cheered their neighbours. And as the Blackpool team – Harry Johnston, the captain, holding the Cup aloft all the way – reached Blackpool Town Hall after a 30 mile tour from Preston, there were roars of triumph. The band struck up 'We Do Like to be Beside the Seaside'.

Blackpool promenade was packed six deep with cheering men, women and children of all ages.

Some of the players were almost overcome by the welcome. One of them, Tommy Garrett, told me a few minutes later: 'As we sat on the roof of the coach the boys could not hold back a few tears of gladness.

'We were prepared for a big reception, but we never bargained for such a wonderful display of feeling from the public.'

The day had a surprise climax for Tommy. As he stepped from the coach at the Town Hall, he was told that his wife had given birth to a baby daughter today.

The Mayor read telegrams of congratulation to the team from two of Blackpool's Freemen – Sir Winston Churchill and Field Marshal Viscount Montgomery.

1954

WEST BROMWICH ALBION 3

PRESTON NORTH END 2

──── ATTENDANCE ────
100 000

──── REFEREE ────
A. W. Luty (Leeds)

──── GOALSCORERS ────
Allen (2) (1 penalty), Griffin
Morrison, Wayman

──── TEAMS ────

West Bromwich Albion	Preston North End
Sanders	Thompson
Kennedy	Cunningham
Millard	Walton
Dudley	Docherty
Dugdale	Marston
Barlow	Forbes
Griffin	Finney
Ryan	Foster
Allen	Wayman
Nicholls	Baxter
Lee	Morrison

──── THE ROAD TO THE FINAL ────

West Bromwich Albion
4th round
v Rotherham United 4–0 (h)
5th round
v Newcastle United 3–2 (h)
6th round
v Tottenham Hotspur 3–0 (h)
Semi-Final
v Port Vale 2–1

Preston North End
4th round
v Lincoln City 2–0 (a)
5th round
v Ipswich Town 6–1 (h)
6th round
v Leicester City 1–1 (a)
Replay 2–2 (h)
2nd replay 3–1 (a)
Semi-Final
v Sheffield Wednesday 2–0

Divot put Allen on Spot – Skid Shot Drama, then Champagne Finish

WBA's Allen makes no mistake with this penalty kick

RONNIE ALLEN CLUTCHED a glass of champagne in one hand and a gold medal in the other as he lived again one of the most dramatic incidents in the history of the FA Cup.

He described the nerve-wracking moments before he scored only the third penalty to be awarded (and converted) in 26 peace-time Wembley Finals: 'When I went to put the ball on the spot, I found there was a deep rut, caused by someone's heel. I tried to stamp it flat, but only managed to sort of tee the ball up. Just as I was running up to take the kick, Cunningham, the Preston right back, complained that the ball was not on the spot. The referee ordered me to replace it. I spotted it again, right behind the divot mark. Then when I kicked the ball it went smack into the hole and skidded along the grass. For a horrible moment I thought I had muffed it, only to see the ball cannon off Thompson into the net.'

The goal which made the score 2-all and

♛

75

Preston's goalkeeper kneels in defeat after WBA's third goal

Man Gave Away Cup Final Ticket

A car broke down so many times on the journey from Manchester to Wembley that the driver was exhausted at Potters Bar, Middlesex, and gave away his Cup Final ticket.

Left: Even a flying goalkeeper is no match for the Preston equaliser

put West Bromwich back into the game came 18 minutes after half-time.

Justice, They Said

Although there was a doubt about the penalty decision, to Albion fans it was justice, for many considered that their team had been the victims when Preston scored their second goal. Centre forward Wayman seemed offside, but his goal, six minutes after half-time, was allowed by referee Luty. Three of the others involved in the incident give their views:

Ray Barlow: 'I still had control of the ball when I dashed into the area; Docherty came across me and hit me with his body.'

Tommy Docherty: 'Barlow went to jump at me and ran into me. At the worst it should have been an indirect free kick for obstruction.'

Mr Arthur Luty (referee): 'Docherty came straight across Barlow and never intended to play the ball.'

I agree with Docherty. I thought an indirect free kick would have served the purpose, especially as the referee had taken no action when Finney was twice brought down in the penalty area in the first five minutes.

I also fault Mr Luty for what seemed to me an extraordinary decision when Wayman was allowed to run on for his goal when standing about two yards offside. The attitude of the nearest players of both sides indicated that they expected a whistle, but taking his cue from the linesman, who saw nothing wrong, the referee allowed the goal.

Enterprising

Nevertheless, despite this controversy, the Albion forwards always looked the more enterprising, and their tireless spirit played a great part in their success. The forwards did much of the work up to the last half-hour on their own, for Barlow was obviously under orders to stay back and harass Finney. But when Barlow did join in the attack, it always looked as if Albion would win. In his second upfield foray, the big left half was checked only at the cost of that all-important penalty.

The Preston players were very disappointed with their showing, and it was the expression 'we never hit our stride' which best summed up their feelings at the end of the game.

Finney Flaw

Tom Finney did many clever things, but was uninspired in captaincy. He was 'blanketed' by three shadowers and got little help from his colleagues. Yet I thought the great winger might have attempted to switch his attacks across the field.

I thought Docherty was Preston's best player, as strong and rugged as was Jimmy Dugdale at the other end of the field.

It was not a classic game, but the goals and controversy made it all very exciting and a match to remember.

'Well done, lads!' Congratulations from WBA's manager

Three Big Cheers for Preston – from the Ref's Wife!

I was talking yesterday to Mrs Maud Luty, of Leeds, whose husband has been chosen to referee the Cup Final.

Mr Luty is, of course, strictly neutral about the teams, but Mrs Luty is going to Wembley heavily biased in favour of Preston North End.

She is a Lancastrian from Southport: 'I say three big cheers for Preston. I think they'll bring the Cup back to Lancashire.'

When the news came through that her husband was to be given 'The highest honour any referee can get', his first words to his wife were 'Get out the wool, darling, and start knitting my stocking tops'.

Season after season, during the years he has been refereeing big football, Mrs Luty has always knitted extra long white tops on his regulation black ref's stockings. The extra length makes them look smarter.

'I only knitted you some new stocking tops a fortnight ago,' said Mrs Luty.

'I know,' said Mr Luty, 'but I must have everything new for Wembley.'

So yesterday she was knitting away, while looking after the baby and answering hundreds of telephone calls.

No wonder she calls herself a football widow. Every Friday during the season her husband goes off to his refereeing and is very often not back until Sunday. He has only been home one weekend this season, and then they went to

watch Leeds United on their home ground.

Every referee gets a free ticket for the match he is refereeing. But Mrs Luty rarely goes, because she has to stay at home to look after the children. She usually has to be content to sit at home and tune into broadcasts of the games he is refereeing.

She quickly summed up her husband: 'He has a strict, neat sort of face which makes some people think he is a detective. He is harmless enough but, make no mistake about it, when he is on the field, he is the boss. He does not like to push himself forward too much, but he makes sure he is always there at the right time.'

1955

NEWCASTLE UNITED 3
MANCHESTER CITY 1

ATTENDANCE
100 000

REFEREE
R. J. Leafe (Nottingham)

GOALSCORERS
Milburn, Mitchell, Hannah
Johnstone

TEAMS

Newcastle United	Manchester City
Simpson	Trautmann
Batty	Meadows
Cowell	Little
Casey	Barnes
Stokoe	Ewing
Scoular	Paul
Mitchell	Spurdle
Hannah	Hayes
Keeble	Revie
Milburn	Johnstone
White	Fagan

THE ROAD TO THE FINAL

Newcastle United
4th round
v Brentford 3–2 (h)
5th round
v Nottingham Forest 1–1 (a)
Replay 2–2 (h)
2nd replay 2–1 (a)
6th round
v Huddersfield Town 1–1 (a)
Replay 2–0 (h)
Semi-Final
v York City 1–1
Replay 2–0

Manchester City
4th round
v Manchester United 2–0 (h)
5th round
v Luton Town 2–0 (a)
6th round
v Birmingham City 1–0 (a)
Semi-Final
v Sunderland 1–0

Cup Was Tragedy Filled for City – Meadows May Never Play Again

A stylish header from Newcastle's Milburn gives his team a goal in the first minute

YOU ARE 23, a picture of health and vitality and first choice for your country. You are playing at Wembley in the Cup Final – something you have looked forward to all your life.

You are, in fact, Jimmy Meadows, Manchester City right back, and you have been presented to the Duke of Edinburgh. That was Saturday afternoon.

Yesterday was another day ... dreary and dismal, full of pain, frustration and anxiety. You are still Jimmy Meadows, but the whole fabric of your life has crashed. Not only have you missed most

79

that 19th-minute incident: 'When Bobby Mitchell beat me and pulled the ball back, I was ready, and turned with him. I went to push off with my right foot, and my studs caught in the grass. In effect, the top half of my leg moved forward and the rest stayed put. The pain was indescribable.

'This morning I went to hospital and a specialist told me I had badly strained the knee ligaments and possibly suffered cartilage trouble. The whole of my right leg is in a plaster cast.

'I have had strained ligaments before, but it's never been so painful as this. I'm going to see the club's specialist when I return to Manchester.'

No detailed examination can be made until the swelling has gone down, but the fear is that Meadows has torn the cruciate ligaments of his knee. If this is so, it could mean the end of soccer for the boy.

Struggling

The Final was spoilt as a spectacle by the loss of Meadows. It left ten Manchester City men with right winger Spurdle at right back, struggling against Newcastle's fit and confident XI.

Yet I think Newcastle would have won against a full-strength side. United snatched the quickest Wembley goal – little more than half a minute after the start – and should have been at least three goals in the lead before half-time.

But City fought back so well that they finished the first half all square, thanks to a magnificently headed goal by Johnstone.

The odds were too heavy, though, and the game died eight minutes after the start of the second half, after Newcastle had

Newcastle's third goal causes mixed reactions

again taken the lead through an incredible goal by left winger Bobby Mitchell.

White cracked the ball from the right wing across to Mitchell, who feinted to chip it back into the middle.

No Chance

As City keeper Bert Trautmann told me: 'Mitchell had no chance to score from the narrowest possible angle I could cut him down to, so I dived to catch his centre. As I did, he drove the ball straight into the net through the space I had left.'

No black marks for Trautmann for this goal, and congratulations to the brainy Scot for the split-second timing which made the score possible.

Trautmann, one of the men of the match, made the save of the season ten minutes before half-time. White, who had a fine game until he turned over his ankle, cut inside Little, and shaped to cross the ball to Keeble.

Suddenly he turned back and whipped in a fierce shot with his left foot. Trautmann, who had been going to cover Keeble, changed direction in mid-air and caught the ball, both hands at full stretch to his left.

The victors and the Cup after the presentation

of the Final, after being half-carried from the field with a leg injury, but you may never again be able to kick a football. Yes, the injury is as bad as that ... at the moment.

How It Happened

Let Meadows himself tell the story of

Talking Point – Demon Lurks in Wembley Turf

That emerald green Wembley turf on which the Cup Final is played has a demon lurking in its plush grass. The evil sprite that put Manchester City's Meadows out of the Final may have put him out of football for good.

There seemed no danger as Meadows moved to cover Newcastle left winger Mitchell. Then Mitchell changed direction and – to quote a downcast Meadows – 'my studs caught in the grass'.

It was as simple as that. Meadows' right leg moved forward but his foot stayed put. Great strain was put on the knee ligaments and grave damage was done. For the last weeks of most seasons, our footballers generally play on hard, balding pitches where the hold on the foot is almost non-existent. Let Wally Barnes, captain of the 1952 Arsenal Cup Final team, explain. He was injured on almost the same spot and was out of the game for a whole season. 'The Wembley pitch is well watered to keep it in its wonderful condition. That gives your studs a hold you are not used to.'

Meadows and Barnes were both out near the corner flag, where new turf is laid yearly, over part of the speedway track.

Would it not be a good idea if each team were allowed half an hour at Wembley the day before important games, to practise on that plush turf?

Trautmann had no chance with either the first or third goals. Milburn raced through from the kick-off and forced a corner off Ewing. White placed the kick perfectly and Milburn headed in off the cross bar.

The third goal came in the 59th minute. Once again Newcastle's tireless captain, Jimmy Scoular, who had a magnificent game, hit a long cross to Mitchell. Like an arrow the ball flew back into the Manchester penalty area and as Hannah said afterwards, 'I just hit it as hard as I could.'

Out – and Up – for The Cup

A prisoner due for release from Dartmoor in May has written to ask Mr Billy Murray, the Sunderland FC manager, for a ticket for the Cup Final. 'He will get his Wembley ticket if Sunderland get theirs,' Mr Murray said yesterday.

Manchester's right back, Meadows, is carried off after an injury

MANCHESTER CITY 3
BIRMINGHAM CITY 1

ATTENDANCE
100 000

REFEREE
A. Bond (Fulham)

GOALSCORERS
Hayes, Dyson, Johnstone
Kinsey

TEAMS

Manchester City	Birmingham City
Trautmann	Merrick
Leivers	Hall
Little	Green
Barnes	Newman
Ewing	Smith
Paul	Boyd
Johnstone	Astall
Hayes	Kinsey
Revie	Brown
Dyson	Murphy
Clarke	Govan

THE ROAD TO THE FINAL

Manchester City
4th round
v Southend United 1–0 (a)
5th round
v Liverpool 0–0 (h)
Replay 2–1 (a)
6th round
v Everton 2–1 (h)
Semi-Final
v Tottenham Hotspur 1–0

Birmingham City
4th round
v Leyton Orient 4–0 (a)
5th round
v West Bromwich Albion 1–0 (a)
6th round
v Arsenal 3–1 (a)
Semi-Final
v Sunderland 3–0

Triumph for Revie

Manchester's first goal goes into the net as the Birmingham goalkeeper dives too late

IT WAS REVIE, Revie all the way in the FA Cup Final. Within three minutes of the start there could be no doubt he was the man for the job. On the sunlit green carpet of Wembley, Birmingham toiled in his shadow.

They could never match the brilliant ball-play of the smooth Don and his teammates. All the winners played their parts, particularly Bill Leivers, who started many moves with his accurate and intelligent passing. Paul and Barnes were the perfect wing halves.

It will long be argued that Birmingham lost the Cup when skipper Len Boyd was switched to left half. He looked like a fish out of water, while Trevor Smith often looked bewildered as he tried to find the man who usually provides him with so much support.

It was some little consolation for Birmingham manager Arthur Turner that in his first Cup tie John Newman got through a tremendous amount of work and never looked over-awed.

Merrick was impeccable behind shaky Birmingham backs. Jeff Hall was indecisive in the early stages and was often beaten by the line-hugging cunning of Roy Clarke.

Whereas the Manchester forwards switched bewilderingly, always playing foot-

Supporters Choose Own Club Songs

It is going to be a Cup Final of songs, if not goals, today. And not just the normal community singing; for each team's supporters have chosen their own club song.

Birmingham City began it in the third round against Torquay; looking ahead to Wembley, the fans sang 'Keep Right on to the End of the Road' and have sung it at every match since.

Manchester City are, as you might guess, retaliating with 'Lassie from Lancashire'.

I am glad to see that the Cup tie song itself, chosen by the conductor Mr Arthur Caiger, is strictly impartial. It begins: 'On the ball, City, take it down, take it down. Don't stop for half backs; you can waltz them around ...'

A last-ditch save right under the feet of the Birmingham attacker

ball, the Birmingham forward line did not exist as such.

The Birmingham five were planless, offering only an occasional lone break by Brown, or a cunningly crossed ball from the wings, to threaten the harmony of the Manchester defence.

Birmingham were all out of form. But praise the winners for the way they so confidently subdued the team who had simply roared to Wembley in a great surge of success.

Birmingham's tackling was surprisingly weak, while Manchester's Iron Man Paul, forthright Ewing and eager Barnes were always on the ball.

Proud Manchester captain Roy Paul holds up the trophy that makes it all worthwhile

Little Lost It!

It was nearly the big sporting story of the year ... it caused a flap in the Manchester City dressing-room at Wembley after the big game on Saturday.

A player's gold medal had vanished: Roy Little, the left back, lost it ten minutes after the Queen had presented it to him.

He thought that he left it in its box on a bench while he went to shower and change; came back ... no medal.

For half an hour there was a search high and low among the confusion of shorts, jerseys, boots, bags and benches.

Then they found it ... Roy had inadvertently rolled it up in his player's jersey and tossed it into the laundry basket!

1957

ASTON VILLA 2
MANCHESTER UNITED 1

ATTENDANCE
---
100 000

REFEREE

F. Coultas (Hull)

GOALSCORERS

McParland (2)
Taylor

TEAMS

Aston Villa	Manchester United
Sims	Wood
Lynn	Foulkes
Aldis	Byrne
Crowther	Colman
Dugdale	Blanchflower
Saward	Edwards
Smith	Berry
Sewell	Whelan
Myerscough	Taylor
Dixon	Charlton
McParland	Pegg

--- THE ROAD TO THE FINAL ---

Aston Villa
4th round
v Middlesbrough 3–2 (a)
5th round
v Bristol City 2–1 (h)
6th round
v Burnley 1–1 (a)
Replay 2–0 (h)
Semi-Final
v West Bromwich Albion 2–2
Replay 1–0

Manchester United
4th round
v Wrexham 5–0 (a)
5th round
v Everton 1–0 (h)
6th round
v Bournemouth 2–1 (a)
Semi-Final
v Birmingham City 2–0

Charge Clumsy, but not Vicious – Boos Made Me Fight Harder, Says McParland

The referee watches McParland, but Wood's injury is the greater – a cracked jaw

AHEAD OF US a police motor-cyclist wove through the after-Wembley traffic as he guided the Aston Villa coach back to London for the triumphal banquet. In the front seat Johnny Dixon, his face one broad beam, sat clutching the Cup. The man next to me on the back seat held his head and said: 'I've had a migraine for two days ... my head aches like Wood's must do.' Then he looked at me and muttered: 'Do you think I should have sent McParland off the field?'

Referee Frank Coultas was reliving the moment of drama which, Manchester will always claim, cost them the fabulous Cup and League double.

Head-On

In the sixth minute a head-on charge by Villa's left winger at Ray Wood, the Man-

McParland's first goal for Villa leaves Blanchflower (centre half turned emergency goalie) quite helpless

chester goalkeeper – who was safely holding McParland's header – sent both players hurtling to the ground. It also caused all this:

Wood is believed to have fractured a cheekbone; was off the field for two spells totalling 38 minutes; played outside right for the rest of the game except for the last seven minutes, when he kept goal; forced United to make four positional changes, including the playing of centre half Blanchflower in goal; and brought a storm of booing each time McParland touched the ball – booing which was redoubled when Villa went up for the Cup.

This is the first time at a Wembley Final that the Royal presentation has taken place under such bitter circumstances.

Not Vicious

Mr Coultas then answered his own question: 'Personally, I saw nothing vicious in the charge,' he said. 'It was clumsy, but with no foul intent. As a matter of fact, if Wood had not gone down, I would not have given a foul.' He added 'I was very sorry to hear the boos against McParland, because I am sure he did not mean to hurt his opponent.'

I, too, am sure that it was only McParland's Irish enthusiasm which made him lose his judgement. He told me afterwards:

Disbelieving faces – and desperate poses – as United snatch a goal back in the closing minutes

'When Wood caught the ball I went in to shoulder charge him. I got a crack in the face myself and will have an X-ray when I get home.'

Of the booing, McParland said: 'It was most unfair. It annoyed me, yet it made me play harder than ever to get a goal. I was upset that Ray had been hurt, and at the end went upfield to shake hands with him. Ray said that it was OK, but that he wasn't feeling so good.'

Unnecessary

Wood, his face swollen and right eye black, said yesterday, 'I had the ball in my hand when the charge came. McParland never had any chance to get it. I picked the ball up at the goal-line, and I had run with it for three or four yards before he charged. I think it was a bit unnecessary.

'Next thing I found myself lying on the grass covered in water, and somebody said: "I think his jaw is broken; he'll have to go off." Then Jackie Blanchflower pulled off my jersey, and they lifted me on to a stretcher.'

The collision rocked any chance United had of winning the Cup, and immediately stirred up a double controversy – whether a) substitute goalkeepers should be allowed in big show matches; and b) that charging of goalkeepers in British football should be abolished.

When United Began to Crack . . .

United battled manfully with their switched side. Blanchflower, complete with peaked cap borrowed from a photographer, made several unorthodox saves; Edwards looked the perfect centre half, and Whelan did nobly at wing half. But there was little rhythm in the four-man forward line.

Then Villa started to exert pressure, and cracks began to appear in United's defence. In the 58th minute McParland sounded the warning when he headed a Smith cross against an upright. The ball came straight back to Blanchflower's clutching fingers, and he looked so grateful that the crowd laughed.

In the 68th minute, McParland struck. Three times Smith fought Byrne for the ball, and finally crossed it.

There was a blur of silk shirt, and McParland's head rocketed the ball high into the United net.

Five minutes later came his second goal. Dixon hit the left upright, and McParland beat team-mate Myerscough to the rebound and hooked in a beauty.

United were not finished with yet. Edwards raced out to take a corner, and his perfectly placed kick was neatly headed in by Taylor – almost his one good deed of the day.

Artist's impression of the Villa team

By Gum!

Johnny Dixon, captain of Cup-winning Aston Villa, blushed a deep beetroot.

'Do you mean to say that millions of telly viewers saw me chewing gum as the Queen was handing me the Cup?' he cried remorsefully.

'Good heavens! I didn't mean any disrespect.

'It's just that ... well, I forgot to part the wodge of gum before I mounted the steps to the rostrum. Do you think she noticed?'

If the Queen didn't notice, millions did. And Johnny wasn't the only offender. The whole team were chewing gum as they filed past the Queen and Prince Philip, like a bunch of cattle in a new, lush pasture.

'We must have looked like a bunch of Yanks from the backwoods,' said Johnny.

'Never gave it a thought,' added Peter McParland, the outside left who scored both of the goals. 'We chew right through our matches to help get our breath.'

LYNN   SIMS   ALDIS

CROWTHER   SAWARD

DUGDALE

SEWELL   DIXON

SMITH   MYERSCOUGH   McPARLAND

The Man in Charge Mr F. Coultas Referee

Nine Pounds for One Cup Final Ticket

Spivs were selling 50 shilling tickets for today's Cup Final at 9 pounds each last night.

Overseas and continental visitors gladly paid up to three pounds, ten shillings for standard tickets worth three shillings and sixpence.

This morning Euston station was all set for the big invasion. The 19 000 fans arriving in 35 special trains – 3 more than last year – found waiting for them 8 000 sandwiches, 5 000 pies and over 900 hot meals. At Wembley – where they say the pitch is in its best condition for 6 years – 100 workmen toiled all night to put up temporary seating for 20 000.

Unhappy man at the match, between Manchester United and Aston Villa, will be Dennis Viollet, United's inside left. He has been dropped because of an injury.

His place will be taken by 19-year-old reserve Bobby Charlton. He has played on the Wembley turf once before – as a schoolboy international.

Aston Villa's prize

1958

BOLTON WANDERERS 2
MANCHESTER UNITED 0

ATTENDANCE
100 000

REFEREE
J. U. Sherlock (Sheffield)

GOALSCORER
Lofthouse (2)

TEAMS

Bolton Wanderers	Manchester United
Hopkinson	Gregg
Hartle	Foulkes
Banks	Greaves
Hennin	Goodwin
Higgins	Cope
Edwards	Crowther
Stevens	Taylor
Parry	Viollet
Birch	Dawson
Lofthouse	Charlton
Holden	Webster

THE ROAD TO THE FINAL

Bolton Wanderers
4th round
v York City 0–0 (a)
Replay 3–0 (h)
5th round
v Stoke City 3–1 (h)
6th round
v Wolverhampton Wanderers 2–1 (h)
Semi-Final
v Blackburn Rovers 2–1

Manchester United
4th round
v Ipswich Town 2–0 (h)
5th round
v Sheffield Wednesday 3–0 (h)
6th round
v West Bromwich Albion 2–2 (a)
Replay 1–0 (h)
Semi-Final
v Fulham 2–2
Replay 5–3

'Slim' Edwards was the Mastermind

Arms flung wide, Bolton's captain celebrates scoring their first goal

NAT LOFTHOUSE WAS holding the FA Cup high. Matt Busby was walking into the tunnel below the Royal Box, head low. And as a dejected little group of red-shirted players trooped off to their dressing-room Harry Gregg took the ball which had twice found the goal behind him and booted it high into the Bolton section of the terraces – a symbolic acceptance that United were second best.

'We were a bad team today, we didn't deserve to win,' skipper Foulkes told me later.

And a century of arguments over Lofthouse's second goal will not alter the fact that United looked a bad team from the moment Lofthouse scored his first – after *three* minutes.

One spectator who has been watching Cup Finals since 1904 told me it was the worst Final he had ever seen.

Speed, Speed

Don't blame Bolton.

They played the game they planned to play, with magnetic marking, speed into the tackle, even more speed in deciding what to do with the ball and sheer lightning in doing it.

Not very pretty, not even very clever, but worthy of high admiration for the power, fitness, persistence and confidence that produced a winning formula. It all stemmed from the absolute mastery which left half Bryan 'Slim' Edwards gained over inside right Ernie Taylor. Shadowing him all over the pitch, Edwards made almost a spectator of the United field marshal.

Edwards was even following Taylor in that vital third minute and was upfield to snap up Crowther's clearance of Holden's corner.

His pass to Lofthouse caught all the United defence on the wrong foot, and Nat was almost jumping for joy as he crashed the ball home.

Horrible Passing

Aided by the horrible passing of opposite numbers Crowther and Goodwin, Edwards and his henchman Hennin could have put a fence round the centre circle and hoisted the Bolton flag, so complete was their hold.

No matter how United forwards switched, the wings were always weak, and full backs Hartle and Banks cantered through the game, hardly breaking sweat. Only one man kept the United flame alight, but even Bobby Charlton couldn't burn the candle at both ends. He was falling back to fetch the ball or racing through the middle looking for a return

Bolton 'keeper Hopkinson dives to save the ball, at the feet of Manchester's Viollet

United 'keeper Gregg is knocked unconscious during the match

pass, but he couldn't be on the wing as well at the same time.

Tragedy

Centre half Cope was United's next best player, but where I expected them to be most reliable they were shakiest. Though he recovered later, Gregg made several early errors.

And it was a Gregg fumble in Bolton's first attack that forced Foulkes to concede the corner from which Lofthouse scored.

That was the vital moment of this game, not the unsatisfactory scramble of the second goal. It robbed United of rhythm, cohesion, accuracy and plan. It did not rob them of spirit; they had too much of this at times.

After Lofthouse had lit such a magnificent fuse, what a tragedy that the game did no more than splutter.

This is Soccer's greatest epic

Out through the long, dark tunnel of the Munich air disaster which killed eight of his Manchester United Babes and almost cost his own life, Matt Busby strides back on to the field of glory.

The performance of his shattered team in getting through to the Cup Final, beating, since that tragedy, such sides as Sheffield Wednesday, West Bromwich Albion and Fulham, will remain the greatest Soccer epic of all time.

The most poignant moment of the whole day at Wembley is likely to be the traditional singing before the match of King George V's favourite hymn, *Abide With Me*.

NOTTINGHAM FOREST 2

LUTON TOWN 1

ATTENDANCE
100 000

REFEREE
J. H. Clough (Bolton)

GOALSCORERS
Dwight, Wilson
Pacey

TEAMS

Nottingham Forest	Luton Town
Thomson	Baysham
Whare	McNally
McDonald	Hawkes
Whitefoot	Groves
McKinlay	Owen
Burkitt	Pacey
Dwight	Bingham
Quigley	Brown
Wilson	Morton
Gray	Cummins
Imlach	Gregory

THE ROAD TO THE FINAL

Nottingham Forest
4th round
v Grimsby Town 4–1 (h)
5th round
v Birmingham City 1–1 (a)
Replay 1–1 (h)
2nd replay 5–0 (a)
6th round
v Bolton Wanderers 2–1 (h)
Semi-Final
v Aston Villa 1–0

Luton Town
4th round
v Leicester City 1–1 (a)
Replay 4–1 (h)
5th round
v Ipswich Town 5–2 (a)
6th round
v Blackpool 1–1 (a)
Replay 1–0 (h)
Semi-Final
v Norwich City 1–1
Replay 1–0

Goal No. 2 – and Forest go two up within 14 minutes

BRENDON McNALLY, THE innocent cause of Roy Dwight breaking his leg in the Cup Final, was himself a victim of the extraordinary run of Wembley injuries. Late in the second half, when Luton were desperately pressing for the equaliser, McNally caught his studs in the holding turf, twisted sharply, and dislocated his right knee. He collapsed in agony, and was half-carried to the touch-line by the trainer. For a few seconds it looked as if McNally was to be the second stretcher case of the day, but the trainer steadied his knee back into position and McNally's injury passed almost unnoticed by the crowd.

Dwight had exonerated McNally when the Luton player ran over to his stretcher. And yesterday he said: 'It was a complete accident – we were both going for the ball and collided.'

Medal Sent to Hospital

At half-time, lying on the dressing-room table as Burkitt led the depleted team out to resume the game, Dwight prompted 'Keep them going, skipper'. Burkitt kept them going.

Later several of his team-mates took Dwight's medal to him in hospital. They all laughed when they heard that a patient said when Dwight arrived: 'We've been watching the game on TV – come on in, we've been waiting for you.' They then made room for the Forest player to watch the last 25 minutes of the game on TV!

It was well for Luton that Forest lost a player; I do not remember any team being

...inal Victim

Players May Boycott Forest Banquet

Angry Nottingham Forest players are threatening to boycott their club's Cup Final banquet at the Savoy next Saturday. One reserve player has returned his complimentary ticket for the Final. A muddle over the banquet angered the players, already upset about the Wembley tickets allotted to them.

The Reserves were invited to the banquet – then, a few days later, their invitations were cancelled. The cancellations were later rescinded, but they are now invited to the banquet – which starts at 8 p.m. – only on condition that they catch the 11 p.m. train home to Nottingham.

One player said: 'They are treating us like babies. The banquet will hardly have started before we have to leave. Some of the boys are so furious, they have decided not to go.'

Bought Seat

The complimentary ticket was returned by goalkeeper Bill Fraser. Said Fraser: 'Fancy sending me a 3s 6d complimentary ticket! I have sent it back and have bought myself a seat. I would look a proper Charlie standing on the terracing. I think I deserve something better than a 3s 6d ticket. I know Fourth Division clubs who give their players better complimentary tickets than I received. This means that on the club's greatest day since they won the Cup in 1898 the reserves will have to stand in the crowd.'

'A Mistake'

Forest manager Billy Walker denied that the invitations had ever been cancelled. He snapped: 'That is completely untrue. There was a mistake over Bill Fraser and his wife, but this was put right.'

Mr Walker added: 'No club could do more for their staff than Forest. Everybody connected with the club has been looked after. The washerwomen, 108 turnstile operators, 26 programme sellers and the St John Ambulance people have all been given a Wembley ticket, a rail ticket, and money for meals.

'What more can we do?'

so on top at Wembley as were Billy Walker's men during that classic first half-hour. But even against depleted opponents, there was no spark of urgency about the Luton players. Skipper Syd Owen tried. Time and again he implored his players to get a move on.

A Long Time to Settle In

Owen summed up his last game before taking over as Luton manager: 'Forest deserved to win. They started off like greyhounds, and it took us a long time to settle in. It's too late to start playing your best when you are two goals down. We were all too placid.'

The Luton players blamed the lush grass for their poor display, as most teams beaten at Wembley have done. Certainly,

Jubilation for Luton as the Forest keeper (in cap) turns to collect the ball he missed

there were a lot more injuries than usual.

Should substitutes be allowed at Wembley? No, definitely not. Spare players would have to be admitted in every game of the competition, which annually proves the biggest lottery of football.

Had a substitute come on for Dwight, we would not have had our memories of an epic struggle.

One reason why it took Luton so long to get to grips with the Forest ten was the clever way in which skipper Burkitt deployed his forces.

Amazing Display

As Dwight was being carried off, Burkitt told his forwards: 'Stay on the wings and spread the line out – you'll all have to take turns going down the middle.' Said Billy Walker: 'It was magnificent. I told Jack it was the most sensible decision he could have taken.'

Luton reeled before Forest's sustained, crisp, attractive moves. The two goals, in the 10th and 15th minutes, were brilliantly and quickly taken.

All played well, but after special praise for Burkitt and McKinlay, I must single out Imlach for an amazing display of energy on the stamina-killing turf. He

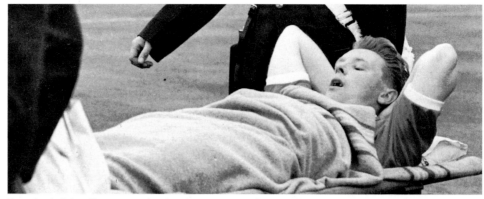

Despite helping Forest to win, the day was to end badly for Dwight – he broke his leg

played a great part in the first goal. Taking Burkitt's shrewd pass, he cleverly flicked the ball round McNally and crossed it at speed. Dwight raced in to hammer home a beautiful left-foot shot.

Then Gray moved to outside left, and his neat centre was coolly headed home by Wilson.

Fairy-Tale End

Luton's goal came 25 minutes from the end. As Bingham took a corner on the left, Hawkes raced up, calling for the ball. His pass eluded the whole Forest defence, and Pacey made no mistake from close in.

He was promptly switched to centre forward, with Morton dropping back.

There was almost a fairy-tale end for the strangely slow Alan Brown. With four minutes left, he roared in to head Bingham's cross just inches past the post. Almost a fairy tale, but not quite.

Forest to Take Pills to Beat Final Jitters

Nottingham Forest players are likely to walk out at Wembley under the influence of a sedative – given them a few hours before the match to break down pre-match tension and strain.

Manager Billy Walker revealed this last night, when he said: 'We used a sedative before our semi-final with Aston Villa – with great effect.'

'It was the club doctor's idea to rid our lads of the jitters. I tried the pill first – it is just as bad watching as playing in these important games – and told them how much happier I felt!

'Then the players were given the pill before the Villa game – most said they noticed an improvement. Let me emphasise this is not any sort of pep pill or wonder drug. But I have played in four finals at Wembley – I know from first hand experience what the occasion can do to a player.

'The first few moments can be vital. Anything that quietens the players before the game and stops them getting jitters must help.

'There is really nothing very unusual or sensational about this. Many clubs have used some sort of sedative before games to get rid of tension.'

Forest players celebrate with dinner at the Savoy. Note the empty chair, in honour of Dwight

1960

WOLVERHAMPTON WANDERERS 3
BLACKBURN ROVERS 0

ATTENDANCE
100 000

REFEREE
K. Howley (Middlesbrough)

GOALSCORERS
McGrath (own goal), Deeley (2)

TEAMS

Wolverhampton Wanderers	Blackburn Rovers
Finlayson	Leyland
Showell	Bray
Harris	Whelan
Clamp	Clayton
Slater	Woods
Flowers	McGrath
Deeley	Bimpson
Stobart	Dobing
Murray	Dougan
Broadbent	Douglas
Horne	MacLeod

THE ROAD TO THE FINAL

Wolverhampton Wanderers
4th round
v Charlton Athletic 2–1 (h)
5th round
v Luton Town 4–1 (a)
6th round
v Leicester City 2–1 (a)
Semi-Final
v Aston Villa 1–0

Blackburn Rovers
4th round
v Blackpool 1–1 (a)
Replay 3–0 (h)
5th round
v Tottenham Hotspur 3–1 (a)
6th round
v Burnley 3–3 (h)
Replay 2–0 (a)
Semi-Final
v Sheffield Wednesday 2–1

'I Thought *My* Leg Was Broken'–Deeley

Blackburn's McGrath (on right) realises he has just scored an own goal

NORMAN DEELEY, THE two-goal Wembley hero of Wolves who was the innocent cause of Dave Whelan breaking his leg, also feared that he had broken his. Not until 6 p.m. yesterday when a specialist pronounced 'no fracture, just very bad bruising' was his mind eased.

Manager Stan Cullis took Deeley for an X-ray straight from the civic welcome the team received on their arrival home yesterday afternoon.

The wee winger, whose alertness and goal sense played havoc with the Blackburn defence, also told me of the awful moment when he knew Whelan's leg was broken. Deeley said: 'It was about two minutes to half-time. I had just pushed the ball forward and was going after it when Whelan came in low and hard, but fair. My right shin met his left shin, and I heard the crack as his bone went.

'As I rolled away, feeling pretty terrible, I yelled to the referee, "Stop the game, he's broken his leg," but I don't think he

The ball sails into the net for Wolves' third goal

Billy Will Be There – Joy Beverley

(Wife of Billy Wright, and one of the singing-act, the Beverley Sisters)

'It would be nice to be able to go to the Cup Final with Billy. We've never been together before. One of us always seems to be working!

There's a matinee booked for this afternoon, so the twins (Babs and Teddie) and I will be on duty. But we'll be there in spirit. Of course I would sooner see Billy out on the field with his beloved Wolves. Or would I?

Now I think I would rather sit beside him and watch his face as the Wolves win. Oh, they'll win, all right. The Wright household won't hear a word about defeat. Billy wants them to win because, of course, he is still a Wolves fan.'

heard me, for play went on for some time.'

Disgraceful Behaviour

The accident came when Wolves had got into their stride and looked likely winners. But the handicap spurred Blackburn to a very fine first 15 minutes of the second half. Eventually, Wolves wore them down and scored four more goals: the only two allowed were those Deeley hammered in with his injured leg.

I thought at the time that the 'goals'

Cup Final Gets Youngest Referee

Kevin Howley, the 35-year-old Yorkshire referee, is to take charge of the Wolves v Blackburn FA Cup Final. He is the youngest official ever to be given charge of Britain's most publicised match.

It is a far cry from Wembley's manicured turf to the frozen, snow-covered ground that greeted him at Barrow before a Cup-tie last season.

Then Howley tore off his jacket and joined the volunteers who worked all morning to make sure the pitch was cleared for a tie with Wolves.

But it is enthusiasm of that sort that gets him such an honour. As he said yesterday, 'It really surprised me. This game is usually given to seasoned referees in recognition of years of service to football.'

when they went down the tunnel after the match.

The tragedy of Whelan was a pure accident. As he was being carried off the field, he waved to Deeley, to indicate that the Wolves player was not to blame.

Immaculate Ball-Play

With a side once again sorely handicapped in a Wembley Final, it is difficult to get a true criticism of collective or individual play.

But in the first half I thought that Wolves had gradually got on top, mainly through the strength of their half back line and Broadbent's immaculate ball-play. There were flashes of talent from Bryan Douglas, but little of note from Dobing, Dougan or Bimpson. Wolves were much better served on the wings.

Wolves' goalkeeper Finlayson coming into close contact with Blackburn's Douglas

Murray and Flowers scored were wrongly disallowed by referee Kevin Howley, who had a very indifferent match.

The match was marred at the end by the disgraceful behaviour of the Blackburn supporters solidly massed over the tunnel leading to the dressing-rooms. They booed Wolves when they went up for the Cup and showered the players and manager with oranges, cartons and other missiles

1961

TOTTENHAM HOTSPUR 2
LEICESTER CITY 0

ATTENDANCE
100 000

REFEREE
J. Kelly (Chorley)

GOALSCORERS
Smith, Dyson

TEAMS

Tottenham Hotspur	Leicester City
Brown	Banks
Baker	Chalmers
Henry	Norman
Blanchflower	McLintock
Norman	King
Mackay	Appleton
Jones	Riley
White	Walsh
Smith	McIlmoyle
Allen	Keyworth
Dyson	Cheesebrough

THE ROAD TO THE FINAL

Tottenham Hotspur
4th round
v Crewe Alexandra 5–1 (h)
5th round
v Aston Villa 2–0 (a)
6th round
v Sunderland 1–1 (a)
Replay 5–0 (h)
Semi-Final
v Burnley 3–0

Leicester City
4th round
v Bristol City 5–1 (h)
5th round
v Birmingham City 1–1 (a)
Replay 2–1 (h)
6th round
v Barnsley 0–0 (h)
Replay 2–1 (a)
Semi-Final
v Sheffield United 0–0
Replay 0–0
2nd replay 2–0

They Still Played to W Leicester Made Wro

Smith shouts for joy . . . but the goal is disallowed

THE FA CUP and the Double belong to Tottenham this morning because Leicester City's manager and players deliberately spurned safety-first tactics with ten fit men at Wembley.

Leicester made their controversial decision at half-time because they thought they could still beat Spurs, and because they did not want to cause a drab Cup Final. Highly commendable – but wrong. I am sure that Leicester could have lived to fight a replay with 11 fit men if they had concentrated on defence.

Manager Gillies said: 'At half-time we really thought we could win by playing attacking football. I knew the strain of losing a man must make itself felt in the last part of the game, but I hoped we could get in front by then. We've no regrets,' he added.

This Final, which promised so much, will be recalled not only for Spurs' double but also for the unusual tactical moves employed by the shrewd Gillies.

Chalmers, the injured back, hobbled uselessly on the left wing for an hour before he retired to the dressing-room. Passengers usually go to centre forward these days. Apparently Chalmers insisted on staying on the field as long as possible.

Utterly Unable to Shine

Leicester's whole tactical plan was geared to three fit inside forwards, able to chase

in, but...
ng Choice

Banks makes an acrobatic effort to stop Dyson's shot, but it's 2–0 to Spurs

and harry Blanchflower and Mackay, the key Spurs men.

It was because this plan was so successful that Spurs fell so far below their customary standard. Mackay, Blanchflower and White – who was also tightly marked – were utterly unable to shine.

These facts add weight to Leicester's belief that their calm and confident football would have won the Cup if Chalmers had not been hurt. History will neither know nor care.

But Leicester must remember that their forwards, ably led by the unknown 21-year-old, McIlmoyle, scarcely produced one real shot at 'keeper Brown.

In contrast, Spurs' Jones had a goal ruled out by a most suspect offside decision, and three or four other great chances were wasted, before stamina finally deserted weary Leicester.

Brilliant Shooting

In the end it was Bobby Smith, whose brilliant shooting has changed the course of a dozen vital games, who steered the anxious Spurs safely into harbour. He produced another great shot in the 68th minute. Smith, who finds Wembley a happy playground, added to his obvious delight when he made the second for Dyson nine minutes later.

Jones and the immaculate Henry, who must surely play for England, were a little ahead of Norman as Spurs' stars. Keyworth and McLintock, covering acres of green turf as emergency wing half and right back, deserved extra medals from Leicester. Tottenham have the Cup, the honour and the sincere congratulations of the soccer world. To Leicester goes most of the glory of this 1961 Cup Final.

A Real Man's Game

Sir,
I have two Cup Final tickets, but I will not be watching soccer at Wembley.

Instead, I shall be going on May 13th to see a real he-man's game – when St Helens play Wigan in the Rugby League Cup Final.

John H. Roberts,
Honiton, Devon

LAST WORD by JON

TOTTENHAM HOTSPUR BOARD ROOM

"It's all very well, but now I've two to polish!"

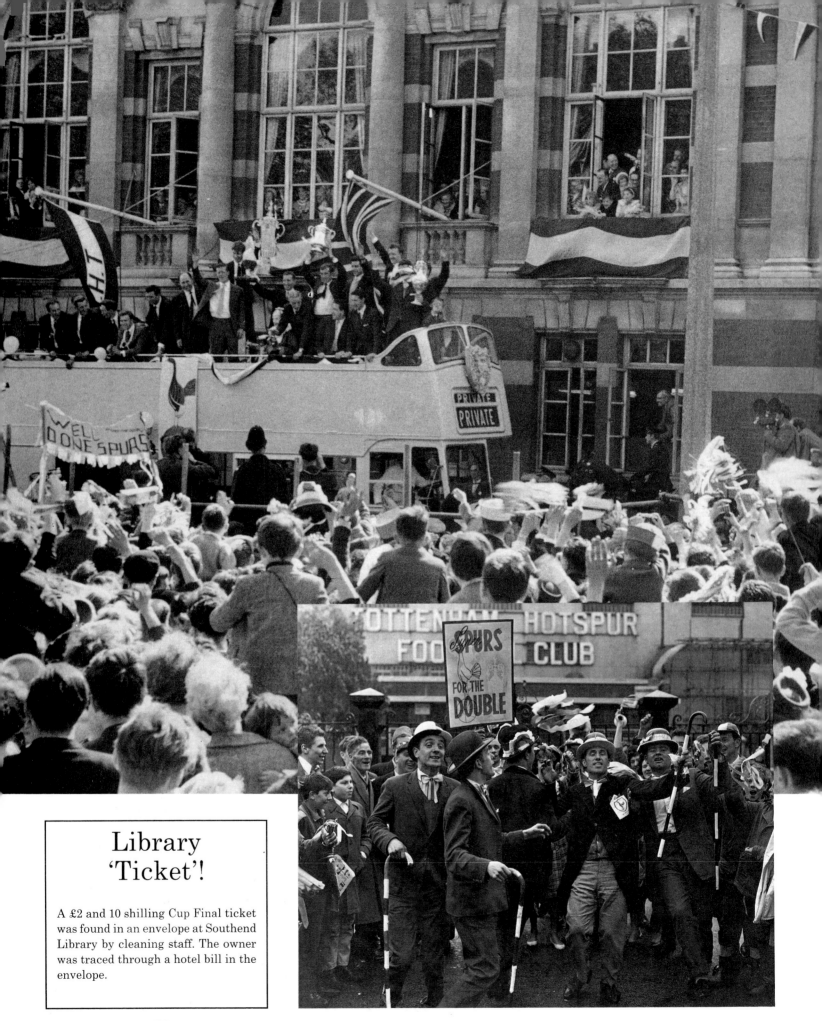

Library 'Ticket'!

A £2 and 10 shilling Cup Final ticket was found in an envelope at Southend Library by cleaning staff. The owner was traced through a hotel bill in the envelope.

7 500 Miles to See Final

George Wright, an ardent Spurs fan all his life, flew into London yesterday and said: 'I just had to come and see Tottenham play in the Cup Final. I'll be back at my job by Tuesday.'

The round trip of 7 500 miles will cost George about £250. 'And it is going to be worth every penny of it to see Spurs win the Cup,' he commented. 'I am confident that they are going to complete the great double.'

He tried to wager on Spurs winning the Cup Final before leaving Toronto. 'But bets on Spurs stopped a week ago,' he said. 'Everybody there is so confident that the Spurs will win.'

We've done the double! Spurs are welcomed home by a huge crowd outside the town hall

Left: dancing in the streets as Spurs fans celebrate the double

...*everyone* has a 'double' when it's Vat 69 FINEST SCOTCH WHISKY
SO IF YOUR GLASSES ARE EMPTY PUT ANOTHER TOTTENHAM!

1962

TOTTENHAM HOTSPUR 3
BURNLEY 1

ATTENDANCE
100 000

REFEREE
J. Finney (Hereford)

GOALSCORERS
Greaves, Smith, Blanchflower (penalty)
Robson

TEAMS

Tottenham Hotspur	Burnley
Brown	Blacklaw
Baker	Angus
Henry	Elder
Blanchflower	Adamson
Norman	Cummings
Mackay	Miller
Medwin	Connelly
White	McIlroy
Smith	Pointer
Greaves	Robson
Jones	Harris

THE ROAD TO THE FINAL

Tottenham Hotspur
4th round
v Plymouth Argyle 5–1 (a)
5th round
v West Bromwich Albion 4–2 (a)
6th round
v Aston Villa 2–0 (h)
Semi-Final
v Manchester United 3–1

Burnley
4th round
v Leyton Orient 1–1 (h)
Replay 1–0 (a)
5th round
v Everton 3–1 (h)
6th round
v Sheffield United 1–0 (a)
Semi-Final
v Fulham 1–1
Replay 2–1

Right To Ign

Smith scores Spurs' second goal

LINESMAN C. A. BROWNLOW did flag for a foul by a Tottenham player on Adam Blacklaw, Burnley's goalkeeper, before Spurs were awarded a penalty for hands nine minutes from the end of the Cup Final.

He then lowered his flag, because when he referees he askes his linesmen not to keep flagging. He raised his red flag again when Tommy Cummings handled Medwin's shot on the goal-line.

I don't agree that there was a foul when Smith and Jones went up with Blacklaw for White's high cross. The referee was near to the incident and I support his instant decision.

Burnley made no protest on the field,

but complained about the foul afterwards. Manager Harry Potts confirmed that the flag was up before the penalty was awarded.

Courageous

Referee Jim Finney said: 'The flag went up, and down again. If a linesman signals he must keep his flag up. I saw no foul, and immediately awarded a penalty when the player handled.'

Mr Finney might have awarded Spurs a penalty in the 34th minute, but ruled soundly that Miller had handled accidentally. This courageous decision could have proved controversial. Burnley went straight downfield and Connelly shot

ore Red Flag

Fair or a foul? Smith goes up with Blacklaw, but the referee said play on

against the side netting. Supposing Burnley had scored!

Bill Nicholson considered it Spurs' worst Cup performance of the season. I find that criticism harsh. Two very fine teams helped make it one of the best games at Wembley since the War.

Nicholson may be right in feeling that Spurs should have won more easily after Jimmy Greaves had scored in the fourth minute.

Crashing

I salute the way Burnley pulled themselves off the floor, forgot their pre-Final weariness and drew level – even though they were lucky to be only one down at half-time.

Burnley had 14 shots – 9 from moves of

JON'S SPORTING TYPES

"Tottenham? But I saw them play here last year!"

up to 3 passes; and 5 from moves of more than 3.

Long passes help to reduce indirect play. Spurs had 54 (36 goal clearances, 18 from midfield).

Burnley had 37 long passes (17 goal clearances, 20 from midfield).

And two of Tottenham's goals (first and third) originated with goal clearances.

Wembley Sell-Out for Spivs

Ticket touts have made their biggest black market fortune on today's Cup Final between Tottenham Hotspur and Burnley. Last night some fans were paying more than 20 times face value.

Five-shilling tickets were selling for £7 and fifty-shilling ones for £25. One London tout said: 'I have just sold a pair of 50-shilling tickets for £50. If I had waited until tomorrow I could have doubled it.'

He added: 'Londoners are willing to pay *anything* to see Spurs win the Cup for the second year running.'

Burnley fans are too! One business-man last night joyfully boasted that he had paid £200 for seven 50-shilling tickets. And another desperate fan even offered a free three-week holiday in his seaside caravan to anyone who could get him two tickets.

Spurs bring back the Cup – again!

1963

MANCHESTER UNITED 3
LEICESTER CITY 1

ATTENDANCE
100 000

REFEREE
K. G. Aston (Ilford)

GOALSCORERS
Law, Herd (2)
Keyworth

TEAMS

Manchester United	Leicester City
Gaskell	Banks
Dunne	Sjoberg
Cantwell	Norman
Crerand	McLintock
Foulkes	King
Setters	Appleton
Giles	Riley
Quixall	Cross
Herd	Keyworth
Law	Gibson
Charlton	Stringfellow

THE ROAD TO THE FINAL

Manchester United
4th round
v Aston Villa 1–0 (h)
5th round
v Chelsea 2–1 (h)
6th round
v Coventry City 3–1 (a)
Semi-Final
v Southampton 1–0

Leicester City
4th round
v Ipswich Town 3–1 (h)
5th round
v Leyton Orient 1–0 (a)
6th round
v Norwich City 2–0 (a)
Semi-Final
v Liverpool 1–0

Final Flop Verdict: Leicester Suicide

Coin-tossing captains at the start of the game

THE 1963 CUP Final will be remembered as the match in which a team was born ... and the 90 minutes in which a side committed suicide on the blade of its own best weapon.

Manchester United, too often a maddening enigma, became fused into the side Matt Busby had laboured to build along the long road from Munich.

Leicester, a team that worked its way to Wembley, were finally destroyed by the monster of their method. Their manager Matt Gillies summed up: 'We created a system, but instead of playing to make it work we leaned upon it. That's why we failed.'

Tactically, Leicester's weakness was clear. They had not the patience to build what they could not instantly create. So Manchester were given the freedom of the centre, liberty that became licence to roam and plunder, producing in their 3–1 victory some of the best football Wembley has seen.

New Parts?

If this was *how* Leicester lost, I still do not know *why*. Gillies, too, grasps for the answer: 'I know what went wrong, but why we couldn't produce our form on the day is another thing. I have got to go into this and find the reason. It will be rather like stripping down an engine, examining everything and perhaps – if necessary – getting new parts.

'This has not changed my conviction that we are on the right path. There is a great feeling of let-down ... but let's not forget what we have achieved. We have not been wrong all the time – only at Wembley,' he added.

The FA, in this hundredth year, were given a good, if not great, Final, but Manchester did not make the occasion – they were made by it.

Brilliant Individuals

United had limped through this long season – and only in the act of taking the Cup did they become great. Much has been recorded of the brilliant individuals – and rightly so. But United's victory was greater than the sum of Law's poise, of Crerand's unflagging command, of Charlton's and Quixall's craft, and of Foulkes' and Setters' defence.

They worked together as a unit – perhaps for the first time. And the knowledge of what this new unity has achieved will be always with them. Something ended when Cantwell went up to accept the Cup, but much more began.

As Matt Busby said: 'It's wonderful to

Busby Orders a Truncheon Guard

Three men carrying truncheons will drive up to Wembley in an armoured car this afternoon, to wait for the Cup Final result.

If Leicester City win, they will just drive back to their London HQ, then go home. If Manchester United win, they are in business – guarding the Cup until it leaves for Manchester.

Leicester are untroubled about responsibility for the Cup. Said Manager Gillies: 'We were approached by a security company to make such arrangements, but we decided we could look after it ourselves.'

But confident Manchester chief Matt Busby said last night: 'With all the celebrations that will be going on, we want to be relieved of the worry of looking after the Cup.'

Jumping for joy as United take a 3–1 lead

win ... and wonderful to be back in the act. This is what top-class football is all about.'

This Manchester United can do brilliant battle for Britain. But that's for the future. At present, we have the memories of the match ...

Spin, Shoot

Of the first 15 minutes, when a confident Leicester nearly scored through Gibson, then Stringfellow ... and a settling United retaliated with a Law pass that Quixall could not quite reach, and a swift Charlton drive that Giles hooked over.

Of the split seconds when the game was turned firmly and finally Manchester's way when Crerand beat Gibson to the ball, cut down the left and crossed for Law to spin and shoot the first goal, after 29 minutes.

Of the Gaskell–Giles–Charlton move in

Manchester United v Leicester City

the 57th minute, that ended with Herd turning in the second goal when Banks failed to hold Charlton's shot.

Of the brief moments of hope for Leicester, when Keyworth put his head where only a boot had a right to be, to smack in their goal.

Of the final crushing United goal. Law had already jumped once to head against the post, when he leapt again – anxious as a boy in a playground kickabout to be always with the ball – Banks watched him and missed Giles' cross, and Herd hammered in the killing goal.

Matt Busby and the boys who did him proud

Manchester 'keeper Gaskell goes full stretch to snatch the ball from Cross

WEST HAM UNITED 3
PRESTON NORTH END 2

ATTENDANCE
100 000

REFEREE
A. Holland (Barnsley)

GOALSCORERS
Sissons, Hurst, Boyce
Holden, Dawson

TEAMS

West Ham United	Preston North End
Standen	Kelly
Boyd	Ross
Burkett	Lawton
Bovington	Smith
Brown	Singleton
Moore	Kendall
Brabrook	Wilson
Boyce	Ashworth
Byrne	Dawson
Hurst	Spavin
Sissons	Holden

THE ROAD TO THE FINAL

West Ham United
4th round
v Leyton Orient 1–1 (h)
Replay 3–0 (a)
5th round
v Swindon Town 3–1 (h)
6th round
v Burnley 3–2 (h)
Semi-Final
v Manchester United 3–1

Preston North End
4th round
v Bolton Wanderers 2–2 (h)
Replay 2–1 (a)
5th round
v Carlisle United 1–0 (a)
6th round
v Oxford United 2–1 (a)
Semi-Final
v Swansea Town 2–1

Europe, Her

Tension relieved – Byrne, Boyce, Brabrook and Sissons celebrate West Ham's winner

ON NOW TO Europe! Amid the tears, champagne, milk and linament of the dressing room, West Ham clasped each other in a sort of stupor, which combined relief with release, joy with anticipation.

But it was noticeable that they did not shout 'We've done it', but 'We're there'. In this outward-looking age the trips, not the trophy, are the real reward.

Change of Style

Already they prepare. Their manager, Ron Greenwood, revealed that the club is trying to arrange a tough Continental tour before next season starts.

'If we are to do well in Europe, we need this sort of practice. Winning at Wembley was the greatest moment in the life of this club, but it is only a stage in development.'

Only the months and matches to come will show how much more Greenwood can draw from this team. One thing is certain – no one could get more. For the name of Greenwood is now written large on the fabric and history of Wembley. It was his hand, when a 15-year-old sign-writer, that scrawled the names on the dressing-room doors.

And it was his handling of his team's talents in the tense, worried minutes of half-time that produced the change of style that finally beat Preston.

'We had been giving Lawton and Spavin too much room. The pitch is so spacious that normal marking systems can be wrecked by the extra yards,' he said. 'So we decided to pitch Bovington against Lawton, Boyce against Spavin and pull Bobby Moore up to take on Ashworth. For the first time we were playing 4–2–4.'

And so the restart was the beginning of Preston's end. The second division side hit a peak in the first minute, which they held until the dragging weight of the impossible pitch took its toll of energy.

Scholarly

At half-time I felt Preston could not play

e We Come!

Jack's Ready for the Ticket Dodgers

Twenty-two men may be playing in the Cup Final tomorrow, but at least twice that number will be playing another sort of game at Wembley. I refer to the sport known as Getting In Without A Ticket. It's a tough game.

Wembley's security man, Jack Smith, has been refereeing it for 17 years. He knows all the dodges.

The staff have all been warned by Mr Smith about fat men. They waddle their way up to the officials' entrance and say 'Couldn't get through the turnstile, so they sent me here.'

'And where, sir, is your ticket?'

'Oh, they took it at the turnstile.'

'Sorry, sir, heard that one before.'

And you won't get by with that act of rushing up to the turnstile minutes before the kick-off waving a pair of boots and yelling, 'Quick, let me through. One of the boys has forgotten his boots.'

They've heard that one before, too.

There are bound to be at least a couple of men posing as piemen. Simple Simons that they are. Piemen, like all the other traders, have special passes.

I can't help feeling that Mr Smith has a sneaking regard for the bogus milkman who arrived in a shining white overall, explaining that he'd brought the milk for the Queen's tea.

No good trying that one this year, though. The Queen isn't going.

The quiet, pipe-smoking Mr Smith is no longer surprised by the number of football fanatics who acquire a sudden interest in greyhounds on the eve of the big day. Along they'll go to Wembley this evening, intending to stay on after the crowds have gone. They'll hide at the back of the dustbins, in the shadows behind the stands, or, if originality is not their metier, in the Gents.

And Mr Smith will round them all up, shake them by the hand, show them the gate and bid them goodnight.

better, while West Ham were spluttering along at 60 per cent efficiency.

Holden easily scored the first after Standen had fumbled the second of Dawson's shots in the tenth minute. The screams of Preston's faithful thousands were still rising when Sissons took a Byrne pass somewhere between knee and neck, strode into a box of four white shirts and somehow squeezed West Ham level.

But Preston's neat and scholarly football deserved more reward. It came when, five minutes from half-time, Dawson strode in from a corner to head. Brown fell over trying to close in. Standen slipped trying to save. The ball settled in the net as the Hammers beat a tattoo of frustration.

But the second half swung, with the change of style, to West Ham. Preston showed the first signs of panic when, after seven minutes, the second equaliser came. Hurst got the goal with his head. Kelly touched the ball briefly with his fingertips but could not stop it stealing in.

Hurst was unstoppable. Collecting a goal-kick he set out on a swerving, surging run past three tired tacklers. At the last second he parted to Brabrook and at the precise moment the winger crossed – and there was Boyce, running in to head a goal. He did it with a precise forward motion of head and trunk as though bidding a polite bow of farewell to Preston, and as such, it was.

West Ham did their lap of honour, Preston trailed sadly away. To be pipped for promotion, then to lose the Cup, was piling agony upon agony. They were too good to be dismissed with polite praise – but sympathy must not cloud the facts. Preston were often good, but not consistent.

Consistency may come. But for now, the ability to play badly and recover, to be scared but to go on believing, are qualities that should warm England – and warn Europe.

The Player Who Didn't Sleep

Alan Spavin, the 'brains' of Preston's Cup Final attack, went to bed last night knowing that he would not sleep more than an hour before the most important football match of his life. He took with him a flask of coffee and a pile of books, including four Westerns, to while away the time.

Inside left Spavin, 22, quietly read his way through the night at a Surrey hotel – his team's HQ until the final with West Ham at Wembley.

Before he went to bed, Spavin said: 'Every game gets me this way. I'm not taut and tense just because it's the Cup Final tomorrow. Sometimes I do doze off for an hour or two. Sometimes the dawn breaks before I manage it. And often the tension makes me irritable on Saturday mornings.'

His room-mate, full back George Ross, slept soundly. Ross said: 'Alan does not sleep, but that does not keep me awake.'

Bobby Moore, flanked by Byrne and Brabrook, on West Ham's victory lap

London's slowest bus journey, and moving due east!

JON'S SPORTING TYPES

" You deserve a thick head, you know you're not used drinking milk "

1965

LIVERPOOL 2

LEEDS UNITED 1

(after extra time)

--- ATTENDANCE ---
100 000

--- REFEREE ---
W. Clements (West Bromwich)

--- GOALSCORERS ---
Hunt, St John
Bremner

--- TEAMS ---

Liverpool	Leeds United
Lawrence	Sprake
Lawler	Reaney
Byrne	Bell
Strong	Bremner
Yeats	Charlton
Stevenson	Hunter
Callaghan	Giles
Hunt	Storrie
St John	Peacock
Smith	Collins
Thompson	Johannesson

--- THE ROAD TO THE FINAL ---

Liverpool
4th round
v Stockport County 1–1 (h)
Replay 2–0 (a)
5th round
v Bolton Wanderers 1–0 (a)
6th round
v Leicester City 0–0 (a)
Replay 1–0 (h)
Semi-Final
v Chelsea 2–0

Leeds United
4th round
v Everton 1–1 (h)
Replay 2–1 (a)
5th round
v Shrewsbury Town 2–0 (h)
6th round
v Crystal Palace 3–0 (a)
Semi-Final
v Manchester United 0–0
Replay 1–0

We Want Success. They Bore Us. Have They Any Real Choice?

Excitement as Leeds equalise

THE LEADEN FOOTBALL of the first 90 minutes has earned the 1965 Cup Final a reputation as the worst Final for years.

This is the price the public must pay for the success it demands. Gates for years have shown that fans will not settle for brave losers; they ought not now complain of the way victories are won. Leeds and Liverpool did not play like this because they were at Wembley. Rather, they were at Wembley precisely because they play like this.

Like it or loathe it, this was the football that got them there. I am astonished to find so many surprised at the style and standard of the play. Almost alone on Saturday, I warned that this method football would come strange to the taste of many. Too late, the English are finding that you cannot have the prize without the play. It is like a man swapping his battered sports car for the efficiency and comfort of a saloon, then complaining he misses the exhilarating rush of wind in his face.

Millions Were Yawning

The trend will continue. Look at the League honours list. With rare exceptions, the method men have won the lot.

Any team with application to match its ambition can create a Leeds or a Liverpool

Again, enjoyment is purely relative. Maybe the neutral millions were yawning, but when Liverpool scored their second goal, can anyone say the red hordes at Wembley were not happy? The fans of Arsenal, Forest or Blackburn would settle for being this dull – to be this successful.

This is not to say that this Final could not have been played better. Leeds, sadly, functioned at two-thirds efficiency.

Storrie was hurt after 20 minutes and as his thigh stiffened so his efforts on one wing grew more feeble. On the other wing, Johannesson seemed crippled in spirit and was no help to a too-static Peacock, or a frustrated Collins and Bremner.

For 90 minutes, the match was virtual stalemate. Liverpool held sway because their foremost forwards, Hunt and St John, were so much more confident and enterprising. This gave chances for

Thompson and Strong to fire wide, for Sprake and Charlton again and again to show their mettle. But it did not give them a goal because Leeds, if feeble upfront, were firm behind. Weariness finally swung a Final that planning had not been able to decide. As extra time was signalled caution was thrown aside with shin-guards.

Defenders Byrne and Stephenson, racing up the left, created a first goal for Liverpool's Hunt. He had only to bow perfunctorily to head the full back's cross past Sprake.

Dropping like Flies

Leeds men were now dropping like flies. Charlton, Giles, Storrie and Hunter were all treated for cramp. The weariness was as much of the spirit as of the muscle. For when Charlton burst upfield to head Hunter's cross just where Bremner could volley an equaliser, Leeds looked new men.

Liverpool's Ian St John crashes in the winning goal

Damp and bedraggled, managers Revie and Shankley shelter from the rain

But Liverpool had done too much to be denied. Callaghan finally crossed well for St John to head the winner. And the songs burst out anew. The Liverpool hordes had not been silent because they were displeased with the way their team played, simply anxious that the play was not producing results.

Do not begrudge them their final roaring triumph. They had seen their team succeed with football that could yet give them the European Cup as well. Method football. Modern football. Football that's easier to decry than overcome.

Football that is here to stay. Football that keeps managers in jobs, clubs in trophies and fans in a torment of hating its ruthlessness, but loving its rewards.

Just Fancy That!

Cup Final referees receive either a 10 guinea fee or a souvenir medal of equivalent value. Mr Clements, like most of his predecessors, will take the medal.

Ian St John and his wife Betty, going home with Liverpool's spoils of war

1966

EVERTON 3
SHEFFIELD WEDNESDAY 2

ATTENDANCE
100 000

REFEREE
J. K. Taylor (Wolverhampton)

GOALSCORERS
Trebilcock (2), Temple
McCalliog, Ford

TEAMS

Everton	Sheffield Wednesday
West	Springett
Wright	Smith
Wilson	Megson
Gabriel	Eustace
Labone	Ellis
Harris	Young
Scott	Pugh
Trebilcock	Fantham
Young	McCalliog
Harvey	Ford
Temple	Quinn

THE ROAD TO THE FINAL

Everton
4th round
v Bedford Town 3–0 (a)
5th round
v Coventry City 3–0 (h)
6th round
v Manchester City 0–0 (a)
Replay 0–0 (h)
2nd replay 2–0
Semi-Final
v Manchester United 1–0

Sheffield Wednesday
4th round
v Newcastle United 2–1 (a)
5th round
v Huddersfield Town 2–1 (a)
6th round
v Blackburn Rovers 2–1 (a)
Semi-Final
v Chelsea 2–0

Everton Beat Keyst

A despairing lunge by Springett fails to stop Trebilcock's second goal

THE HELL-FOR-LEATHER, hair-raising and hilarious Cup Final of 1966 spilled a few drops of *dernier cri* football into an old bottle of British blood-and-guts. The result, as I recall, was Everton Wednesday 5, Metropolitan Police 2.

This was arrived at by the referee's liberal interpretation of the law. He allowed Springett and the Keystone Kops, loving every minute of this audience-participation game, to arrest their men in any old low dive they could lay their hands on.

Finally, however, the professionals took the prize. A goal struck with the chilling timing of a karate chop gave Everton a 3–2 victory and the FA Cup in payment for their poise.

Sheffield captain Don Megson whipped his defeated team to one more effort, to tread a losers' lap of Wembley that was without precedent and beyond reproach.

Megson said: 'I have watched many Cup Finals. I have seen players give every-thing, then slink away in ones and twos to the dressing-room as though they were ashamed. Why should this be? I am not ashamed of how I played, or of the team. We were beaten, but we had let nobody down. They had done all they could – I was not going to let those lads crawl off the pitch.

'I called to them, and they came. The crowd rose to us, and I am not ashamed to say I was nearly crying. But we DESERVED a cheer; we could not have done more.'

A Match Lost with Honour

I prize honesty above formal modesty, and Megson's words summed up the spirit of the dressing-room. Filled with regret, of course, but alive, too, with the satisfaction of a match lost with honour.

I wish that we pressmen had joined in a lap of penitence; willingly I would have led it. For, almost without exception, we who sit in judgement had dismissed this

one Kops

their destruction. Two up, Wednesday tried to play containing football to a level that their youngsters could not quite attain.

How Everton, having never lost their heads, moved into the spaces they were given and created the half-chances for Trebilcock to score twice in six minutes.

And how, finally, Gerry Young's one miskick gave the Cup to Merseyside. Temple slipped behind him to gather the ball, ran on with Young in helpless pursuit and judged Springett's advance before shooting with calculation that I

have never seen equalled in a moment of such importance.

Wednesday mounted raids enough to have five more shots at saving the game torn so ruthlessly from their grasp. But Everton were home because in every position they had a professional. In too many places, Wednesday had men whose best years are yet to come.

Wembley has staged few greater recoveries than this. As the right-hand sweep of the Stadium erupted into a wall of sound and Everton trooped up for the trophy, we knew the result was fitting.

Brown Wins Wednesday Ticket Clash

Sheffield Wednesday manager Alan Brown has won his stand against what he called 'excessive demands' by five of his players for FA Cup Final tickets. For their match with Everton, his team will receive only what they are allowed under Cup rules.

Brown said: 'Each man has listened to me and apologised. In future they will accept without question my decision on tickets.'

Now he will share the Wembley tickets on the basis of appearances in

the 5 games which have taken the club to their first Final for 31 years.

Brown had accused his players of being greedy, and had threatened to resign.

'I am not going to have anything that means business blackmail,' he said. But yesterday he conceded: 'They are only young, and they made their decision in a hurry. They did not mean they would not support me football-wise.'

Brown himself will receive four tickets – as allowed by the rules.

Final as dull in prospect. We were utterly wrong. Wednesday emerged before us as a side of deep thought, of undoubted merit. Everton played, and won, with resource and restraint.

The peak moments of the match – its points of crisis, its instants of drama and decision – have now been charted:

How Wednesday struck in five minutes with a McCalliog goal that flew off Wilson's heel.

How this goal drove Everton out of the cautious camp they had begun to establish around their goal and sent them seeking the equaliser.

How Wednesday survived Alex Young's sharp threats – a justified appeal for a penalty, a 'goal' that could have been barely offside – to lead still at half-time.

How McCalliog and Eustace busily built a midfield command that threatened to overwhelm Everton.

How Ford and Fantham created a second goal that was to be the start of

Temple scores Everton's winning goal

Sunday morning, so it must be Euston station for the trip home. Harry Catterick, Everton's manager, holds the Cup

Jubilant Everton players hold the Cup aloft

The Morning after the Night Before

The morning after the night before at Wembley ... and there, abandoned on the terraces, was a perfectly good pair of tweed trousers.

They must, I suppose, have belonged to an Everton supporter, too excited to notice the draught.

In his own way, he helped to swell the pile of Cup Final rubbish cleared away yesterday – eight lorry loads of rubbish and a sackful or two of lost property.

An expert groundsman can tell what sort of team has been playing by the kind of rubbish their fans leave behind. A London team's supporters will leave four times as many evening papers as anyone else, while the youthful fans who go along to Schoolboy Internationals have a gerbil-like habit of tearing all their bits of paper into confetti size. Fans from the north-east always leave more beer bottles than anyone else, while those from the north-west always leave most mufflers and scarves.

Mount Everest of Litter

Reg Butler, the maintenance department foreman, could have told you that both teams this year came from within 50 miles of Manchester, even if he'd just come back from six months on Mars. One look at the number of red and black cans on the ground was enough. These were tins of a Manchester-made rum and cola drink ('not more than 2 per cent alcohol').

Mr Butler had a team of 50 cleaners at work by 8 a.m. amassing the Mount Everest of litter. It was too dirty this year to be pulped, so it will just be dumped. And 14 electricians were reconnecting the dog-track lights which had been dismantled to give a clear view of the football. On the roof, other men were taking down the 70 flagpoles which are used only for big events.

But in all the litter of milk bottles, bus tickets, railway timetables, funny hats, whisky bottles and streamers, inside the Stadium and out, you couldn't see a programme anywhere. Several people were looking for one. But, as a cleaner put it, 'After the battle to get here, people won't ever drop them. They take them home to show they've actually been to the Cup Final.'

Trousers, of course, are easier to come by.

1967

TOTTENHAM HOTSPUR 2
CHELSEA 1

ATTENDANCE
100 000

REFEREE
K. Dagnall (Bolton)

GOALSCORERS
Robertson, Saul
Tambling

TEAMS

Tottenham Hotspur	Chelsea
Jennings	Bonetti
Kinnear	A. Harris
Knowles	McCreadie
Mullery	Hollins
England	Hinton
Mackay	R. Harris
Robertson	Cooke
Greaves	Baldwin
Gilzean	Hately
Venables	Tambling
Saul	Boyce

THE ROAD TO THE FINAL

Tottenham Hotspur
4th round
v Portsmouth 3–1 (h)
5th round
v Bristol City 2–0 (h)
6th round
v Birmingham City 0–0 (a)
Replay 6–0 (h)
Semi-Final
v Nottingham Forest 2–1

Chelsea
4th round
v Brighton & Hove Albion 1–1 (a)
Replay 4–0 (h)
5th round
v Sheffield United 2–0 (h)
6th round
v Sheffield Wednesday 1–0 (h)
Semi-Final
v Leeds United 1–0

Man of Destiny Now Joins the Greats

Chelsea's keeper Bonetti slides to his knees after Spurs score their first goal. Jimmy Greaves on left

SPURS WILL BE led again into Europe next season by a man whose only security is the team's success. Manager Bill Nicholson has no contract. He will not accept one. So a man who has spent a fortune to amass for Spurs a wealth of fame is tied only by the same terms as the office boy.

This was revealed on Saturday night after Nicholson's team and tactics had given Spurs the FA Cup for the third time in six years.

Mackay, puffed with pride, walked up to take the trophy. I believe that Nicholson, man of destiny, is the person who had done most to earn it.

In the small hours afterwards when the champagne and confidences had burst out, Spurs' chairman Fred Wale said: 'When I asked Bill if he wanted to try his hand at managing he simply answered "yes". Money was not mentioned, no contract was talked about. It has been the same with this man ever since.'

The hand that Nicholson agreed to try has proved both steady and skilled. Contract or not, Nicholson has joined the greats by his own merits.

Tactical Switch

Never has his acumen been more clearly proved than in his instructions to this year's Cup Finalists.

Mullery, it was thought, would continue to be the back marker in defence. Mackay would continue to romp unfettered midfield.

Nicholson changed all that on Friday afternoon. As a result, Mullery became the main instrument of Chelsea's destruction, Mackay the all-seeing prop of a defence. Mullery told me: 'I was surprised at this. But not so surprised as Chelsea seemed to be. They had worked on the theory that Dave would be charging upfield. They never seemed to get over the fact that he didn't.'

Magnificently Marked

It should have been altered as soon as it became obvious that Gilzean was winning every ball. No goals came from his stream of flicked headers, mainly because Greaves was magnificently marked by Ron Harris. But Gilzean's play was like a persistent, prodding finger into Chelsea's midriff, making them twist and twitch uneasily. They were never without the pressure of his presence.

Cooke gave the game its greatest skills, with swift dribbles for Chelsea. They were robbed of reward by his lack of support and the cunning selection by Spurs of the 'killing grounds', where Venables, Mackay or Robertson waited to pounce.

Academic Match

I rated this a good, if academic, match but an unemotional Final. After the first 20 minutes, the crowd drifted into silent acceptance of what seemed certain to happen – Spurs fans didn't need to cheer, Chelsea's following knew it would be no use.

Spurs' control and professionalism were so overwhelming it was like watching a high-wire act practising a foot above the ground. They would not slip, and it did not matter if they did. This Final died not for lack of interest but for lack of hope.

The emotion was saved for the celebrations. Then Nicholson told his team: 'Enjoy yourselves. In winning the Cup you did more than I thought likely when the season started.' He meant that.

He added: 'But don't get big-headed. You still have to win in Europe to be as good a team as the last.' He meant that too.

Not Showbusiness

'We're not going there to entertain anyone, we're going to win this match. People are saying it will be a great game, but I don't know about that. We'll attack if the game goes that way, or we'll defend. I know it will be a great occasion, there will be royalty there, but we won't be there to entertain them.'

Tommy Docherty,
Chelsea Manager

England outjumps Hately to head the ball clear

Two Letters in a Million

Sir,
Please find enclosed one 10 shilling Cup ticket.

I have heard and read of the rackets in tickets and that people will pay ridiculous prices to see their only soccer game of the year.

I would like you to find a disappointed fan (from either side) who is unable to obtain a ticket and most deserves to see the match.

Name and address supplied

Sir,
I enclose a 10 shilling Cup Final ticket and hope you will pass it on to a deserving soccer fan.

I cannot use it and I would hate to think that it reached some unscrupulous person whose main idea would be to make a profit.

Name and address supplied

Spurs victorious – the suited gatecrasher followed the team into the dressing room for a share of the champagne

A fan's dream come true . . . a Spurs' supporter (he's the one in the suit) gatecrashes the lap of honour

3 a.m. at the Hilton – and the Spurs players are still celebrating, with their partners

Boyle's Nightmare

Chelsea's John Boyle relived an FA Cup Final nightmare at Wembley on Saturday. On Friday night, at Chelsea's Hendon Hotel, he had dreamed vividly that Chelsea would lose to Tottenham ... 2–1.

'When I woke up I felt really terrible,' said Boyle. 'I told my room-mate, Peter Osgood, about it and he had a right go at me for being pessimistic.'

Osgood said yesterday: 'I tried to make him put it at the back of his mind and I don't think it had any effect in the match. But afterwards he felt twice as sick. It was like having a nightmare twice over.'

1968

WEST BROMWICH ALBION 1

EVERTON 0

ATTENDANCE
100 000

REFEREE
L. Callaghan (Merthyr Tydfil)

GOALSCORER
Astle

TEAMS

West Bromwich Albion	Everton
Clark	West
Astle	Wright
Lovett	Hurst
Hope	Labone
Collard	Wilson
Brown	Kendall
Williams	Ball
Kaye	Harvey
Talbut	Husband
Fraser	Royle
Osborne	Morrissey

THE ROAD TO THE FINAL

West Bromwich Albion
4th round
v Southampton 1–1 (h)
Replay 3–2 (a)
5th round
v Portsmouth 2–1 (a)
6th round
v Liverpool 0–0 (h)
Replay 1–1 (a)
2nd replay 2–1 (at Maine Road)
Semi-Final
v Birmingham City 2–0

Everton
4th round
v Carlisle United 2–0 (a)
5th round
v Tranmere Rovers 2–0 (h)
6th round
v Leicester City 3–1 (a)
Semi-Final
v Leeds United 1–0

Plea for the Finalists: Not Guilty of Murder

After 90 goal-less minutes, Everton goalkeeper West is taken by surprise

AT LEAST THEY did not do it on purpose. Football, at Saturday's Cup Final, fell victim to a clumsy attempt at the kiss of life rather than a calculated killing.

After two hours at this awful anticlimax, I am convinced that West Brom and Everton bore the Final no malice. This sole mitigation of a match that seemed so much worse, because it had promised to be so much better, deserves to be offered. It is easier to forgive incompetence than planned destruction.

Both teams were beset by one factor beyond their control: the pitch demanded from the forwards a fine judgement of pace that few could produce. And it gave the defenders the chance to make comprehensive sweeping tackles, so easy to launch, so hard to elude. It was no coincidence that nearly every defender appeared a better man than the man he marked.

28 Fouls

The attacking exceptions would certainly include Everton's Ball and Albion's Hope, but both moved easiest midfield where marking was less rigid and tackling less imminent. When Ball finally forced himself to play nearer the tip of Everton's raids he began to suffer like the rest.

Much has been made of the 28 fouls of the match, less of the fact that most were for obstruction or tripping, few for real

All eyes on the ball as WBA's Kaye heads it off the line

pieces of foul play. Comment has also been made on the fact that attacks on opponents well outnumbered attacks on their goal, but less of the statistic that shots came as freely as in all but the very best of League matches.

West Bromwich won a match I could never see Everton being about to lose. The Merseyside team had seemed more alert and more dangerous in the few raids that survived the first half. And Everton mounted the one sustained burst of attacking midway through the second, when Husband began to compile a list of misses that will haunt him for years.

Albion survived this battering, apparently at the cost of their remaining strength. Just before full-time, Brown, Collard and Hope were standing wearily, watching the play flow about them. Ball's industry must have filled them with a sense of doom.

Strength from Somewhere

After the cramp had been massaged from their calves at 90 minutes, and hope dinned into their ears, Albion found strength from somewhere. The figures prove it. In the last 30 minutes they managed as many shots as in the first 90.

One, finally, was enough.

It came from Astle, whose previous contribution had been one single fine header in the 93rd minute. For the first time he took a pass with no Labone to hamper him and in a flash he set upon the Everton defence.

His first right-foot shot was blocked, and his instant swing with his left drove the ball high over West's shoulder.

Perhaps for this one act of instinct Albion deserved to win. But for Everton's entire defence, manful but unlucky to the last, carrying away a loser's medal was a clear injustice.

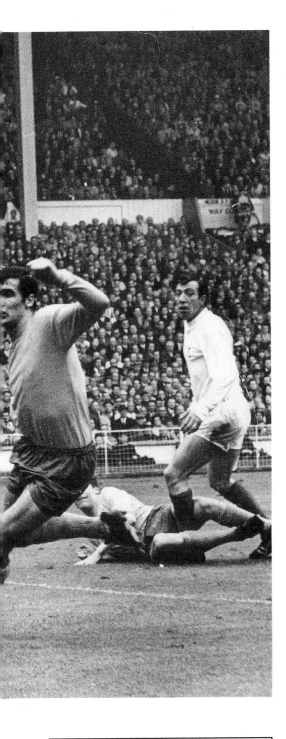

It took 93 minutes – but we did it! Jeff Astle celebrates his winning goal

Fans make use of every possible viewpoint to see their heroes

Cup Hero's Wife Backed Everton

Laraine Astle, 22, the blonde wife of Jeff Astle, scorer of West Bromwich Albion's winning goal in Saturday's FA Cup Final, confessed yesterday that she had a £1 bet – on Everton.

She said: 'I always bet for the Albion to lose, so that they will win. It's superstition, really.'

MANCHESTER CITY 1
LEICESTER CITY 0

ATTENDANCE
100 000

REFEREE
G. McCabe (Sheffield)

GOALSCORER
Young

TEAMS

Manchester City	Leicester City
Dowd	Shilton
Book	Rodrigues
Pardoe	Nish
Doyle	Roberts
Booth	Woollett
Oakes	Cross
Summerbee	Fern
Bell	Gibson
Lee	Lochhead
Young	Clarke
Coleman	Glover

THE ROAD TO THE FINAL

Manchester City
4th round
v Newcastle United 0–0 (a)
Replay 2–0 (h)
5th round
v Blackburn Rovers 4–1 (h)
6th round
v Tottenham Hotspur 1–0 (h)
Semi-Final
v Everton 1–0

Leicester City
4th round
v Millwall 1–0 (a)
5th round
v Liverpool 0–0 (a)
Replay 1–0 (h)
6th round
v Mansfield Town 1–0 (a)
Semi-Final
v West Bromwich Albion 1–0

Mercer Gives Bad News after the Good

Tony Book holds aloft the precious Cup; Mike Doyle supports his captain on his shoulders

THE FOOTBALL WITH which Manchester City raised this Final nearly to the level of its promise was one of the best things to happen to soccer in years.

And the forecast by Joe Mercer about the way City must now develop was one of the worst.

Mercer said that City were going to be a very good side. Nobody, in the minutes after this match, was going to argue. 'But,' he added, 'you'd be kidding yourself if you thought you could always play that way.'

'We have got to learn to be as good going back as going forward. We have got to learn to contain. This is not going to be good for the public, but it is going to be good for the club.'

So cling to the memory of the best of Manchester's Wembley football – we may not see so much of the like in future.

Never in Doubt

Only the impossibly demanding could have been dissatisfied by the score. For the chances were there for a 3–3 draw, or a 4–3 victory for either side ... and the fact that the shots went wide does not detract from the moves that created the openings.

But though Leicester might have scored

Referee Kicks Off Decimals

Referee George McCabe will make history today on the Wembley pitch before he starts the Cup Final.

Just before 3 p.m. he will put a new 50 pence piece into circulation for the first time.

The seven-sided ten shilling bit will not become legal tender for six months, but captains Book and Nish will officially win and lose today's toss with the first coin of its kind to be put into public use.

McCabe received the coin yesterday from the Minister for Sport at the House of Commons. He does not plan to spend it after October 14th, though by then it will be legal to do so and in this case worth even more than the face value of a Cup Final ticket.

Princess Anne meets the Manchester captain before the game. The chairman of the FA looks on

A moment of anxiety – and acrobatics – for Manchester

Dejection from Leicester just after Manchester had scored the match's only goal

before Young gave the Cup to Manchester, though Leicester might later have pulled level, had the chances been made *for* Clarke rather than *by* Clarke, the winners were never in doubt.

Having walked the pitch, I know that the criticism of the surface was justified and, therefore, the level of precision in the play was remarkable.

The losers were not left without heroes. Clarke, of course, created more with less than any colleague or rival; Cross was a superb sight in defence and Lochhead lost only with his shooting the applause he deserved with his aggression.

The mood was equal to the match. Fear was hardly evident, bad fouls were few, and the sight of Manchester men clapping the losers provided a warm afterglow.

Manchester City, no matter how they develop, are among the best Cup-winners of past decades. Leicester, no matter whether they now survive, are far from being the worst losers.

Cross Your Fingers, Hope to Win

It is not just skill, fitness and quick thinking which wins Cup Finals. Ask almost any of the 22 players today.

Says Manchester's Joe Mercer: 'Footballers are a superstitious lot.' And Leicester's manager Frank O'Farrell states: 'I believe in luck – the luck of the Irish.'

Even referee George McCabe declares stoutly: 'I have no superstitions – but I always pack my bag the same way.'

Unlike Leicester's Allan Clarke, Mike Summerbee WILL walk under a ladder before a big game. But he still uses the shinguards he has had eight years. 'That's habit, not superstition' – he says!

Leicester's winger Len Glover is frank about his superstition. 'You name it and, blimey, I do it. I never go under ladders, I'm careful with mirrors and I go out looking for black cats!'

A lucky coin and two St Christopher's medals will be in Manchester skipper's Tony Book's jacket pocket in the dressing room while he is on the field.

Peter Rodrigues will be putting on his right boot first. Andy Lochhead never puts his boots on the dressing table. Graham Cross will be wanting to be last out of the tunnel.

Peter Shilton always puts his shirt on before his shorts, while Alan Woollett goes back home if he has forgotten to say goodbye to his collie dog Kim. Let's hope he hasn't forgotten today!

TV Trouble

The Cup Final clash is still raging – for the BBC and London Weekend Television at least.

The rival TV teams clashed as they tried to get interviews with Manchester City and Leicester players after the match at Wembley.

Mr Jimmy Hill claimed yesterday that his team of LWT staff were manhandled by BBC men.

Mr David Yallop, LWT floor manager, says he lost a tooth in the scuffles. 'I'm considering suing the BBC and the man concerned,' he added.

But the company did admit to dressing three of their men – including Mr Yallop – in tracksuits to try to deceive the BBC.

Mr Bryan Cowgill, head of sports programmes, said in a statement: 'We had an exclusive contract to interview the Manchester players, which was known to all concerned, including ITV, who had been beaten by the BBC in competition for these rights.'

But LWT retorted: 'There is no question of the BBC having exclusive rights.'

1970

CHELSEA 2

LEEDS UNITED 1
(replay, after extra time; following a 2–2 draw after extra time)

ATTENDANCE
100 000
(Replay) 62 078

REFEREE
E. Jennings (Stourbridge)

GOALSCORERS
Houseman, Hutchinson
Charlton, Jones
Replay: Osgood, Webb
Jones

TEAMS

Chelsea	Leeds United
Bonetti	Sprake
Harris	Madeley
McCreadie	Cooper
Hollins	Bremner
Dempsey	Charlton
Webb	Hunter
Baldwin	Lorimer
Cooke	Clarke
Osgood	Jones
Hutchinson	Giles
Houseman	Gray

(Harvey replaced Sprake in the replay)

THE ROAD TO THE FINAL

Chelsea
4th round
v Burnley 2–2 (h)
Replay 3–1 (a)
5th round
v Crystal Palace 4–1 (h)
6th round
v Queen's Park Rangers 4–2 (a)
Semi-Final
v Watford 5–1

Leeds United
4th round
v Sutton United 6–0 (a)
5th round
v Mansfield Town 2–0 (a)
6th round
v Swindon Town 2–0 (a)
Semi-Final
v Manchester United 0–0
Replay 0–0
2nd replay 1–0

Leeds Won, Chelsea Didn't Lose

A tense moment as Webb and Gray duel for the ball

THE GAME HAD gasped to its finish. Wembley, now a place of rustling, wind-blown papers, was miles behind the Chelsea team coach speeding steadily towards central London. Then at a strip of dual carriageway, the coach carrying the Leeds team drew alongside. And for 100 yards Bremner & Co. smilingly toasted their rivals with raised glasses.

That moment will remain with me. For to fight as Leeds and Chelsea did through the longest of Cup Final afternoons, and then to pass away to different venues to talk over different memories with such a gesture, was magnificent.

Let us speak plainly. Leeds were not toasting their equals. They won this Cup Final as well as if it had been won. It was just that Chelsea didn't lose.

Flair and Instinct

Counting chances, nominating heroes, seeking fallen idols is not the way to assess the margins of the match. Simply, in all things, Leeds played at their best. And at their best they are England's greatest team. Simply, Chelsea, marvellously resolute, somehow endured, and know next time they can be, must be, better.

Gray, tearing at the right flank of Chelsea's defence, knowing Cooper was ready to take over if he should ever tire, was the man who should have won it for Leeds.

Bonetti, diving gloriously, was the man who saved it for Chelsea.

And the others; Charlton and Dempsey showing what centre half play is about; Giles and Bremner making Houseman and Hollins play heroically just to avoid being overwhelmed; McCreadie's fatigue, Harris's fading strength, Madeley's endless power.

The goals: Charlton inelegantly and Jones crisply. Houseman luckily, and Hutchinson despairingly. The misses: Gray

Chelsea's goalkeeper (centre) is caught well out of position as Jackie Charlton heads in a goal

and Clarke against the bar, Dempsey and Osgood over and wide.

Football played with flair and instinct, with spirit and sportsmanship. And finally, Don Revie asking the question no one can hope to answer. Standing in his dressing room, he said quietly: 'And just think what sort of game would it have been on a pitch?'

Goalkeeper Bonetti is grounded as Leeds score their second goal

Jackie Charlton about to intercept Peter Osgood's goal attempt. The match ended in a draw – the first time this had happened in a Wembley Final

REPLAY
Stop-Start Final

THE PATTERN set by two hours at Wembley was re-established in the first minutes of this FA Cup Final replay at Old Trafford, with Leeds pounding through on attack and Chelsea living breathlessly from escape to escape.

Webb, who had seen too much of Gray in the first match, was relieved to be shifted into the centre. But Gray came booming unexpectedly through the middle and he and Webb renewed their acquaintance.

Hutchinson, boring in from the right, swung Chelsea's first shot wide of goal. Then Osgood brilliantly beat Bremner and Hunter on the edge of the penalty area to make room for their second. That, too, was wide.

Mass Protest

Players from both sides were cut down by awful tackles, and referee Jennings, seeking peace in his final important match, was content to wave the odd reproving finger.

Leeds were storming ahead between the stoppages and Jones moved on to meet a cross from the quick and agile Gray to scrape the outside of a post with a shot. Then Bonetti was lured from his goal and beaten to the ball by Lorimer on the right of the area. It took the quick insight of

McCreadie to get back on the line and clear a certain goal.

The match was halted for nearly three minutes when Bonetti was laid out by a late and pointless charge from Jones. The incident brought a mass protest from the Chelsea team and an angry mass attack when the game restarted.

This reaction can be said to have cost Chelsea a goal. For they were all up pushing desperately when Leeds played their way coolly out of trouble to where Clarke picked up the running on the halfway line. He beat three men before sending Jones on a long run at the Chelsea goal. And, despite having to squeeze between both Dempsey and McCreadie, Jones's persistence and strength earned him the room to shoot a brilliant goal.

Cooke and Clarke were involved in a brisk kicking match soon after the restart and, like all the earlier nastiness, it went unpunished. But finally, there came an incident which could not be ignored. Charlton and Osgood were involved in a scramble near the touch-line and the floored Charlton got up and ran three yards before knocking Osgood flat.

This time Mr Jennings did have a long chat with the two concerned. Jennings finally decided on sterner action in the

They may have had to wait for the replay, but these Chelsea players are convinced the Cup has found its rightful home at last

65th minute. Osgood and Bremner had tangled and when Bremner appeared to be hacking at the fallen Chelsea man, the referee thought it worth only another cool glance. So Hutchinson rushed up impetuously to knock Bremner flat and was booked.

Leeds' grip on the game had seemed unshakeable when Chelsea again displayed their capacity to save themselves with an equaliser 12 minutes from time.

Cooke made the goal. From an inside right position half-way to the line, he produced a magnificent pass over the Leeds defence. And Osgood, sprinting free at last, dived to head a magnificent goal.

Bremner was constantly in trouble in the last few minutes. First he was kicked unconscious by a wild and dangerous clearance from Baldwin. Then he appeared to have been booked after a skirmish with Hutchinson, and finally he was brought crashing to the ground as he charged in on goal and lay screaming his protest at the refusal of a penalty.

Just before the end of the first period of extra time came the seventh goal of this saga – and for the first time, Chelsea

were ahead. A long throw from Hutchinson on the left brought the Chelsea defenders up in support. Dempsey got to the ball to back-head it under the bar and it was there the lunging Webb forced the ball home.

The last 15 minutes of this incredible Final were almost unreal. With Hinton on to reinforce Chelsea's defence, almost the entire period was spent with Leeds pounding away in and around the Chelsea area.

Finally exhausted, it was all over.

For another year.

1971

ARSENAL 2
LIVERPOOL 1
(after extra time)

ATTENDANCE
100 000

REFEREE
N. Burtenshaw (Great Yarmouth)

GOALSCORERS
Graham, George
Heighway

TEAMS

Arsenal	Liverpool
Wilson	Clemence
Rice	Lawler
McNab	Lindsay
Storey	Smith
McLintock	Lloyd
Simpson	Hughes
Armstrong	Callaghan
Graham	Evans
Radford	Heighway
Kennedy	Toshack
George	Hall

THE ROAD TO THE FINAL

Arsenal
4th round
v Portsmouth 1–1 (a)
Replay 3–2 (h)
5th round
v Manchester City 2–1 (a)
6th round
v Leicester City 0–0 (a)
Replay 1–0 (h)
Semi-Final
v Stoke City 2–2
Replay 2–0

Liverpool
4th round
v Swansea City 3–0 (h)
5th round
v Southampton 1–0 (h)
6th round
v Tottenham Hotspur 0–0 (h)
Replay 1–0 (a)
Semi-Final
v Everton 2–1

Gunners Double! – Graham, George do it in Extra Time

The ball slips out of Clemence's reach as Graham equalises for Arsenal in the 100th minute

IT'S THE DOUBLE for Arsenal. Extra-time goals by Graham and George gave the League champions a magnificent victory in the Cup Final this afternoon.

What a comeback by Arsenal! Having dominated the first goal-less 90 minutes, they had the shattering experience of a goal by Liverpool's Heighway after a minute of extra time. Yet they picked themselves off the floor.

As Liverpool had been allowed to retain their all-red strip, Arsenal were in their lucky change of gold shirts and blue shorts.

McLintock won the toss and decided to kick towards the goal behind which were the Arsenal fans. So Liverpool were facing their own supporters – normally they like to play towards them in the second half.

Aggressive Start

Liverpool were off to an aggressive start. Toshack headed a long, high pass from Smith into the area, where Simpson partially cleared.

Storey bowled Heighway over to a reproving admonition from the referee, but Smith's free kick was wasted by Hughes, who put a centre behind.

There was a hectic scramble in the Arsenal goalmouth as Evans tried to force a way through. George stopped the run and then calmly looked up to send Kennedy away, completely free of the opposition. Unfortunately for Arsenal, he was on the left, and his angled shot flashed wide of the far post.

It's a Habit ...

Tommy Smith throws the ball across the dressing-room to Emlyn Hughes, who puts it under the bench until he has finished changing. Smith goes to the lavatory and leaves the match programme there.

There are a whole lot of super-stitions at Liverpool before a big match ... Smith has a massage ... Lawler throws a brush – the same one before every match – to Smith, who runs it through his hair, then throws it back.

The team always try to go out on the field in the same order – there's trouble if anyone steps out of turn. Hughes always waits behind to make sure he is last.

The relief was only temporary. Back came Liverpool, sharper on the ball, alert to the opening and accurate in the pass. Arsenal's midfield men, notably Graham and George, were forced right back and could give little help to the men in front. When McNab slung across a high centre, Lloyd climbed above Storey to head clear, his height invaluable.

not his head, so it came to nothing.

Graham headed a corner by Armstrong back into the middle, Lloyd partially cleared and Storey hit the clearance on the half-volley just over the bar.

George startled the Liverpool defenders by suddenly letting fly from 30 yards and Clemence clawed in vain as the ball screamed over the bar. But once more it was

had a chance to put Arsenal in the lead, but Clemence smothered the shot with brilliant anticipation. A minute later Liverpool came the closest they had been to a goal, after Simpson had fouled Evans. Callaghan pushed the free kick wide to Lindsay, whose fierce shot was turned wide by Wilson at the foot of the right-hand post. Wilson flung himself to

Six nerve-wracking minutes later, it was glory for Charlie George

Hughes, his long stride eating up the ground, was very dangerous with his sudden runs on goal. Once he tried a two by one shot which was deflected by McLintock, but safely gathered by Wilson.

More Composure

Arsenal were playing with more composure now, as you would expect of the League champions. Another quick break through the middle, this time led by Radford, caused Clemence to come outside the area to kick into touch. A brilliant, curling pass by George put Radford away on the left. Over came a long centre and Lindsay headed for a corner as Storey came careering in.

A foul by Graham on Heighway led to another uneasy siege of the Arsenal goal as Lloyd headed the free kick back into the middle. Once more George ended the danger with an astute clearance.

Heighway's sudden bursts were always dangerous, despite being closely watched, mainly by Rice. He put over an inviting centre, but it was to Toshack's feet and

a case of promise rather than execution.

Brilliant Anticipation

Two minutes from the interval, Armstrong

concede a corner as Lawler tried to centre from the clearance.

The miss of the match came after 50 minutes, and the culprit was Kennedy, at

Bill Shankly's Guilty Secret!

Mention the name of Arsenal to Bill Shankly, the shaggy, craggy Liverpool manager, and he is apt to snarl.

Suggest the Gunners have a chance to win at Wembley and he'll give you a withering glance.

'Arsenal? Who are they?' he'll ask with studied sarcasm.

Bill is a great lover of Liverpool. And a great hater of the opposition. This time, it's Arsenal. So now we reveal a fact which will bring blushes to Mr Shankly's weatherbeaten face.

Once he was proud to play for Arsenal ... and regularly!

That was 28 years ago, when Bill was a Leading Aircraftsman. And we have the evidence to prove it. It's all there in the programme of the day – No. 4, LAC Shankly, an Arsenal guest when stationed in the south.

Highbury was an Air Raid Warden's post during the War – Arsenal shared White Hart Lane with Spurs – and young Shankly would stay overnight with the wardens. One of them complained to Jimmy Logie after the War: 'Shankly got on my nerves. He never stopped talking about football.' So he hasn't changed THAT much!

19 the youngest player on the field.

A corner by Armstrong was cleared with difficulty and Liverpool broke away when Hughes brilliantly anticipated a pass by Simpson.

Disappointing Finishing

George was the forward who threatened most often to break the deadlock. He hit a tremendous first-time shot which was too close for Clemence's comfort. Toshack managed to head a centre back into the middle, but Rice was too quick for Hall. Storey had developed a limp and after 62 minutes he was replaced by Kelly.

By this stage Arsenal were the more threatening, using the wings well, the quick one-two through the middle, and were prepared to shoot, though their finishing was disappointing.

Liverpool made a change at 67 minutes, bringing on Thompson to replace Evans. In the 77th minute Arsenal almost cracked the remarkable Liverpool defence when Graham back-headed a long throw by Radford on to the bar, with Clemence beaten. A corner followed, and Graham rose for a fine header which Lindsay blocked at the foot of a post.

With four minutes to go, yet another chance for Kennedy, squeezed out by Radford. The shot was from an angle, admittedly, but Kennedy put it wide. So it was extra time, and even referee Norman Burtenshaw looked exhausted.

Heighway Robbery

After 91 minutes Liverpool at last ended the deadlock when Heighway put them in front. He was put clear by Thompson, cut in along the byeline and beat Wilson from the narrowest of angles, with a shot along the ground. Heighway robbery, as Arsenal had completely dominated the match up to this point.

Miraculously, Arsenal equalised after 100 minutes, Graham slipping the ball past Clemence to round off a move between Kelly and Radford.

The excitement which had perhaps been lacking in the first 90 minutes was now crowded into extra time, with both teams flat out for the winner.

Liverpool looked the more tired – several players had cramp, even Hughes. This had immediate effects, such as the point when Smith broke up an Arsenal attack, came out with the ball and set up an attack for Heighway, who failed to exploit it because he too had cramp.

Finally, George put Arsenal in front

No doubt about this home's allegiance!

Showbusiness Says ...

Sorry, Arsenal, but the showbusiness world favours Liverpool.

In fact, Anthony Booth from *Till Death Us Do Part* and *Oh! Calcutta!* says: 'They can send them the Cup now. Liverpool are the better side, and have the greatest manager in the world.'

Mind you, Booth, like Cilla Black and Jimmy Tarbuck, who share his supreme confidence, is just a shade biased. He is President of the London branch of the Liverpool Supporters' Club.

Non-committed Eric Morecambe picks Liverpool, too. Says he: 'They wear our reserve colours, so it's a foregone conclusion they'll win,' before adding with the dignity of a Luton Town director: 'They have strength in every position.'

Arsenal have support, of course, like

regular Highbury fan Bernie Winters, who forecasts a 3–1 win, and that cheerful Cockney Tommy Steele, who says: 'If they'd lost on Monday, Arsenal would have annihilated Liverpool. Now, as League Champions, I think they'll breeze to victory in the Cup.'

There is heavyweight support for Arsenal from British boxing champions past and present – Henry Cooper, an Arsenal fan for several years, and Joe Bugner – but former Minister for Sport and ex-referee Denis Howell joins the majority view behind Liverpool.

'Arsenal have done magnificently, but I saw Liverpool come back to win against Everton in the semi-final. Until then I didn't think they were quite mature enough, but clearly they are. They have skill plus a powerhouse of effort.'

with a great goal after 106 minutes. He had moved up as a striker, took a return pass from Radford and cracked his shot irresistably past Clemence.

He fell down and lay full length with exhaustion. Half his team-mates had no

energy left to congratulate him.

How Arsenal came back so magnificently at the end of such a gruelling match, at the end of a gruelling season, I will never understand. What a tribute to their strength of character.

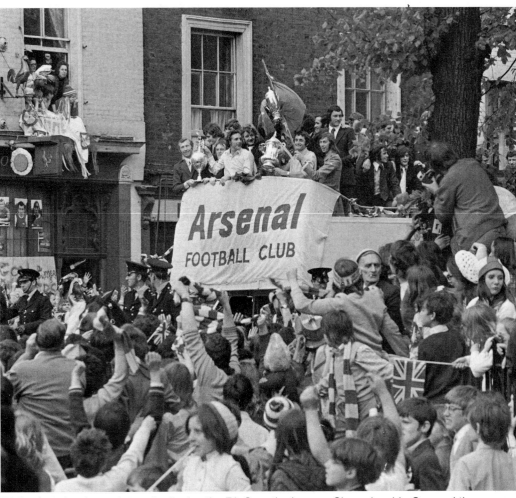

'Can I hold it for a minute?' A young fan at Islington Town Hall with Frank McLintock

Triple triumph – Arsenal proudly display the FA Cup, the League Championship Cup and the FA Youth Cup, won by their boys' team

GOALGRAPH, a Sportsmail Special, shows the Build-up and Talks to the Men Involved in the Winner

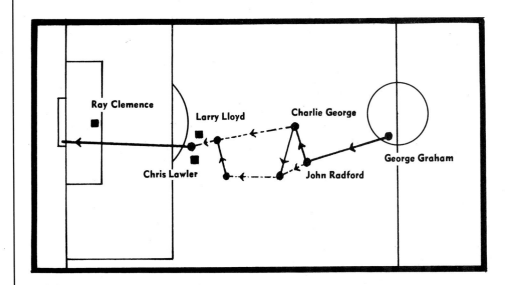

George Graham, the man of the match, started it. He said: 'This high clearance from their goalkeeper came downfield and I got under it to head it back to Radford.'

Over to **John Radford**: 'I played the ball inside to Charlie George, got it back first time, ran on and played it back. He dummied, went on a pace or two and shot.'

Come in **Charlie George**: 'When I get the ball like that I'm supposed to have a go round the edge of the box and I whacked it. No difficulty at all. In it went. Fabulous!'

The ball deflected off **Larry Lloyd's** left foot. Said Lloyd: 'I was two feet away from him going in with a tackle when he shot and the ball just caught my foot.'

Did the deflection make any difference? Said goalkeeper **Ray Clemence**: 'No, it might have dipped a bit, but it came straight on.'

LEEDS UNITED 1
ARSENAL 0

ATTENDANCE
100 000

REFEREE
D. Smith (Gloucester)

GOALSCORER
Clarke

TEAMS

Leeds United	Arsenal
Harvey	Barnett
Reaney	Rice
Madeley	McNab
Bremner	Storey
Charlton	McLintock
Hunter	Simpson
Lorimer	Armstrong
Clarke	Ball
Jones	George
Giles	Radford
Gray	Graham

THE ROAD TO THE FINAL

Leeds United
4th round
v Liverpool 0–0 (a)
Replay 2–0 (h)
5th round
v Cardiff City 2–0 (a)
6th round
v Tottenham Hotspur 2–1 (h)
Semi-Final
v Birmingham City 3–0

Arsenal
4th round
v Reading 2–1 (a)
5th round
v Derby County 2–2 (a)
Replay 0–0 (h)
2nd replay 1–0 (a)
6th round
v Orient 1–0 (a)
Semi-Final
v Stoke City 1–1
Replay 2–1

Violent, Yes, But Never Vindictive

Charlie George and Jack Charlton battle for the ball as the wind creates havoc with their hairstyles

THE MILLIONS WHO watched and shuddered through the Centenary Cup Final's host of fouls will need no convincing that soccer is a violent society.

What matters is that the world should know the spirit in which Leeds wrested a major honour from Arsenal to support their status as the best team in the country.

There was nothing vicious or vindictive about most of the physical assaults which had Wembley's 100 000 and the world's televiewers wincing.

This Final did more than bring Leeds the first leg of their double seal of greatness. It laid bare the physical concept of the game.

Arsenal and Leeds – the retiring and the elect double champions – accept that success is the privilege of those prepared to administer and take their punishment.

Peter Storey – Arsenal's personification

135

Delighted fans – and players – after Leeds score the winning goal

of that philosophy in the way he stifled the genius of Johnny Giles, said: 'Who was badly hurt other than Mick Jones, who fell on his own elbow?

Suddenly, It's The Last Walk

Let's open up the Wembley scene by starting at the most exclusive spot – the dressing-rooms.

Club dressing-rooms are warm and well-used. Wembley's are austere, cold in character, tiled and clinical like a hospital. There are a lot of strange faces about, security men, CID, uniformed officials.

The noise seeps down to you, but you don't recognise the tunes the band are playing, although you hear your supporters shout.

The dressing-rooms are on two levels with a big bath, showers and individual baths up some steps. The ceilings are high, there's too much room and too much time for some.

Then you're brought out into the tunnel to line up. It's dark and a bit damp and you feel you're preparing for the last walk.

Your thoughts are only for yourself and your job; how you are going to react to the noise, colour and light of that amphitheatre up there.

'Our teams respect each other. And if the game seemed hard, well that was down to finding out the truth of each other's qualities. Where's the satisfaction in playing well just because you've been allowed to?'

Leeds and Arsenal sorted each other out in the first half, then Leeds got on with sorting out the destiny of the FA Cup with their better football in the second half.

Their hunger for the battle and the glory – particularly of their strikers – was much sharper than Arsenal's.

The result was a fascinating contest – but not a memorable Final.

The frighteners were on from the 1st to the 46th minute, in which Bob McNab, Norman Hunter, Billy Bremner and Charlie George were booked in that order.

Miraculous

McNab said jokingly: 'Peter Lorimer laid it on a bit thick. I only mistimed my tackle right under the Royal Box and when I went up for my medal the Duke of Edinburgh said he would appear for me at a personal hearing.'

The first half was otherwise notable for David Harvey's fine save from Frank McLintock's powerful and deflected shot, Paul Reaney's miraculous clearance from the line of probably the best shot Alan Ball has hit in his life, Geoff Barnett's scrambling unsighted save from Lorimer and Allan Clarke's prodigious header against the Arsenal crossbar.

Clarke – surprisingly voted man of the

JON'S SPORTING TYRES

'Mr Bremner, can't you put it down just for 90 minutes?'

Leeds players celebrate their victory, won
in FA Cup centenary year

match in view of Hunter's second great
Wembley performance in a week and
Simpson's magnificent defensive effort for
Arsenal – headed the 53rd-minute glory
winner from Jones's cross.

Angry McNab Will Fight Booking

Arsenal defender Bob McNab is to
appeal against his first-minute Cup
Final booking – the quickest ever at
Wembley. Referee Dave Smith cautioned him for a badly-timed tackle
on Peter Lorimer.

'Right in front of the Queen and
the Duke of Edinburgh,' said McNab
angrily. 'I am not going to let that
go. Obviously the referee was out to
make an impression.'

Leeds' manager Don Revie and captain Billy Bremner share their joy

SUNDERLAND 1
LEEDS UNITED 0

ATTENDANCE
100 000

REFEREE
K. Burns (Stourbridge)

GOALSCORER
Porterfield

TEAMS

Sunderland	Leeds United
Montgomery	Harvey
Malone	Reaney
Guthrie	Cherry
Horswill	Bremner
Watson	Madeley
Pitt	Hunter
Kerr	Lorimer
Hughes	Clarke
Halom	Jones
Porterfield	Giles
Tueart	E. Gray

THE ROAD TO THE FINAL

Sunderland
4th round
v Reading 1–1 (h)
Replay 3–1 (a)
5th round
v Manchester City 2–2 (a)
Replay 3–1 (h)
6th round
v Luton Town 2–0 (h)
Semi-Final
v Arsenal 2–1

Leeds United
4th round
v Plymouth Argyle 2–1 (h)
5th round
v West Bromwich Albion 2–0 (h)
6th round
v Derby County 1–0 (a)
Semi-Final
v Wolverhampton Wanderers 1–0

No Mystery About Stokoe's Miracle

Sunderland – the first Second Division team to win the Cup in over 40 years – celebrate their winning goal

IN A WORD, honesty made Sunderland the impossible winners of the FA Cup.

Not a man shirked a tackle, not a player failed to summon up the spirit for yet another long-burning run. Even the less gifted of their men kept trying to play football.

It would not be honest to say they were brilliant. It would not be truthful to deny that Leeds, for the first time, lacked real aggression and ravenous hunger for the battle and contributed to their own sorry downfall. It would not be proper to pretend this was a great game of pure football.

But it would be less than fair to deny Sunderland all the credit for raising themselves to produce an unforgettable occasion, for bringing back the days of high drama to the amphitheatre of Wembley.

The richest moment of all belonged to Jim Montgomery, the goalkeeper who plucked a save from the Pele-defying repertoire of Gordon Banks to resist the most menacing of all the Leeds attacks.

Montgomery was still prostrate after beating out a diving header from Trevor Cherry when Peter Lorimer stroked the

The final clearance as Malone boots the ball away

Lorimer shoots, but Montgomery swoops acrobatically to save

ball at an open goal from six yards. Montgomery sprang like some flying fish to divert the ball up against the crossbar and out to safety.

Montgomery had so defied all natural laws of agility and gravity that most of Wembley's cacophonous 100 000 believed Lorimer had shot directly against the bar.

No Justice

Much of the rest of the action revolved

around Dave Watson, once a centre forward, now transformed into potentially the most commanding centre half in England.

Watson defied Mick Jones and Alan Clarke, arguably the best pair of forwards in the land, almost single handed. Three times in the first half Watson had to

forsake the arduous task of marking Jones to make last-second saving tackles on a goalbound Clarke.

In the second half Watson luckily escaped conceding a penalty for tripping Bremner. There was no justice in one of referee Ken Burns's many bewildering decisions, only in the irony that perhaps

Stars say Leeds

The stars broadcast messages which are sometimes strong and clear, sometimes faint and difficult to decipher.

On 31 March, the day of the 1973 Grand National, the message was loud and unmistakable: 'Favourites to win.' And the first three in the betting swept home clear of the field.

Sunderland are in the Cup Final today as outsiders to everyone except their strongest supporters and there is no clear-cut factor favouring outsiders today. The indications are neutral.

So Sunderland do not start the match with any special help or encouragement from the stars. Sunderland are the older, longer-established of the two clubs. They were founded in 1879, although they didn't take their present title until 1881 and turned professional five years later.

For astrological purposes, Sunderland are under the rulership of Leo. Leeds started out as Leeds City in 1904 and were reorganised in 1920, when the present Leeds United came into being.

Leeds are under the rulership of Cancer.

So far as competitive success is concerned, the current planetary set-up is altogether more favourable to Cancer than to Leo.

Leeds have been tempered and hardened by success in recent years, by achieving so many honours and by experience of the big occasion.

Combining this with their indication that luck is on their side and that form favours them, they seem to have everything going for them.

That's why we expect to see a proud and excited Billy Bremner lead his team on the traditional lap of honour around Wembley Stadium today.

The Leeds victory should be a convincing one, their score running to more than one goal.

David beating Goliath is one of the most appealing stories and certainly one close to the hearts of most British sportsmen. But there is no indication of it happening today.

The Sunderland players' wives get their chance to hold the Cup

Leeds were punished this time for crying wolf so often in the past.

Strangely Static

Once England's Clarke was subdued, Watson out-tackled every Leeds man who came forward and vindicated manager Stokoe's plan to force Leeds into long, high forward passes by winning everything in the air. .

Bobby Kerr, the tiny captain, was vital to Sunderland. He had to help right back Dick Malone cope with Eddie Gray – the potential Leeds match-winner who in the event looked anything but match fit.

This half-pint figure played like two men – no, make that three. And Kerr, Montgomery, Watson, the arrogant Billy Hughes – who like Clarke was booked – and the dependable Ron Guthrie were rewarded by the 32nd minute match winner by a player whose Sunderland career was in decline under Alan Brown.

Ian Porterfield volleyed an historic goal through a strangely static Leeds defence after Vic Halom's aggression had won a vital touch to Hughes's corner.

That goal confounded all of us who said Sunderland could not win.

I was in good company in expecting Leeds to prevail with style and goals to spare. But perhaps I should have known better.

1974

LIVERPOOL 3
NEWCASTLE UNITED 0

ATTENDANCE
100 000

REFEREE
C. G. Kew (Amersham)

GOALSCORERS
Keegan (2), Heighway

TEAMS

Liverpool	Newcastle United
Clemence	McFaul
Smith	Clark
Thompson	Howard
Hughes	Moncur
Lindsay	Kennedy
Hall	Smith
Callaghan	McDermott
Cormack	Cassidy
Keegan	Macdonald
Toshack	Tudor
Heighway	Hibbitt

THE ROAD TO THE FINAL

Liverpool
4th round
v Carlisle United 0–0 (h)
Replay 2–0 (a)
5th round
v Ipswich Town 2–0 (h)
6th round
v Bristol City 1–0 (a)
Semi-Final
v Leicester City 0–0
Replay 3–1

Newcastle United
4th round
v Scunthorpe United 1–1 (h)
Replay 3–0 (a)
5th round
v West Bromwich Albion 3–0 (a)
6th round
v Nottingham Forest 4–3* (h)
Replay 0–0
2nd replay 1–0
Semi-Final
v Burnley 2–0

*FA ordered replay because of crowd invasion. Second and third games both played at Goodison Park.

A Triumph for the Professionals

Intense concentration on every fan's face as Keegan puts Liverpool a goal up

THE PROFESSIONALS ARE firmly back in control of English club football. And that much-abused description need no longer wrinkle the public nose with distaste.

Liverpool's Wembley walkover endorsed all the thrilling football Leeds played earlier in the season to win the League Championship.

Two teams of professionals built by managers Bill Shankly and Don Revie have achieved such supremacy that they at last feel able to let their talent run free. That could be the best thing to happen to English football for years.

Liverpool capsuled into a glorious last hour of Saturday's FA Cup Final all the qualities that the word professionalism ought to encompass. They were fit, tough, disciplined, determined and skilful.

Significantly it was Shankly – and not even two-goal Kevin Keegan – who was singled out for hero-worship by the fans.

Liverpool are not a team to trust everything to individual inspiration – though their skills stand comparison with any in the country. Shankly is the symbol of their dedication and togetherness.

So the TV cameras focused on the hand signals he used to direct tactics ... then conduct the Kop choir. So the fans came on at the end to kiss his feet.

Surrender

It was not Liverpool's fault that this Final failed to mature from an exhibition into a thrilling contest.

Newcastle's belief in free-wheeling flair and reliance on individual talents amounted to nothing better than surrender.

Manager Joe Harvey seemed content to make a marginal adjustment in his use of Malcolm Macdonald and trust the hordes of Geordie fans to will his team to victory.

Perhaps there was a moral in the way the teams prepared for Wembley. Liverpool were billeted well away from London – at St Albans. They were also kept well away from the pre-Wembley week round of social engagements. Shankly took Ian Callaghan in and out of dinners in record time to receive his Footballer Of The Year awards.

Relaxed Run-Up

Newcastle had opted for the relaxed, social run-up ... so relaxed that some of them never woke up.

Liverpool had men of the match everywhere. Newcastle played a system which

Mixed feelings in the goalmouth as Keegan (extreme right) scores Liverpool's third goal

allowed Tommy Smith and Alec Lindsay to run riot from full back ... which gave young Phil Thompson the chance to emerge as a central defender of the highest class ... and which failed to cope with Callaghan and Hall in midfield.

Newcastle's defenders were hounded to death by Keegan's lethal darts and Steve Heighway's punishingly quick long runs so that even John Toshack's fumbling form passed largely unnoticed.

By the end of the first half Liverpool were threatening to destroy them. Five minutes into the second half a linesman – quite rightly, despite the Merseyside arguments – delayed the slaughter by giving Keegan offside as he helped create a volleyed goal for Lindsay.

After another six minutes nothing could save Newcastle. Smith crossed from the right, Hall caused confusion by missing his header and Keegan had time and space to volley Liverpool ahead off Ian McFaul's uncertain fingers.

There was a rush later to pin the blame on Newcastle's young full back Alan Kennedy. But in truth the whole team were culpable. As evidence, Newcastle did not force their first corner until two minutes before Liverpool's 75th minute second goal.

Waiting

Then Toshack headed on a long clearance by goalkeeper Ray Clemence. Heighway cut to the right across Newcastle's leaden defenders and shot back across McFaul, inside the left post.

A minute from time Liverpool signed off with an 11-pass move from which Keegan turned in Smith's low cross for the third goal. And Clemence was still waiting to save his first shot when he collected his winner's medal.

That makes it hard to say anything complementary about Newcastle ... except that they met their doom with good grace and sportsmanship.

Ear-Splitting

Up in the black-and-white world of Tyneside they know what gritty dedication to the cause of winning is all about.

Geordie nationalism knows no compromises and a Tynesider friend told me in all seriousness that there will be a revolution in Britain if they don't win.

In Newcastle, anything black and white is right for the occasion. The most common form of dress is a black and white striped football shirt with 'Howay The Lads' written on the back, black and white hat and a black and white scarf trailing from the trouser pocket. Optional extras are a school blazer – black, of course – and black and white walking stick. I even saw a black and white CND badge.

Liverpudlians admit that they have never heard such a volume as that produced by the Newcastle fans at the Cup replay against Nottingham Forest at Goodison Park.

The musical confrontation has already begun. Liverpool have labelled Newcastle 'The Wombles' and a football shirt on sale in Liverpool reads 'FA Cup Final – Liverpool FC versus The Wombles'. Newcastle fans hit back with 'I'd Rather Be A Womble Than a Scouse', to the tune of *She'll Be Coming Round The Mountain*.

Each team could fill Wembley with their own supporters, but among those who have managed to get a ticket, the contest to outshout and outsing the other crowd will be as impressive as anything that goes on in the game itself.

Lung Power
Could Carry off The Cup

On to the Wembley terraces today will step two of the most awe-inspiring, goal-inspiring sets of fans that football has ever seen.

It's Liverpool's celebrated Kop versus Newcastle's formidable Leazes End; it's *You'll Never Walk Alone* against *Blaydon Races*.

There is a mystical quality about the Kop, a sense of belief. The Kop first made *You'll Never Walk Alone* their own song and, when other supporters sing it, they sing back 'Sing your own song'.

They sing 'Oh Come Ye To Anfield' to the tune of *Oh Come All Ye Faithful* and when some dedicated Liverpudlians die the funeral cortege drives around Anfield as an act of homage.

One of the strangest things about the Kop is how 28 000 people can apparently decide to sing the same song at the same time. It's almost as though Koppites have a sixth sense.

In a game against Everton the fog was so thick that the Kop could not see when Liverpool scored a goal at the other end.

'Tell us who scored,' the Kop sang in unison.

'Tony Hateley,' the crowd at the other end chorused back.

'Thank you very much,' sang the Kop.

They break spontaneously into songs they have never sung before. Once, when Liverpool scored five goals against Spurs, the entire Kop sang *London Bridge Is Falling Down*.

Who knows what they will come up with today?

Shirt-swapping time as Liverpool show off the Cup

1975

WEST HAM UNITED 2
FULHAM 0

ATTENDANCE
100 000

REFEREE
P. Partridge (Bishop Auckland)

GOALSCORER
A. Taylor (2)

TEAMS

West Ham United	Fulham
Day	Mellor
McDowell	Cutbush
Lampard	Fraser
Bonds	Mullery
T. Taylor	Lacy
Lock	Moore
A. Taylor	Mitchell
Paddon	J. Conway
Jennings	Busby
Brooking	Slough
Holland	Barrett

THE ROAD TO THE FINAL

West Ham United
4th round
v Swindon Town 1–1 (h)
Replay 2–1 (a)
5th round
v Queen's Park Rangers 2–1 (h)
6th round
v Arsenal 2–0 (a)
Semi-Final
v Ipswich Town 0–0
Replay 2–1

Fulham
4th round
v Nottingham Forest 0–0 (h)
Replay 1–1 (a)
2nd replay 1–1 (h)
3rd replay 2–1 (a)
5th round
v Everton 2–1 (a)
6th round
v Carlisle United 1–0 (a)
Semi-Final
v Birmingham City 1–1
Replay 1–0

Fings ain't Wot They Were at Wembley

Alan Taylor shoots through Mellor's legs to put West Ham one goal up

THE FIRST TIME West Ham went to Wembley, in 1923, one police horse managed to clear the pitch of invaders.

On Saturday, it would have needed 100 police dogs to allow the Cup Final and its rituals to run their course unimpeded. How times change! There was a time, for example, when players decided on their footwear for the Final in the bootroom, and not the High Court.

They would walk up that long tunnel and stamp a few testing paces across the turf only in their most familiar boots.

As Fulham appeared, their feet clad in uniform and gleaming black, we became aware that the size of the contract is now more vital than the degree of comfort. But at least they had done a better job with their aerosols than Sunderland two years ago, when rain washed the disguising paint off the stripes!

Even the football looked different. Wembley, with its wide spaces and its code of no crippling kicks from defenders, has always been an attackers' paradise. Fulham and West Ham defenders abided by the code, but the forwards weren't good enough to take advantage.

The Pitch

But I suppose we mustn't complain. Great defenders – like Moore and Mullery, Lock, Fraser, McDowell and Lampard – dominated the Final but without them, how else could these teams have got there? The lack of class among the six forwards

in attack was exposed even by this pitch.

EVEN this pitch? That's another thing that has altered with the years. They used to say 'If you can't play at Wembley, you can't play.' When Wembley authorities, greedy for gain, allowed horses to stamp the old turf into a morass, that legend lost its meaning.

As Fulham's Les Barrett said: 'If they want us to nip down these wings, they'd better give us motor-bikes.'

The Hooligans

With the wings slowed, and the middle

contorted, we were beginning to think about a replay.

Then Taylor struck. Twice. That's one thing about Finals that doesn't change – the creation of a hero. Now let's hope he doesn't go the way of some of the Sunderland 'giants' and forget that a few weeks ago the height of his dreams was two Wembley tickets rather than two Wembley goals.

After the game ended, there was a time, I seem to remember, when the winning team went to the crowd. On Saturday the crowd, or at least its youngest element, went to the team.

The invading rush of kids visibly disturbed the bandsmen, one of whom got away with the best bit of blind-side retaliation of the afternoon – a quick bang with a euphonium on a tormentor's ear.

The Reporters

This Final was different below stairs, too. Ron Greenwood, who now has the habit of being as ungracious in victory as he is calm in defeat (more practice?) banned the Press from his dressing room. 'This is the players' day,' he is reported to have said.

I should have thought that the public – who are represented behind the scenes only by reporters – might also have felt they had a share in the Final.

Brian Clough is Lost for Words

For once, Brian Clough is lost for an opinion. Sportsmail asked all the managers of clubs who were beaten by Fulham and West Ham in the Cup this season who they thought would win the Final.

Opinions differed, but Clough, manager of Nottingham Forest (who were knocked out by Fulham after two replays), said: 'I just can't make up my mind. Having played Fulham so often I can say that anyone who writes them off must be crackers. It's anybody's game – typical of this season.'

This fan had just managed to reach Trevor Brooking and give him a kiss

Brooking is mobbed by fans after West
Ham's win

Stop! It's Bobby Moore

Bobby Moore, the most awe-inspiring obstacle in football, stands between West Ham and the FA Cup.

West Ham learned everything about Moore down the years. They know the limitations he is supposed to have – yet they know the way he thinks around the problems. Above all, they know Bobby Moore to be the sort of big occasion player who does not allow his team to lose Finals at Wembley. What concerns them now is that his team is Fulham.

The trouble for West Ham is that this is Boy's Own day for Bobby Moore. He says: 'A lot of the letters I've received have come from West Ham fans who can't help saying they hope I pull it off. That's lovely. Honestly, I'm touched.'

The trouble for West Ham is that this time the Second Division team are less likely to freeze in the Wembley atmosphere than their own First Division players. The trouble for West Ham ... is Bobby Moore.

1976

SOUTHAMPTON 1
MANCHESTER UNITED 0

ATTENDANCE
100 000

REFEREE
C. Thomas (Treorchy)

GOALSCORER
Stokes

TEAMS

Southampton	Manchester United
Turner	Stepney
Rodrigues	Forsyth
Blyth	Greenhoff
Steele	Buchan
Peach	Houston
Holmes	Daly
Gilchrist	Macari
McCalliog	Coppell
Channon	McIlroy
Osgood	Pearson
Stokes	Hill

THE ROAD TO THE FINAL

Southampton
4th round
v Blackpool 3–1 (h)
5th round
v West Bromwich Albion 1–1 (a)
Replay 4–0 (h)
6th round
v Bradford City 1–0 (a)
Semi-Final
v Crystal Palace 2–0

Manchester United
4th round
v Peterborough United 3–1 (h)
5th round
v Leicester City 2–1 (a)
6th round
v Wolverhampton Wanderers 1–1 (h)
Replay 3–2 (a)
Semi-Final
v Derby County 2–0

We Won ... because We Did It Our Way

Manchester's Daly has the advantage as Southampton's Steele slides to the ground

TWENTY HOURS CAN tell you a lot about a man no less special because a month ago half the country had never heard of him, and the other half weren't quite sure how to spell his name.

Saturday Night and Sunday Morning with Lawrie McMenemy deserves documentation for those who have ever wondered how they might deal with one of Kipling's twin imposters ... triumph.

You begin as his Southampton team become the talk of the country. Celebrate at the Talk of the Town. Sleep too little, then meet at breakfast and talk.

Or rather listen as, utterly composed, totally in control, he weaves through encounters in hotel suites and streets, TV studios and restaurant toilets. Always with something to say:

About the Mood Before the Match

'I knew we'd got it right when Mickey Channon started rollicking the coach driver. 'Cos he does every week ... it's a ritual ... and it had to be kept.

'When I woke on Saturday morning I was tired to death. So I sat on the bed for two hours putting myself into shape. The manager sets the mood ... on a day like this they didn't need me miserable, and they didn't need me cocky. They didn't need me nervous, indecisive, moody. They needed me, me ... just like we were on our way to York instead of Wembley.'

About the Emotion

'I have never watched two managers come out for a Final without a lump in my throat ... for them, imagining how they must feel. When it happened to me I felt ... nothing.

'And I haven't been hit by it since. I've done all these interviews, shaken a million hands, and it is as though I am

The referee closely follows a confrontation between Coppell and Peach

outside myself watching myself, wondering about my own control, always saying the right things. This may not go on. Maybe Wednesday I'll sit down and cry like a babe.'

About the Game

'The referee came in and told the lads that Wembley or no Wembley, if they showed dissent he'd have 'em. Soon as he'd gone I said: "He's got it right, and if I see any of you shoving passes about with his elbows in the air, posing, then I'LL have you."

'We had to play the stuff that got us there. I told Mel Blyth: "I don't care if the Queen is watching. If it's dangerous stick it in the Tyne," in other words belt that ball anywhere. That's why we won – because we were us.'

About Wembley

'They talk of the pageantry of it all, but what about the pettiness? It's quite a

surprise. Did you know there's a little bloke that comes into the dressing-room an hour before the start and asks you to order your drinks?

'Tea or lemonade, he tells you, you get free. But if you want beer, or cider, or champagne, you'll have to pay. He must

have a signature. You ARE the manager and entitled? You are sure your club will foot the bill? Incredible, there is, what, £400 000 coming into Wembley for the afternoon, and they're worried someone'll nick off leaving them to pick up the bill for a lager!'

Friendly Match

Whatever happened to that 'Red Army of the Ticketless Ones'? Where did 'The Terror of the Terraces' disappear to?

All we saw at Wembley was an incredibly exciting game of football played between two skilled and sporting sides.

Very few fouls. No sulks. The fans in glorious voice. And two managers of outstanding wit, grit and charm.

Why wasn't the Queen allowed to shake hands with Monsieurs Docherty and McMenemy? Come to that, why isn't she allowed to put them in her government?

It's nice to be reminded that football can be fun. Underdogs can win. And you can have a great day out without taking your courage in both hands.

Winning Wembley ... in 300 Points

In the tradition of all fairy stories, there is a secret behind Southampton's triumph against Manchester United, the odds and the logical assessment of even the most romantic students of football.

Southampton's greatest day was planned for them in microscopic detail by courtesy of a man with no official involvement in their club.

England and former Leeds manager Don Revie volunteered the intelligence which guided Southampton through the treacherous straits of Saturday's FA Cup Final. His knowledge enabled them to cope with everything from the seating arrangements to the psychology of a smooth operation at Wembley.

Revie's dossier on how to deal with the problems of a Wembley final ran to no fewer than 300 points.

The face of dejection – Tommy Docherty helps two of his players off the pitch after Manchester's surprise defeat

Putting a brave face on it. The losers were given a civic reception in their home city

JON'S SPORTING TYPES

'There's no drought in Manchester.'

MANCHESTER UNITED 2

LIVERPOOL 1

ATTENDANCE
100 000

REFEREE
R. Matthewson (Bolton)

GOALSCORERS
Pearson, J. Greenhoff
Case

TEAMS

Manchester United	Liverpool
Stepney	Clemence
Nicholl	Neal
Albiston	Jones
McIlroy	Smith
B. Greenhoff	Kennedy
Buchan	Hughes
Coppell	McDermott
J. Greenhoff	Keegan
Pearson	Case
Macari	Heighway
Hill	Johnson

THE ROAD TO THE FINAL

Manchester United
4th round
v Queen's Park Rangers 1–0 (h)
5th round
v Southampton 2–2 (a)
Replay 2–1 (h)
6th round
v Aston Villa 2–1 (h)
Semi-Final
v Leeds United 2–1

Liverpool
4th round
v Carlisle United 3–0 (h)
5th round
v Oldham 3–1 (h)
6th round
v Middlesbrough 2–0 (h)
Semi-Final
v Everton 2–2
Replay 3–0

Albiston Gets It Right

Coppell, on the left, struggling for control of the ball with Ray Kennedy

ARTHUR ALBISTON CAME unflinching through all the fears that his inexperience might be Manchester United's undoing. None of the more celebrated names contributed more than the 19-year-old Scot to the spectacle of the 1977 FA Cup Final.

Boisterous

But while Albiston was busy justifying Docherty's boisterous belief, it became painfully clear that Bob Paisley had picked the wrong team.

A gentler spirit, Liverpool's manager had settled for the soft option, that of rewarding the 11 players who had finished the League Championship season. It was the wrong alternative of the several available within his enviable squad.

The point was driven home by Paisley himself in the last 25 minutes. For that last thrash, he sent Ian Callaghan to replace David Johnson, a man whose considerable talents remain a square peg in Liverpool's rounded pattern of play.

All too late.

That six-minute goal burst had put them behind. The substitute was already on. There was no David Fairclough to come high-stepping to Liverpool's rescue with his improbable goals.

It was a small and essentially human error by Paisley which must not be allowed to obscure his long season of shrewd management. But the treble is won and lost by the finest of margins and Paisley suffered cruel confirmation of my warning that his regular team were running out of goals at the vital moment.

Masterly

That was bad enough, even without Heighway's failure to respond to the occasion.

Stepney cuts a lonely figure as he fails to stop the equalising goal

He was mastered by Albiston and Jimmy Nicholl. The young full backs did their job with sharp, early tackles which were merely an appetiser for the close-marking Heighway will have to endure from Borussia's Berti Vogts.

So with Alex Stepney in better form than Ray Clemence, with Albiston, Martin Buchan, Brian Greenhoff and Nicholl in more resolute mood than Emlyn Hughes and Tommy Smith, with the breaks for once going against them, Liverpool surrendered a romantic victory to Manchester United.

In truth, United barely got going in the Wembley heat. But their exciting contribution to the game in this country in the past two seasons made them overdue for a major trophy.

They got the better of the flurry of goals between the 50th and 55th minutes. First Pearson sprinted behind Hughes's hesitancy, on to Greenhoff's flick, and shot powerfully inside Clemence's near post ... not a memory England's goalkeeper will cherish.

Case equalised with a neat turn and a typically fierce, rising right-foot shot which scorched Stepney's fingertips on its way to the United net.

Then Nicholl weighted a forward pass, Macari headed on, Greenhoff wriggled away from Smith and as the ball ran loose, Macari was following up in alert fashion. His shot was going wide until it struck Greenhoff in the ribs and veered sharply past Clemence.

New Era

There was time for Callaghan to come round and show Liverpool what might have been, for David McCreery to take up United's running from Gordon Hill, for Stepney to save Case's shot at the feet of Keegan.

Then it was time for the legions of Liverpool and United to cheer each other's teams in a demonstration of sportsmanship which put the behaviour of the hooligan fringe into a more muted perspective.

For United, it marked the dawn of a new era of success. Liverpool were left to drag themselves away, dog-tired.

I never thought it would be necessary to feel sorry for the Anfield machinery ... until now.

Just too late to stop Manchester's ball going into the net

Jones and Greenhoff tussle for the ball in a close-fought Final

Sportspeak Has a Field Day

Manchester United supporters must have cheered up no end when, at half-time, Don Revie said that Liverpool were 'as men playing against boys'.

This virtually guaranteed two goals from the boys before the words had finished vibrating. For an iron law of televised sport is that pundits will be confounded – dear old David Coleman had only to bark *gotta* be a penalty' for the referee to wave on play while some player trotted away with a sheep-ish grin.

And, of course, it is the day when sportspeak comes into its own. Frank Bough married the sonorous ('its own accolade') and the colloquial ('looks in grand nick') in the same sentence without stripping his gears.

From a world of his own an interviewer cried: 'The left peg and all that, the double and all that, are you feeling it a bit?' Stalls had sold out of 'glory', 'adrenalin' and 'tragedy' long before kick-off.

Switching sides can be confusing, however. ITV opined that the pitch was patchy, while the BBC thought it like – you've guessed it – a billiards table.

As always, there were some insights, such as Jack Charlton's unfeigned hunger when he muttered: 'I'd like to go on playing, though.' And Malcolm Macdonald's disclosure that foot-ballers walking out to the biggest day of their careers are first struck by Wembley's 'tremendous smell of hot dogs'.

Television's real success at Wembley, however, is to take an enor-mously complex outside broadcast and make it work so well that the nation gets a day out by proxy – and takes it for granted.

IPSWICH TOWN 1
ARSENAL 0

ATTENDANCE
100 000

REFEREE
D. R. G. Nippard (Christchurch)

GOALSCORER
Osborne

TEAMS

Ipswich Town	Arsenal
Cooper	Jennings
Burley	Rice
Mills	Nelson
Talbot	Price
Hunter	O'Leary
Beattie	Young
Osborne	Brady
Wark	Sunderland
Mariner	Macdonald
Geddis	Stapleton
Woods	Hudson

THE ROAD TO THE FINAL

Ipswich Town
4th round
v Hartlepool 4–1 (h)
5th round
v Bristol Rovers 2–2 (a)
Replay 3–0 (h)
6th round
v Millwall 6–1 (a)
Semi-Final
v West Bromwich Albion 3–1

Arsenal
4th round
v Wolverhampton Wanderers 2–1 (h)
5th round
v Walsall 4–1 (h)
6th round
v Wrexham 3–2 (a)
Semi-Final
v Orient 3–0

Arsenal Go Limping Home

Jennings tips the ball over the bar as Ipswich put on the pressure

THEY SANG *Abide With Me* with enough of the old reverence to put a lump in your throat and the Ipswich end was a vivid reminder that blue is a spiritual colour.

It was going to be one of Wembley's good days. Awash with sunshine, brimful with psychology, soaked in sentiment.

Arsenal were afloat for five minutes, treading water for five minutes more, drowning in emotional crises thereafter.

The first evidence came even as Arsenal

were savouring O'Leary's close half-volley from Hudson's opening cross. Liam Brady came out of a mild tackle with Roger Osborne … limping.

Brady, of all people, was lame.

Panic. Who else had been out recently? You wondered about Rice, and Woods was soon to expose him. You had misgivings about Sunderland, and Mills was in quick and hard to confirm them.

Like an animal scenting the kill, Kevin Beattie thundered in pursuit of the initiative. They had been draining water from his knee by the bucket but there was nothing wrong with his heart. A pair of great, lunging victories in the tackle took the steam out of the less competitive elements in the Arsenal side.

Beattie, Hunter, Mariner and the rest of the Ipswich crocks appeared to have been strengthened by some miracle of bionic surgery. At the very least, they had come to terms with their injuries.

On the Run

Arsenal were made of more fragile stuff. They could find no answer to Beattie's challenge. Alan Hudson, for all his skilled fencing with the game, settled Arsenal

Talbot, on the left, leaves Arsenal's Hudson behind

into a mood which was too esoteric, insufficiently explosive.

One elaborate square ball too many left Young exposed. Geddis intercepted, Osborne confused what was left of Arsenal's defence and Mariner hit the crossbar.

Initiative surrendered. Ten minutes and already the favourites were on the run. From that mistake on, a dismayed Young was like a combine harvester out of control, threshing in all directions.

Osborne's liquidation of the hobbling Brady encouraged Talbot and Wark to take powerful control of the midfield, Mariner and Woods to play themselves into England contention by ravaging Arsenal's defence, Beattie, Mills and Hunter to obliterate Stapleton, Sunderland and sad Supermac.

Ipswich even won the tactical battle. David Geddis became an overnight sensation as Whymark's replacement, playing unusually wide, thereby blocking Nelson's crucial runs from left back and exploiting the space.

Fifty-two minutes and the Sunday newspapermen in the Press Gallery were rating the players out of ten. Ipswich were easy, everyone a star.

'But who are Arsenal's best players?'

'I give in.'

'Come on, there must be a couple playing well.'

'O'Leary and the woodwork.'

Sixty-five minutes and Brady could barely walk. Graham Rix came on.

Seventy-one minutes and Wark hit the post again with an even better effort …

Osborne: 'I'm No Star and Never Will Be'

Those of us who feared that the ritual mobbing of a goal-scorer might lead to injury saw it happen at Wembley.

Roger Osborne was exhausted when he shot Willie Young's misplaced clearance past Pat Jennings in the 77th minute, but it was the after-effects of having Messrs Geddis, Mills, Woods, Mariner and Burley jump on his back which really floored him.

'I just couldn't breathe,' he said. 'There was no air. I'm not used to scoring and having people jump all over me. The emotion of it got to me as well. Me, scoring the winner at Wembley!

'The doctor wanted me to go to the dressing-room to put some ice on my neck but I got halfway round the track and turned back because I didn't want to miss the presentation. I could have played on. I felt a bit of a fool.'

Son of Cowhand

Osborne, the 28-year-old son of a cowhand from a Suffolk village of 500 inhabitants, must rank as the unlikeliest hero of Wembley.

It was only his tenth goal in seven years as a professional. 'I'm not a star and never will be,' he said in his broad Suffolk accent. 'I'm a hard worker.'

Until he was 21 Osborne – one of a family of 12 – was a labourer. 'I used to go down to Portman Road to watch my brother David train,' he said. 'He played in the Ipswich Youth side. I played for a local side and one day I was invited to train with Ipswich. They were a man short and I got a game.' In 1971 Bobby Robson signed him.

The Osborne family hired a bus to bring them to Wembley. 'I only just managed to get enough tickets for them all,' Roger said.

After scoring Ipswich's winning goal, Osborne left the field, overcome by the emotion of the moment

74 minutes and Burley's header was saved incredibly by Jennings ... 77 minutes and ecstasy.

Unlikely Hero

Geddis outflanked Hudson and Nelson, poor Young could only tee up the low cross for Osborne and one of the unlikeliest heroes in Wembley history hit the winner. There was a hint of that hidden ankle injury in Jennings's despairing dive, but Osborne was so overcome by his own achievement that he had to be substituted by Lambert.

Before the Final, Terry Neill said he hoped above all that the game would be good for football. It may not have worked out exactly as he planned, but he got his wish.

ARSENAL 3
MANCHESTER UNITED 2

──── ATTENDANCE ────
100 000

──── REFEREE ────
R. Challis (Tonbridge)

──── GOALSCORERS ────
Talbot, Stapleton, Sunderland
McQueen, McIlroy

──── TEAMS ────

Arsenal	Manchester United
Jennings	Bailey
Rice	Nicholl
Nelson	Albiston
Talbot	McIlroy
O'Leary	McQueen
Young	Buchan
Brady	Coppell
Sunderland	J. Greenhoff
Stapleton	Jordan
Price	B. Greenhoff
Rix	Thomas

──── THE ROAD TO THE FINAL ────

Arsenal
4th round
v Notts County 2–0 (h)
5th round
v Nottingham Forest 1–0 (a)
6th round
v Southampton 1–1 (a)
Replay 2–0 (h)
Semi-Final
v Wolverhampton Wanderers 2–0

Manchester United
4th round
v Fulham 1–1 (a)
Replay 1–0 (h)
5th round
v Colchester United 1–0 (a)
6th round
v Tottenham Hotspur 1–1 (a)
Replay 2–0 (h)
Semi-Final
v Liverpool 2–2
Replay 1–0

This was Just a Five-Minute Final

Brian Talbot gives thanks as his team-mates celebrate their luck

IF CUP FINALS lasted five minutes, then 1979 would have witnessed the greatest of them all.

If a handful of sublime touches were the sum total of genius, then Liam Brady could consider himself a football immortal.

And if pigs could fly they would have caused Arsenal more trouble on the wings than Manchester United did on Saturday.

Here, in this brief interlude between Wembley's overwhelming climax and memory's loving lip service to a fabled occasion, let's have it right.

What that unforgettable finish did for Arsenal was prove they deserved to win a Final which they had little right to be leading 2–0 in the first place.

Character

What it did for Brady was to suggest that Arsenal have found a way for him to exploit his remarkable gifts without exposing the occasional human flaw inevitable in a developing personality.

What it did for United was endorse their strength of character but question their common sense.

No match can be called perfect when it is successfully stifled for 80 minutes by cautious strategy, almost thrown away by what looked suspiciously like a sentimental substitution, then won again on a tide of unprofessional delirium.

Had Alan Sunderland not scored with his last, injurious lunge, he would have been at best a crippled passenger in extra time with no substitute left and United favourites to win a Cup they had lost once already.

Instead, the Highbury management can take credit for the tactics which enabled Arsenal to steal two goals from a first half in which they did not otherwise manage a single corner.

United's cavalry were sucked into a

Greenhoff's Dilemma

Manchester United's FA Cup Final team will be decided today by the professional honesty of striker Jimmy Greenhoff.

Greenhoff, leading scorer and as near indispensable as one man can be, will be asked to tell manager Dave Sexton whether he can run the whole 90 minutes of tomorrow's Final against Arsenal.

After a month of doubt, yesterday's encouraging fitness test had to be the last one. All that remains now is for Greenhoff to own up if, after a night's rest, he suffers any reaction from the pelvic strain.

Sexton trusts him to take no chances. 'I would not take the slightest risk, even if it meant missing the game,' vowed Greenhoff.

Stapleton appears to somersault as his kick goes over the bar

smothering midfield, drawn on to a battling defence ... and crucified on the break by the controlled power of Brady's runs and subtlety of his vision.

I have never known opinion so divided after a big match, but I have to insist that if United had played like Arsenal, we would have been left with a Final to forget, not a finish to remember.

Frustrated

When Arsenal give thanks for deliverance, they should remember not so much who scored their goals but who frustrated United.

Their foundations were the way Pat Rice and Sammy Nelson rose above Steve Coppell, Mickey Thomas and their critics,

Arsenal goalkeeper Pat Jennings kneels in the goalmouth after McQueen's goal

Steve Coppell lets his feelings show at the end of the match

touch-line as Gordon McQueen and Sammy McIlroy ripped the lid off the coffin. Bobby Charlton said: 'They forgot one of the oldest maxims of the game, that you're at your most vulnerable immediately after you score.'

Arsenal must have known that, with the exception of Lou Macari, United played badly but might have won.

That's why the Highbury recruitment drive continues ... and why the mourning in Manchester can be limited to regret at being out of Europe next season.

O'Leary Rocket Brings Partner to Earth

One of the abiding memories of the Five-Minute Final was the sight of young David O'Leary giving his defensive partner, Willie Young, a rocket in the 86th minute.

'He's Scottish and gets a bit excitable, so I had to tell him to calm down,' said O'Leary. 'We were giving the game to them. It was a total lapse in concentration, not just Willie, but me and everyone else.

'We were thinking about walking up those steps and behind handed our winners' medals by Prince Charles. We gave away two terrible goals. After leading for so long, we were blowing it.'

Surprised

On the bench, out of hearing, Arsenal manager Terry Neill and coach Don Howe were signalling frantically. 'I was dreading extra time,' said Neill. 'Those goals lifted United right up and we were down. They had to be favourites if it went to extra time.'

Neill defended his decision to send on Steve Walford for David Price in the 85th minute, saying it wasn't a sentimental gesture. 'Dave was knackered,' he said. 'We needed a new face.'

Walford was so surprised, he asked Neill: 'Are you sure you want me to go on?'

Afterwards he said: 'I hope no one is blaming me for what happened. I only got one kick. You can't get into a game in five minutes.'

the way David O'Leary lived up to Jimmy Greenhoff's fears and everyone else's expectations, the way Willie Young stuck at Joe Jordan and the immaculate positioning of Pat Jennings.

The fulcrum of their team was the way Brian Talbot chased, fought and footballed to give Brady and Graham Rix enough leisure time to exercise their skills.

Brady's foot was in all three Arsenal goals, Rix's imperative to the winner.

But the greatest justice of the Final came yesterday with official confirmation that Talbot has been officially credited with the first goal. Brady was beautiful but Talbot, who had helped Ipswich harry Arsenal to defeat a year earlier, was the man who made the winning of this match possible. Talbot ... and the way United forgot Bobby Moore's advice 'Leave the celebrating until we're in the bar'.

Even the thoroughly responsible Dave Sexton was dancing with delight on the

1980

WEST HAM UNITED 1
ARSENAL 0

ATTENDANCE
100 000

REFEREE
G. Courtney (Spennymoor)

GOALSCORER
Brooking

TEAMS

West Ham United	Arsenal
Parkes	Jennings
Stewart	Rice
Lampard	Devine
Bonds	Talbot
Martin	O'Leary
Devonshire	Brady
Allen	Sunderland
Pearson	Stapleton
Cross	Price
Brooking	Rix
Pike	Young

THE ROAD TO THE FINAL

West Ham United
4th round
v Orient 3–2 (a)
5th round
v Swansea City 2–0 (h)
6th round
v Aston Villa 1–0 (h)
Semi-Final
v Everton 1–1
Replay 2–1

Arsenal
4th round
v Brighton & Hove Albion 2–0 (h)
5th round
v Bolton Wanderers 1–1 (a)
Replay 3–0 (h)
6th round
v Watford 2–1 (a)
Semi-Final
v Liverpool 0–0
Replay 1–1
2nd replay 1–1
3rd replay 1–0

Instant Justice

The yellow card goes up . . . and Arsenal's chances go down even further

WE MAY NEVER know for certain, but to those of us with accurate watches it seemed George Courtney was playing God when he terminated the 1980 FA Cup Final with West Ham clinging to their one-goal lead.

Judgement – in the form of a short second half also shorn of injury time and any allowance for West Ham's time-wasting – may well have been delivered on Arsenal because of Willie Young's professional foul.

If so, the referee deserves our gratitude, because instead of the legend of a conclusive 87th-minute goal from the Cup's youngest finalist, the watching world was consigned to a sour memory of the beaten Young's cynical trip on Paul Allen.

Big, blunt Willie is not to blame.

This most straightforward of centre halves is conditioned to the modern game. Had he not floored young Allen on the brink of glory, he would surely have brought the wrath of Arsenal's management down upon his own head.

That reaction would have been con-

Keep Your Shirt On!

Arsenal and West Ham will be told before today's kick-off that they must not exchange shirts on the field after the match. The FA have decided that, as with England Internationals, shirt swapping must wait until the players are back in the dressing rooms. Last year Arsenal's Liam Brady collected his winner's medal wearing a Manchester United shirt.

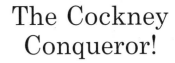
West Ham United v Arsenal

The Cockney Conqueror!

It should have been an embarrassing moment for Paul Allen, the titch of a 17-year-old whom the nation took to its heart in the Cup Final. He was the first West Ham player out on the balcony at Newham Town Hall yesterday, after a tumultuous East End welcome for the team.

He looked round to find that the other players hadn't yet followed him up the stairs. He was on his own, facing thousands of cheering fans in claret and blue.

But the youngest player ever to appear in a Wembley Final responded with the aplomb he'd shown facing the Arsenal team. He raised his arms aloft and smiled that permanent smile that hadn't left him since walking off the Wembley pitch.

'What a lovely little lad,' said one of the tea ladies. 'He don't look old enough to be a footballer.'

'Ever so Disciplined'

Paul's parents, Rene and Ron, were at the Town Hall, too, to share their son's hero's welcome.

Rene, who works in a restaurant, said proudly of the youngest of their four children, 'He's ever so disciplined. He's in bed for ten most nights. Ever since I can remember he's wanted to be a footballer. It's a footballing family.'

Ron's brother is Les Allen, the former Spurs and QPR player, whose son Clive is a striker with QPR.

At the end of the Final, a fan threw Paul a giant teddy bear, which he is keeping as a souvenir.

As the Duchess of Kent gave him his winner's medal, he burst into tears. 'So did I,' said Rene. 'We all did.'

Thousands of delighted fans cheer their team home

ditioned in turn by football's devouring insistence on victory at all costs.

Authority

Nevertheless, someone in authority somewhere has to do something to restrain that philosophy. And either by accident or design Mr Courtney, who spends his working life as deputy headmaster of a Durham primary school, whistled an end to Arsenal's last push for an equaliser with most watches still ticking off the 89th minute.

It was a long way from being the greatest Final of all time, but it was certainly the shortest.

Any referee would be mad to admit as much. Perhaps, also, Mr Courtney was regretting merely showing Young the yellow card instead of the quickest route to the Wembley dressing rooms.

For unfair as it might have been for Young to carry the can for one of foot-

ball's most contagious ills, a booking was not punishment enough for an act which deprived a mediocre spectacle of a consoling climax.

Allen might have missed. But once he had pushed the ball through Young's legs, he certainly looked confident enough to score one of Wembley's most memorable goals.

Instead, we are left with the story of Trevor Brooking's solitary match-winner, a valid memorial to a gifted gentleman who might well have been Footballer of the Year ... but one of Saturday's few moments to savour.

I find it hard to remember the last time Brooking headed the ball at all, let alone into the net. But, perhaps spurred by criticism from the other notable godhead figure, Brian Clough, he stooped to divert Stuart Pearce's 13th minute cross-shot into disaster for Arsenal.

It was appropriate that both these

players should be involved in West Ham's moment of unexpected but finally deserved triumph.

Brooking was the dominant figure in a midfield which Liam Brady and Graham Rix were supposed to control. Pearson rose far above his injury-hampered form in the Second Division to overshadow that hitherto lethal but now exhausted pair of Gunners, Frank Stapleton and Alan Sunderland.

In company with Allen, who gained ten years' precious maturity in one sunny afternoon, and the West Ham back four of Alvin Martin, Billy Bonds, Frank Lampard and Ray Stewart, they impaled Arsenal on the very strategy which had overcome Liverpool in that marathon semi-final.

Just as Arsenal had done to reach Wembley, West Ham stole their early goal and then fell back in orderly defiance of all the opposition's possession.

Both sides show their gymnastic prowess in a close-fought game

1981

TOTTENHAM HOTSPUR 3
MANCHESTER CITY 2
(replay following a 1–1 draw)

ATTENDANCE
100 000
(Replay) 92 000

REFEREE
K. Hackett (Sheffield)

GOALSCORERS
Hutchison (own goal)
Hutchison
Replay: Villa (2), Crooks
MacKenzie, Reeves

TEAMS

Tottenham Hotspur	Manchester City
Aleksic	Corrigan
Hughton	Ranson
Miller	McDonald
Roberts	Caton
Perryman	Reid
Villa	Gow
Ardiles	Power
Archibald	MacKenzie
Galvin	Reeves
Hoddle	Bennett
Crooks	Hutchison

(Henry replaced Hutchison in the replay)

THE ROAD TO THE FINAL

Tottenham Hotspur
4th round
v Hull City 2–0 (h)
5th round
v Coventry City 3–1 (h)
6th round
v Exeter City 2–0 (h)
Semi-Final
v Wolverhampton Wanderers 2–2
Replay 3–0

Manchester City
4th round
v Norwich City 6–0 (h)
5th round
v Peterborough United 1–0 (a)
6th round
v Everton 2–2 (a)
Replay 3–1 (h)
Semi-Final
v Ipswich Town 1–0

The Skill that Didn't Work

A classic 'who, *me*?' look from Graham Roberts as Gerry Gow shows his feelings

IN A FOOTBALL world in which it is becoming all too easy to settle for second best, the 100th FA Cup Final could be said to have given 100 000 customers passable value for their £703 250.

If it is enough that a team of uneven ability applied themselves to the extremities of their potential, then Manchester City should have possession of the trophy this morning to go with all their praise.

If it is acceptable for a team of genuine talent to stroll decorously about Wembley waiting for class to exercise some mythical privilege over effort, then Tottenham deserve their second chance in Thursday's replay.

Diverting Drama

Between them, on Saturday, City and Spurs might have amounted to one tremendous football team ... even though the combination of the two produced a drama more diverting than many Wembley has endured of late.

On the day, however, you had to pay your considerable amount of money and take your choice.

For what they are worth to the bewildered Tommy Hutchison, the defiant Joe Corrigan, the prodigious Nicky Reid and the inspiring John Bond, my sympathies are with City.

At least they gave their all for 90 minutes and then dredged up a little extra for the additional half-hour.

With the heroic exception of Graham Roberts, Tottenham's approach to the first half was a disgrace.

As Keith Burkinshaw and every other manager in the world will tell them, the justification of skill is the effort applied to its expression.

Until the second half at Wembley, the hardest work of Tottenham's Cup Final

A mighty kick from Glen Hoddle takes the ball . . .

Burkinshaw talked so mysteriously about a 5–4 Final, that his players thought that he was referring to the score over two or three matches?

Admittedly, there would have been times on Saturday when had I been Burkinshaw I would have thought my team were playing a mediocre referee as well as a highly-motivated Manchester City – not least when Garth Crooks was refused a penalty as Bobby McDonald interrupted his advance on to Ardiles's lovely pass, or when Gow, Hutchison and Power failed to join Roberts, Caton and Crooks in Keith Hackett's book.

Nevertheless, Spurs would not have saved the day had Villa not been sent on his long, dramatic walk to the tunnel by the injection of Garry Brooke.

Brooke, on fresher legs, also kept running through extra time while all about him collapsed with cramp or fatigue in a manner which made mockery of all that propaganda about ours being the hardest League and toughest players in the world.

Never have so many potentially good and rank bad footballers been jumbled together in one Wembley Final. But while City deserved to win on Saturday, Spurs are the team with scope for raising their game.

Hopefully, by Thursday, they will remember that their first duty is to Spurs fans paying another fortune to fill Wembley.

week had been devoted to the myriad of commercial activities undertaken by the players to supplement their meagre income of little more than £1000 a week over the season.

City, at least, were prepared to earn their rewards the hard way, willing to run until the last man dropped to implement the briefing with which Bond gave them the maximum chance of glory.

It may not be the football that dreams are made of – although they had their moments of inspiration – but City were not to blame because too many Spurs were slow off the mark and second in the tackle.

The lionising of Gerry Gow – who finds it considerably easier to control the man than the ball – may tell us much that is wrong with English football. But it was not his fault that Osvaldo Ardiles and Glenn Hoddle took so long summoning up the nerve to shake him off or that Ricardo Villa was caught in possession more often than Casanova at the ball.

Had Steve MacKenzie added to Hutchison's headed lead instead of hitting the post in the 58th minute, there would have been no way back for Spurs, not even through Hutchison's luckless deflection of Hoddle's shot.

Mediocre Referee

Who would have guessed, when Keith

A Whistle to Stop a Bus

The shrill of referee Keith Hackett's whistle would halt the rush hour traffic in Rome. The one Hackett will use today is the type usually blown by Italian police!

'A couple of seasons ago, Brian Baker, a former League linesman who travels with me to matches, said my whistle couldn't be heard,' said the referee from Sheffield. 'He suggested I try an Italian police whistle which he received as a gift, and I haven't had any complaints since!

'I'll be using Brian's whistle at Wembley. But, as usual, I'll have a spare – the old Thunderer – just in case.'

. . . to Hutchison's head, and from there scores the equalising goal

Fantastic!

Spurs' opening goal, scored by Villa

THE 100TH CELEBRATION of the most fantastic showpiece in England's sporting tapestry surrendered last night to the macho charms of a South American.

Ricardo Villa, the Argentinian who took the long and tearful walk of a public failure in Part One of this technicoloured dream of a Cup Final, came back to Wembley as Tottenham's conquering hero.

Masterpiece

He launched the replay into giddy orbit with its opening goal, then scored a 77th-minute masterpiece worthy of any trophy in football history.

The stately home of the most English of all games throbbed at the end to the Latin cry of the reigning world champions: 'Argentina, Argentina'.

No one had felt more ashamed than the man substituted on Saturday by the accusations that Spurs failed that day to reinforce their multi-national talents with enough honest toil.

City did their best, but could never beat Spurs' sheer strength of will

After the match, this fan (on the ground) feels even more squashed than most

No one, not even in this pair of teams motivated to the eyeballs, was hungrier for a battle of uncommon ferocity.

No one was better equipped to decide, at the shattering last, that Tottenham's class would tell against Manchester City's fanatical devotion to John Bond's revivalist crusade.

It has cost £2 million to give the FA Cup Final to the people and as Wembley was filled at last by 92 000 genuine supporters, Villa set about making sure that they got double – if not treble – their money's worth.

The first goal was largely Argentinian, significantly Scottish also, in its creation. Ardiles declared Tottenham's willingness to take whatever punishment City might be ready to dish out by bewildering Manchester's lunging hit-man Gow.

Ardiles's own shot struck Archibald but fell kindly for the Scottish centre forward to essay a shot of his own against Corrigan.

This time the ricochet fell to the grateful Villa not far from an open goal.

Although Spurs were to be unsettled by City's stirring and immediate comeback, the mood was set irrevocably in their team for a performance as challenging as it was at times enchanting.

City were quicker about taking their turn to equalise than Spurs had been on Saturday. Within three minutes Ranson's high ball was met by only half a clearance and Mackenzie volleyed from 20 yards what we thought would be the goal of the match.

This time, with the chips down, Hoddle accompanied his Argentine playmates in a performance so committed and creative that it should confirm him as an international player of the highest English order.

Their appetite for the fray matched City's so closely that referee Keith Hackett's determination to impose stricter control on the replay necessitated five bookings.

Booked – Again

Tommy Caton, City's inspiring young defender, set some sort of unenviable record by being booked for the second time in one FA Cup Final. But neither he nor Ranson, Galvin, Archibald or, inevitably in the end, Gow, had cause for complaint.

The temper of the game was most visible after a 50th minute penalty gave City the lead. There was no denying Miller's push on Bennett, no resisting the ensuing and remarkably composed despatch of the penalty by Reeves.

But Spurs seemed outraged that the Cup might be won and lost on one penalty instead of the many which were looming at the end of extra-time if the final stage deadlocked.

Spurs demanded a penalty of their own when Caton's panicking arm made contact with Hoddle's deep corner in the 70th minute.

The referee was unsighted but Hoddle was not finished with that particular spasm of pressure and his immediate pass left Corrigan unprotected against Archibald's straining touch and a final prod at the ball by Crooks.

Then came Villa's moment of glory. Galvin's pass was short and orthodox; but it set the big, bearded man off on a mesmerising run past Caton twice and Ranson once before delivering the goal of his life.

Keith Burkinshaw called now for calm in the Spurs ranks. Bond sent on Tueart for McDonald in a last effort. Tueart almost obliged when his, the final shot of the match, sailed just outside a post. Then it was Perryman's, not Corrigan's, moment to collect the Cup in reward for a lifetime of one-club devotion.

Then Villa went round to receive his ovation. In the end, it was not so much the Year of Tottenham's Cockerel as the Night of the Pampas Bull.

1982

TOTTENHAM HOTSPUR 1
QUEEN'S PARK RANGERS 0
(replay, following a 1–1 draw)

ATTENDANCE
100 000
(replay) 90 000

REFEREE
C. White (Harrow)

GOALSCORERS
Hoddle
Fenwick

Replay: Hoddle

TEAMS

Tottenham Hotspur	Queen's Park Rangers
Clemence	Hucker
Hughton	Fenwick
Miller	Gillard
Price	Waddock
Hazard	Hazell
Perryman	Neill
Roberts	Currie
Archibald	Flanagan
Galvin	Micklewhite
Hoddle	Stainrod
Crooks	Gregory

(Allen replaced Micklewhite in the replay)

THE ROAD TO THE FINAL

Tottenham Hotspur
4th round
v Leeds United 1–0 (h)
5th round
v Aston Villa 1–0 (h)
6th round
v Chelsea 3–2 (a)
Semi-Final
v Leicester City 2–0

Queen's Park Rangers
4th round
v Blackpool 0–0 (a)
Replay 5–1 (h)
5th round
v Grimsby Town 3–1 (h)
6th round
v Crystal Palace 1–0 (h)
Semi-Final
v West Bromwich Albion 1–0

Fates Haunt Unhappy Spurs

An action-packed Final – with no winners at the end

EVEN NOW, deep into May and stretched to their 66th game of a season which refuses to end, Spurs still seem cursed to play all the football yet to win nothing at all.

Here, right down at the fag end of what started as a Grand Slam campaign, they find an overrun Second Division side still clinging to what should be Tottenham's consolation prize ... if such the FA Cup can be called.

Will Thursday's replay, their sixth journey to Wembley in a year, produce the happy ending?

Not if Peter Hucker has another game in goal for Queen's Park Rangers as inspired as the one he played on Saturday.

Not if Steve Archibald and associates continue to miss chances as if there will always be more Cups to come. No, most disconcertingly of all, if their script for glorious failure has been written from the start.

How else do you explain why a team with so much to offer – not least to the public – should still be scavenging for the last crumb from this season's table of honours?

Judging by events in the Cup Final so far, Rangers should return to Wembley expecting nothing more than their share of another near £1 million gate ... and grateful for it. The suspicion lingers, however, that they are fated to profit

The fans rise as Glen Hoddle falls to his knees after scoring for Spurs

still further from Tottenham's misfortune.

Not even the suspension of Glen Roeder from the replay, a punishment out of all proportion with a misdemeanour in a Second Division game, can compare with Tottenham's loss of two Argentines.

Terry Venables is more than cute enough to accommodate Roeder's absence with some new strategy, while Keith Burkinshaw finds his honourable decision to release Ossie Ardiles to Argentine's World Cup preparations repaid by a war in which Ricardo Villa has become an ancillary casualty.

And even the one apparent mistake Venables has made as manager of QPR is rebounding to his spectacular advantage. Had he not been tempted to go back to Crystal Palace to sign John Burridge, Venables would have bought another goalkeeper and the incredible Hucker might never have had the chance to become Saturday's hero.

Instead, the tense relationship between Venables and Burridge broke down again and Hucker was hurried out of the reserves in time to conquer Wembley at the age of 22.

Not Boring

When Archibald, Crooks and Hazard hit the target, Hucker responded with the kind of saves which England's Ray Clemence admitted he would have been proud to make at the other end. So, although Currie, Hazell and Waddock acquitted themselves with distinction, it is hard to conceive a less nervous Rangers conceding so much territory and possession of the ball second time around.

Spurs, in fact, had more than enough attempts at goal to refute accusations of a boring final. Not profoundly exciting, maybe, but not boring.

Hucker's most accomplished save was low to his right from Archibald in the 82nd minute, the most eye-catching when soaring to touch over from Crooks in the sixth minute and from Hazard before he was substituted by Brooke.

He was beaten, 11 minutes from the end of extra time, only after Waddock's intended tackle on Hoddle was impeded by the referee and when Hoddle's subsequent shot was deflected off the inside of Currie's left knee.

Equaliser

That should have been the end of that. But Stainrod's long throw and Hazell's help-on header presented Fenwick and Queen's Park Rangers with the equaliser and a replay.

Unless something goes unexpectedly right on Thursday, then this is just not meant to be poor old Tottenham's year, after all.

The goal which meant a replay – scored by QPR's Fenwick

A *pas de deux* between Spurs' goalkeeper Clemence and QPR's Stainrod

REPLAY

Spurs ... At Last! but it's Tough on QPR as Spot Kick Settles It

A ball's eye view of Hoddle's winning penalty shot

LEGIONS OF TOTTENHAM fans rose as one man last night to salute the Second Division players who came so close to leaving their season in total ruin.

QPR, the youngest and one of the most remarkable teams ever to contest the FA Cup Final, went off to the kind of ovation which Wembley normally reserves for conquering heroes.

The entire congregation of 90 000, irrespective of the colours they wore, realised that Tottenham's luck had turned at last, and with a vengeance, against the underdogs from the other side of London.

The generosity of that crowd sweetened the tears on QPR's cheeks. For once, in a match played after even their marathon season ought to have ended, Spurs were comprehensively outpaced at their own attacking game.

For once, when it really mattered, Spurs' were given the benefit of the vital decision and enjoyed the kindest bounce of the ball. And for once it was Spurs who went home with the Cup.

Ironies

This replay, their 66th game of the season, offered Spurs positively their last chance of salvaging a trophy from what might have been a grand slam season.

And as they came down to the bottom line of their diminished ambitions, they won by an orthodox penalty in the first Cup Final which might otherwise have been decided by a penalty shoot-out.

Those ironies will not be lost on Spurs' manager Keith Burkinshaw, but neither will they cost him any sleep. He has suffered more than his share of disappointments in recent weeks.

For Terry Venables, his counterpart at QPR, it remains a magnificent achievement that he should rightly be able to claim a moral victory after having to patch up his underrated side.

Unlike Saturday, when Spurs struggled to get 11 fit and available men to Wembley, it was the turn of Venables to replace Rangers' key players, either injured or ruled out of this Final.

In replacing his punitively suspended captain Glenn Roeder and his principal goal-scorer Clive Allen with the 19-year-old Warren Neill and the 20-year-old Gary Micklewhite, he reduced the average age of his side to 23, yet still succeeded in convincing them that they could outclass the country's most attractive football team.

Nothing would demoralise the young Rangers, not the emotional intensity aroused in Tottenham's players and fans by the appearance of Argentina's Ricardo Villa on the bench, not even the penalty which put them behind after only six minutes.

There was no denying, however, the justice of referee Clive White's decision. Graham Roberts had broken into open country behind Bob Hazell's rash and inconclusive tackle and Tony Currie, an otherwise immaculate captain for QPR on the night, reached the man but not the ball, in his attempt to retrieve the situation.

Justice

Glenn Hoddle, mindful that when he last took a penalty it had been saved by Nottingham Forest's Peter Shilton, wasted no time over this one, despatching it low into the corner of the net almost before Peter Hucker had time to crouch on his goal-line.

On such an occasion, many a more experienced side might have surrendered in the face of such an early calamity. But for QPR, that goal was the signal to raise their game, to carry the fight to Tottenham with far greater conviction than at any time in Saturday's 120 minutes.

Spurs were to become so stretched and alarmed that Roberts was reduced to felling Currie long after the ball had been played and Paul Miller was booked for an appalling lunge at Gary Waddock.

Then Spurs were to need all the help that referee White could give them to cling on to their lead. Micklewhite thought he had equalised but Simon Stainrod was flagged offside.

Hazell and Currie both believed they were badly fouled close to Ray Clemence's goal but in their case no penalty was forthcoming.

Most frustratingly of all for Rangers, John Gregory steered Stainrod's dropping, angled pass deliberately over Clemence at the height of their domination, only to see the ball bounce off the crossbar.

Heroics

So complete was QPR's commitment to attack that they risked being caught on the break and Hucker was given the chance by Archibald's running shot to confirm that his heroics on Saturday had been no flash in the pan.

It would have been unjust had Archibald scored instead of hitting the post in the last minute ... just as it would have been heartbreaking for Tottenham to have ended their season empty-handed.

Because Spurs have fallen narrowly short of so many honours themselves, they knew how QPR felt and were the first to commiserate with the youngsters who collapsed, crying, at the end.

Tired and emotional, Spurs' Hoddle and Archibald hold the Cup aloft

I'm so Proud of My Lads, says Venables

QPR manager Terry Venables claimed a moral victory after Wembley's replayed Cup Final yesterday.

'You don't win many medals for that,' he said. 'But if you're going to lose that's the way I want to lose it.

'I'm proud of my players. I thought they were unlucky. We were the better side. The only thing we didn't do was get a result.'

Venables claimed QPR could have had two penalties when Terry Fenwick and Bob Hazell were brought down. He said: 'The linesman had his flag up but the referee didn't take any notice. I was a bit upset about that.'

Spurs' manager Keith Burkinshaw said: 'I'm not as elated as I might be. The last replay we won with style and panache and tonight I didn't think we played as well as we could have done. But we've had a great season and deserve to win something.'

Burkinshaw praised the 90 000 crowd for the magnificent reception given to watching Argentine player Ricky Villa. He said: 'I asked Ricky afterwards what reception an Englishman would have got in Argentina. He replied: "There wouldn't have been one."'

Spurs' skipper Steve Perryman said: 'Ricky has won the Cup for us as much as anybody else and has told me he wants to come back here next season.'

MANCHESTER UNITED 4

BRIGHTON & HOVE ALBION 0

(replay, following a 2–2 draw after extra time)

ATTENDANCE
100 000
(Replay) 92 000

REFEREE
A. W. Grey (Great Yarmouth)

GOALSCORERS
Stapleton, Wilkins
Smith, Stevens

Replay: Robson (2), Whiteside, Muhren

TEAMS

Manchester United	Brighton & Hove Albion
Bailey	Mosely
Duxbury	Gatting
Albiston	Pearce
Wilkins	Grealish
Moran	Ramsey
McQueen	Stevens
Robson	Case
Muhren	Howlett
Stapleton	Robinson
Whiteside	Smith
Davies	Smillie

(Foster replaced Ramsey in the replay)

THE ROAD TO THE FINAL

Manchester United
4th round
v Luton Town 2–0 (a)
5th round
v Derby County 1–0 (a)
6th round
v Everton 1–0 (h)
Semi-Final
v Arsenal 2–1

Brighton & Hove Albion
4th round
v Manchester City 4–0 (h)
5th round
v Liverpool 2–1 (a)
6th round
v Norwich City 1–0 (h)
Semi-Final
v Sheffield Wednesday 2–1

The Tiger Wins Back His Smile

Manchester United's first goal, by Stapleton

FOOTBALL'S INFINITE CAPACITY to replenish its love affair with the British public produced a Cup Final of heroic splendour just when we needed it most.

Brighton first and last – both in the pattern of scoring and the proportion of their endeavour – made nonsense of the game's inclination to rupture itself in a tangle of litigation and recrimination.

Manchester United, having accepted the biting challenge in the manly spirit of true champions, may yet commit on Thursday the massacre predicted for Saturday.

Wembley, its playing surface swamped by incessant rain, was flooded finally by footballers of substance creating moments to cherish.

Great theatre demands one paramount performance and it was Gary Stevens who came of age. Brighton's 21-year-old defender not only scored the goal which required extra time and a replay for the third year running, but also withstood

United's heavy artillery with such aplomb that all the fuss about Brighton's captain, Steve Foster, seemed irrelevant.

Brighton's captain, of course, abounds with initial delight that his team have earned him the right to appear in the Cup Final.

So brave and resourceful were Stevens and Steve Gatting in his absence, however, that Foster could return only to be impaled on the sword of comparison, wielded by United's determination to take one honour from their ambitious season.

Brighton played so mightily above their relegation form that United had to apply all hands to the pumps to stave off another of Wembley's sensations.

It is probable, however, that the Seagulls have had their chance to fly into history. Gordon Smith, scorer of the opening goal, shot at Gary Bailey instead of into the record books in the last seconds of extra time.

Even as they set off on a mutual lap of

well-deserved honour, United were grateful for the reprieve and conscious that a few more ounces of their own application in the preceding 119 minutes would surely have pushed Brighton over the cliff.

Brighton, with the controlled ferocity of Jimmy Case's tackling reinforcing Stevens and Gatting, and with Gary Howlett and Neil Smillie finding spasmodic ways forward, claimed a fair shair of the crucial incidents.

Talent

But Frank Stapleton and Norman Whiteside, Bryan Robson and Ray Wilkins, even young Alan Davies when his natural talent was not betrayed by inexperience, maintained such constant pressure for such lengthy periods that Brighton were stretched to the limit of countless straining interceptions.

Wilkins, whose goals have become collector's items, scored the best of all with a shot swung deliberately over and around Mosley to hit its designated square of the netting.

When Stevens equalised three minutes from the end of normal time, Wilkins flung down his shinguards in dismay that his masterpiece would not be remembered as one of the greatest goals ever to win the Cup.

His consolation is to have played his part in a Final that will be treasured by

Brighton, hardly believing their luck, celebrate their equaliser

us all, a contest enriched rather than tarnished by the aggression of Case, which United survived, and of Whiteside, which required Gerry Ryan to substitute for Chris Ramsey.

Thanks to Brighton & Hove Albion, a smile is back on the face of the tiger of English football.

All cameras in focus in the dying seconds of extra time

Daily Mail Comment: Why We Won't Take Sides!

Now the British people are really gripped by the excitement. All over Europe, too, ordinary men and women wait in fascination for the result.

From the pubs in Accrington to the bars in Athens, they talk of little else. Against the odds, could a left winger snatch victory for the underdogs? Forget the pundits. Anything is possible.

Could a disastrous miscalculation on the right wing wreck the hopes of the favourites?

Soon we should know.

So what advice does this newspaper give to its readers? We have no doubt where we stand. We remain, as we have been in this comment column from the beginning, utterly impartial. We refuse to take sides.

In tonight's FA Cup Final replay between Brighton and Manchester, we can only say: May the best team win!

REPLAY

Happy Birthday, Sir Matt

On Sir Matt Busby's 74th birthday, Manchester United present him with four goals. This is the second

MANCHESTER UNITED celebrated the 74th birthday of the man who made them famous with a Wembley victory of historic magnitude.

Not for 80 years, and never in this noble Stadium, has the FA Cup been won by four clear, crushing, unanswerable goals.

Sir Matt Busby, father of the greatest United team of all, sat among the directors content that Ron Atkinson has begun the creation of a side to compare with his tragic Babes.

Overwhelming

United's red army of supporters turned briefly away from the slaughter of Brighton's Seagulls to sing 'Happy Birthday, Sir Matt'. No football man could have wished for a better present. The new United delivered the Cup in the overwhelming style we had expected of them on Saturday.

It was as if Busby's club had waited the five intervening days for the perfect occasion on which to ratify the expanding quality of Atkinson's team. The extra-time dramatics of the first game gave way to the jubilation of a replay which restored form and order to the 1983 Final.

Steve Foster's headband, which had been the symbol of the Cup campaign with which Brighton had relieved their relegation season, waved like a white flag of surrender as the United tide washed over their dream.

Foster, who had dragged through the High Court his vain appeal for the right to appear in Saturday's match, must have wished that his suspension had been extended to the replay. It was the opposing captain, Bryan Robson of United and England, who proved himself worthy of climbing the steps to the Royal Box and lifting the trophy from the hands of Princess Michael of Kent.

Robson scored two of the three first-half goals which left Brighton with little more than the memories of their epic struggle five days earlier.

Then with a penalty offering him the chance to become the first finalist for 30 years to complete a hat-trick, Robson had the humility to leave the honour of United's fourth goal to Dutchman Arnold Muhren.

Class, in every sense, finally told. Even so Brighton, the team already condemned to relegation, will be haunted in the Second Division by Smith's miss in the last minute of Saturday's extra time.

Jimmy Melia, Brighton's manager, will be left to reflect also on the adjustments made to his defence to accommodate Foster's return. The centre half may not have deserved the taunts of United's fans – 'What a difference Foster made', they chanted – but it was inevitable that he would suffer by comparison with the resourcefulness of the Stevens–Gatting partnership which had taken Brighton to a second game.

Foster made some timely interceptions in an opening 25 minutes which kept the faint whiff of a sensation in the night air.

Then United nagged at Gatting's unfamiliarity with his new role at right back and Brighton's sandcastle fell. Whiteside's shin-high cross was laid back to the edge of the penalty area by young Alan Davies, and Robson swept the first goal low into the far corner of the net.

Four minutes later Davies, an unknown before the Final, turned one of Muhren's inswinging corners back into the goal-mouth and Whiteside's lunging header made it 2–0.

As if in relief at shaking Brighton from their heels, United relaxed and Gary Bailey had to produce an acrobatic save to keep out Case's wickedly deflected shot. Grealish, in a gesture which typified the sportsmanship which never deserted the Final even in its most ferocious moments, was the first to congratulate the United goalkeeper.

Punished

In contrast, Foster's gruesome foul on Whiteside was punished to the full two minutes from half-time. Robson headed on Muhren's resulting free kick and turned to nudge Stapleton's responding header over the line.

Brighton were lucky not to concede one penalty when Whiteside's return pass in the direction of Muhren ran up Foster's arm. But a linesman was perfectly placed to see Stevens, Saturday's hero, wrestle Robson to the ground in the 62nd minute. Robson declined all appeals to embellish his personal triumph and Muhren dispatched the penalty with customary Dutch calm.

Bryan Robson leads the United celebrations

1984

EVERTON 2
WATFORD 0

ATTENDANCE
100 000

REFEREE
J. Hunting (Leicester)

GOALSCORERS
Sharp, Gray

TEAMS

Everton	Watford
Southall	Sherwood
Stevens	Bardsley
Bailey	Price
Ratcliffe	Taylor
Mountfield	Terry
Reid	Sinnott
Steven	Callaghan
Heath	Johnston
Sharp	Reilly
Gray	Jackett
Richardson	Barnes

THE ROAD TO THE FINAL

Everton
4th round
v Gillingham 0–0 (h)
Replay 0–0 (a)
2nd replay 3–0 (h)
5th round
v Shrewsbury Town 3–0 (h)
6th round
v Notts County 2–1 (a)
Semi-Final
v Southampton 1–0

Watford
4th round
v Charlton Athletic 2–0 (a)
5th round
v Brighton & Hove Albion 3–1 (h)
6th round
v Birmingham City 3–1 (a)
Semi-Final
v Plymouth Argyle 1–0

Everton Clean Up

The winning Everton team

EVERTON ENDED YEARS of torment, failure and a season of dramatically changing fortunes by carrying off the FA Cup.

This Final cannot be regarded as a soccer classic but in days of hooliganism and cynical professionalism it must be saluted as a triumph for good, old-fashioned sportsmanship.

There were just 20 fouls recorded by referee John Hunting of Leicester, and there was not a bad one among them. At the end of 90 minutes of cut-and-thrust action, Everton applauded Watford and the losers responded with a similar gesture.

Effective

Watford manager Graham Taylor, who along with flamboyant chairman Elton John, has urged the club along a yellow brick road stretching from the depths of the Fourth Division to the Wembley showpiece, will undoubtedly be back.

And they could so easily have tri-umphed on their first appearance. It was Watford, producing their controversial all-action attacking style, who created the early goal-scoring opportunities.

Captain Les Taylor twice surged clear only to shoot wide. John Barnes, too, will surely reflect on the way he strained the quality of mercy after wrecking Everton's defences with brilliant footwork.

But the youngest team to appear in an FA Cup Final were to be destroyed by their own innocence and inexperience.

In the 38th minute, the 18-year-old Lee Sinnott provided a weak response to a left wing centre from Everton's Kevin Richardson.

His headed clearance dropped straight to Gary Stevens and although the Everton defender could only poke the ball back in the general direction of the Watford penalty area, it was to prove devastatingly effective.

Graeme Sharp, totally unmarked, made maximum use of his opportunity and

Everton's Southall makes an important one-handed save from John Barnes

Only Sad Songs for Elton

As Everton paraded the FA Cup around a Wembley ringed with blue, the electric scoreboard flickered out a brief commercial.

It recommended that we purchase Mr Elton John's new record, a fetching ditty entitled 'Sad Songs'.

High on the terraces, the sombre ranks of yellow and red might have offered their chairman a chorus or two. But they hadn't the heart.

As Everton's celebrations began, the blue legions gave voice to a jaunty little chant: 'Tell Me Ma to Put the Champagne on Ice'.

The Watford loyalists looked on silently. A marvellous effort was at an end, and songs were beyond them. Even sad songs.

Graham Taylor and players show that Watford never forget their fans

swept a shot into the Watford net off the inside of the post.

Not even the persuasive tongue of Taylor at half-time could possibly succeed in resuscitating Watford when their goalkeeper, Steve Sherwood, tragically confirmed his susceptibility to high crosses in the 51st minute and presented Everton with a two-goal advantage.

There appeared to be little imminent danger when Trevor Steven centred from the right for Everton. But Sherwood clearly panicked under the pressure presented by Andy Gray.

Sherwood took his eye off the ball for a split second and Gray was in like a flash. Even he isn't sure whether he headed the ball or the goalkeeper's hand, but the power of his challenge sent the ball over the line.

Watford immediately sent out substitute Paul Atkinson to replace Neal Price. But by then it was too late.

Maurice Johnston, who has provided 24 goals since his £200 000 transfer from Partick Thistle, believed that he had scored in the 79th minute. But he was clearly offside when he sent a header past Everton goalkeeper Neil Southall.

It was a sweet victory for Everton manager Howard Kendall. The same supporters who just six months ago were demanding his dismissal were now providing a massed Wembley salute.

Taylor Blasts the Ref

Watford manager Graham Taylor blasted Cup Final referee John Hunting last night in a bitter outburst over Everton's crucial second goal.

Furious Taylor claimed Hunting should have disallowed the goal because scorer Andy Gray knocked the ball out of goalkeeper Steve Sherwood's hands.

And he claimed the controversial decision probably cost Watford the match.

Taylor stormed: 'Ninety-nine times out of a hundred, Gray's goal would have been disallowed. He came on to Sherwood and made no contact with the ball whatsoever.

'You cannot blame Sherwood. It was impossible for him to hold the cross with Gray making that sort of challenge.

'After that it was all too much for us. We lost our shape and our balance.'

Sherwood backed his boss as the controversy boiled on long after the match was finished.

He said: 'I am very, very, upset. I had the ball in my hands and Andy Gray headed my hands. There was nothing I could do to prevent the ball going in.

'I told Andy he had headed my hands and he admitted it was true. He said it was the only way he could get the ball in. I tried to appeal to the referee but he raced away too quickly.

'I am upset because from other parts of the ground it may have looked as though I had made a bad mistake.'

MANCHESTER UNITED 1

EVERTON 0

ATTENDANCE
100 000

REFEREE
P. N. Willis (Meadowfield)

GOALSCORER
Whiteside

TEAMS

Manchester United	Everton
Bailey	Southall
Gidman	Stevens
Albiston	Van den Hauwe
Whiteside	Ratcliffe
McGrath	Mountfield
Moran	Reid
Robson	Steven
Strachan	Sharp
Hughes	Gray
Stapleton	Bracewell
Olsen	Sheedy

THE ROAD TO THE FINAL

Manchester United
4th round
v Coventry City 2–1 (h)
5th round
v Blackburn Rovers 2–0 (a)
6th round
v West Ham United 4–2 (h)
Semi-Final
v Liverpool 2–2
Replay 2–1

Everton
4th round
v Doncaster Rovers 2–0 (h)
5th round
v Telford United 3–0 (h)
6th round
v Ipswich Town 2–2 (h)
Replay 1–0 (a)
Semi-Final
v Luton Town 2–1

Poetic Justice Is Done

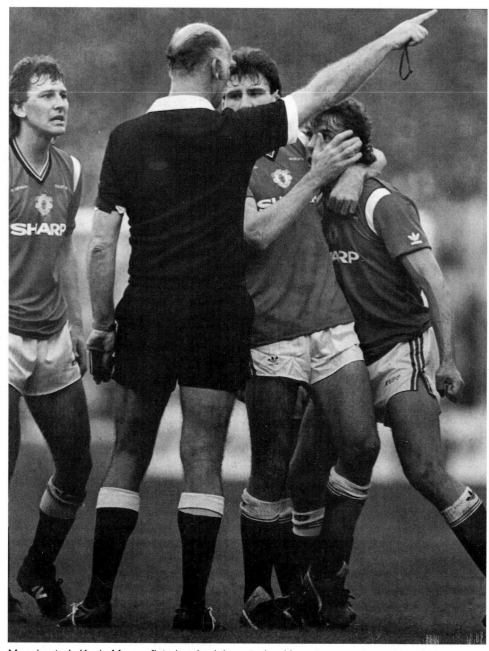

Manchester's Kevin Moran, fist clenched, is restrained by a team-mate as the referee orders him off

FOR WRETCHEDLY MISJUDGED reasons, referee Peter Willis unlocked a match of unbearable compression when he condemned Kevin Moran to be the first player sent off in over 100 FA Cup Finals.

It was more than mere anger at an historic injustice which inspired Manchester United to rise up and smite Everton's mighty dreams of a domestic double and the unique treble.

Liberated

Given a reasonable excuse for losing, United's football became liberated from the fear of defeat which has stifled so many Finals of classic potential.

As Moran sat on the touchline, cursing, grieving and waiting for television to exonerate his challenge of Peter Reid, the rest of United played like men with a burden lifted from them.

Seventy-eight minutes of strategic stalemate gave way to 42 minutes of ten-man heroics, and by the end of extra time, there was no denying United deserved victory.

Even during Saturday's first long hour of mutual nullification, it had seemed that United would be the team either to reach out for the winning goal ... or expose themselves to error and eclipse in the process.

Everton, physically shattered perhaps and mentally dulled by the winning of the League Championship and the Cup-Winners Cup, were just waiting for destiny to decide the issue.

This Is the Show with the MOST!

Exclusive, by Brian Clough

At around 3 p.m. this afternoon, I expect to be sitting comfortably in a jet at 32 000 feet en route to my holiday destination, which I've no intention of revealing.

My one hope is that the aircraft has cleared the English coast when the 1985 FA Cup Final kicks off. When Everton and Manchester United get to grips, the air above Wembley promises to be turbulent!

The outcome I refuse to predict. But one forecast I will make ... this will be THE most aggressive, THE most competitive Final you've seen for over a decade. It is a contest between two of the best teams in the land: a confrontation either side is capable of winning.

Both teams are geared to produce the highest level of individual and team skills guaranteed to keep the public on the edge of its seat for a whole afternoon.

Just imagine it! Those hard-tackling United centre backs against Gray and Sharp; Robson against Reid; Bailey v Southall. They're all dynamite characters, and it could be explosive entertainment.

How about this Everton team? Howard Kendall has assembled all the right ingredients – an exciting young collection of players with a dash of experience in the right places.

People have asked me to analyse their success. It's no great mystery. You don't have to look any further than the goalkeeper and back four. A sound defence has always won and will continue to win Championships and get to Cup Finals.

The scene is set; the cast is marvellous – hope you enjoy the show. I'm off ... ta-ra.

Everton's Andy Gray in action

Goal! The Manchester bench leap to their feet in unison

Fate's messenger proved to be a referee from neutral and distant County Durham.

Willis had done well enough in the opening exchanges, pouncing on every hint that two of English football's juggernaut teams might try to batter each other into submission.

But when he booked Bryan Robson, the England captain no less, for a moderate offence, there was a danger the referee was becoming the central personality of the day.

So it transpired when Reid threatened to break clear. Moran went in desperately but with the ball as his objective. Everton's star flew through the air, and Willis eventually pointed to the benches.

A caution would have sufficed. And for all that the decision did the day a favour, the referee can count himself fortunate it was United's morale and ambition which prevailed.

Had Everton taken advantage of the extra man, it is highly doubtful that a day notable for its faith-restoring mood of humour and goodwill would have ended

in such harmony on and off the pitch.

United's grudge was forgotten as they lifted the Cup, and even Everton's fans booed the referee from the scene.

One moment of skill and cunning made sure sanity prevailed on a day when football could ill afford another televised disaster.

Twenty minutes into extra time, Robson and Mark Hughes conspired to spirit Norman Whiteside through an airlock in Everton's suffocating defence. So early in his career did this Northern Irishman begin acquiring experience that his is an old head on young shoulders.

Poignant

Whiteside used the jockeying presence of Pat Van den Hauwe to obscure Neville Southall's view ... and curled his shot round both those Wales World Cup men.

It was a goal worthy of winning any Final and one made all the more poignant by Southall's earlier, valedictory save at the feet of the same United player.

Although Reid had one early shot

deflected against a post by John Gidman, there was no denying the merit of the result, especially with the referee excusing more serious offences by Kevin Ratcliffe and Gary Stevens either side of Moran's miscalculation.

Frank Stapleton, the most creative element on the pitch for an hour, then a magnificent makeshift in Moran's defensive vacuum, deserved nothing less than his winner's medal. The same applied to Gordon Strachan, Jesper Olsen and Robson for their respective contributions of passion, skill and unselfish toil.

Moran should have his gong, too. It is to be hoped that the FA will be guided by the Fates when they sit down on Wednesday to decide whether to make an exception to the rule which prevented the sent-off player receiving his medal on Saturday.

Moran is honestly hard, not malicious, in his football and there should be scope for compassion at the end of the season of exceptional endeavour by both clubs.

1986

LIVERPOOL 3
EVERTON 1

── ATTENDANCE ──
98 000

── REFEREE ──
A. Robinson (Waterlooville)

── GOALSCORERS ──
Rush (2), Johnston
Lineker

── TEAMS ──

Liverpool	Everton
Grobbelaar	Mimms
Lawrenson	Stevens
Beglin	Van den Hauwe
Nicol	Ratcliffe
Whelan	Mountfield
Hansen	Reid
Dalglish	Steven
Johnston	Lineker
Rush	Sharp
Molby	Bracewell
MacDonald	Sheedy

── THE ROAD TO THE FINAL ──

Liverpool
4th round
v Chelsea 2–1 (a)
5th round
v York City 1–1 (a)
Replay 3–1 (h)
6th round
v Watford 0–0 (h)
Replay 2–1 (a)
Semi-Final
v Southampton 2–0

Everton
4th round
v Blackburn Rovers 3–1 (h)
5th round
v Tottenham Hotspur 2–1 (a)
6th round
v Luton Town 2–2 (a)
Replay 1–0 (h)
Semi-Final
v Sheffield Wednesday 2–1

Superman Rush Is On

Ian Rush on the way to scoring his first goal

IAN RUSH, THE greatest goalscorer in Europe and possibly the world, applied the final irreversible touches to a momentous FA Cup and League Championship double for Liverpool.

If ever the real worth of a truly magnificent marksman had to be personified, this was surely it. As usual, Rush was not found wanting.

And that worth is being assessed by the fabulously wealthy Juventus even as you read these words.

Giampiero Boniperti, the president of the Italian giants, sat in the Royal Box along with his entourage.

Individual Brilliance

The Duchess of Kent was close by, but Mr Boniperti had eyes only for Rush and they must have been popping out of their sockets at the climax of a fabulous individual performance.

Whether Rush's contribution to the destiny of this the first-ever all-Merseyside FA Cup Final will prove to be an unforgettable parting gift remains to be seen.

For the moment, the whole of football should mourn the fact that one of the few greats in the game will not be on show in the World Cup finals because of the sad failure of Wales to qualify for Mexico.

One man who will be there and hopefully firing England to great heights is Gary Lineker.

His irresistible pace left Liverpool captain Alan Hansen in his wake and although goalkeeper Bruce Grobbelaar should have done better than merely block the shot which placed to his left, Lineker was able to follow up and score easily.

There was precious little sign of any kind of recovery from Liverpool. Even before the goal they had enjoyed outrageous fortune in escaping a penalty when Steve Nicol hauled down Graeme Sharp.

Everton's international midfield of Trevor Steven, Peter Reid, the splendid Paul Bracewell and Kevin Sheedy, continued to produce exquisite examples of inventive, controlled, attacking movements.

In sharp contrast Liverpool's attempts to examine the quality of their opponents' defences and the true fitness of centre half Derek Mountfield, who had been cleared to play just before the start of the game, lacked the normal clinical construction for which they are so renowned.

Their nervousness emanated perhaps from the continued fumbles and foibles of their extrovert goalkeeper and it must be said that his competence was questionable on too many occasions.

But just when it seemed to all but the most strictly partisan Anfield supporter that further Everton goals were inevitable, Rush stepped forward to whip off his cloak of anonymity.

It was as though Superman had arrived in the nick of time to rescue another impossible situation.

Incredible Collection

Jan Molby provided the inch-perfect pass in the 57th minute and Rush did the rest.

Fake Ticket Threat to The Final

A flood of forged tickets could cause chaos at today's all-Merseyside FA Cup Final.

Thousands are on the black market in Liverpool, but Scotland Yard warned that the fakes would not beat the stringent turnstile checks at Wembley. More than 80 000 Liverpool and Everton supporters began the great trek south last night, thousands of them without tickets.

Touts, despite police warnings that they will be arrested if they deal near the Stadium, were making a killing, getting up to £300 for a £25 seat.

A major security operation will be mounted for the match, but police are expecting a friendly Final.

Those left at home plan to celebrate the game, the first all-Merseyside Cup Final, in style. Hundreds of street parties are planned and 500 pubs have afternoon extensions.

But, according to a computer in neutral Manchester, the result is cut and dried. After being fed 500 000 facts and figures on both teams, it predicted a 2–1 win for Liverpool.

With breathtaking aplomb, he sidestepped goalkeeper Bobby Mimms and squeezed in a shot from an oblique angle. Craig Johnston dashed in to apply any finishing touch that might be necessary. It wasn't.

But Johnston didn't have to wait too long for his moment of glory. Just seven minutes later a cross from Molby was

Everton's Lineker deftly slots the ball past Grobbelaar

Doubles all round! Dalglish and Lawrenson show off the First Division Trophy and the FA Cup

missed by Kenny Dalglish and Johnston scored easily from close range.

Maybe Liverpool had become unexpectedly inspired to even greater heights by a sudden dash of brilliant expertise by Grobbelaar in the 61st minute, when he produced a sensational back-bending save to keep out what would have been a headed equaliser from Sharp.

Not even the introduction of 'Supersub' Adrian Heath in place of England right back Gary Stevens could influence the situation.

Liverpool merely plugged the ball into the gap Stevens had vacated and wrapped it all up.

And what a marvellous way it was to clinch only the third FA Cup and Championship double this century.

Rush, in his own half of the field, started the movement in style and concluded it with deadly accuracy.

His pass to Molby was transferred from the centre of the field out to Ronnie Whelan on the left. His cross came in and Rush glided forward to examine the strength and durability of the back stanchion of the netting.

'My Conscience is Clear,' says Ref

Cup Final referee Alan Robinson yesterday described Everton's suggestion that he had conducted a vendetta against them as 'absolutely preposterous'.

Everton manager Howard Kendall was convinced his team had been denied a penalty when leading 1–0. But Robinson said: 'I can look back on the match with peace of mind. I met a lot of Everton supporters afterwards and they said, "Well refereed". There was no animosity, and it is rubbish to say I've got something against Everton.'

Kendall, whose side lost 3–1, said: 'We were denied a blatant penalty by the same referee when Alan Hansen handled on the line in the Milk Cup Final two years ago.

'We could have gone in at half-time on Saturday with a two goal lead if the penalty had been given. My players also felt that the Liverpool equaliser was offside.'

Football Association officials are studying Kendall's comments, made immediately after the match, and are likely to ask for an explanation.

Robinson waved play on after Liverpool right back Steve Nicol collided with Everton's Scottish International striker Graham Sharp in the 18th minute.

'It was a free header – suddenly I was pulled back,' said Sharp.

But Robinson, a 48-year-old civil servant from Waterlooville, said: 'I was in a good position and it was a case of two players challenging for the ball and colliding. There was a TV set in our dressing room and at half-time I saw the replay and was satisfied.'

1987

COVENTRY CITY 3
TOTTENHAM HOTSPUR 2
(after extra time)

ATTENDANCE
98 000

REFEREE
N. Midgley (Salford)

GOALSCORERS
Bennett, Houchen, Mabbutt (own goal)
Allen, Mabbutt

TEAMS

Coventry City	Tottenham Hotspur
Ogrizovic	Clemence
Phillips	Hughton
Downs	M. Thomas
McGrath	Hodge
Kilcline	Gough
Peake	Mabbutt
Bennett	C. Allen
Gynn	P. Allen
Regis	Waddle
Houchen	Hoddle
Pickering	Ardiles

THE ROAD TO THE FINAL

Coventry City
4th round
v Manchester United 1–0 (a)
5th round
v Stoke City 1–0 (a)
6th round
v Sheffield Wednesday 3–0 (a)
Semi-Final
v Leeds United 3–2

Tottenham Hotspur
4th round
v Crystal Palace 4–0 (h)
5th round
v Newcastle United 1–0 (h)
6th round
v Wimbledon 2–0 (a)
Semi-Final
v Watford 4–1

Wembley Heroes Show the World English Game Is Back at Its Best

After 111 seconds of play, Allen hammers in Spurs' first goal

ENGLISH FOOTBALL IS alive and well and on television for the whole world to see.

This FA Cup Final offered dazzling evidence that our football is worth playing for its own sake. Coventry could not have won more valiantly nor celebrated more euphorically, Tottenham lost more magnificently nor wept more freely had qualification for one of Europe's cups also been at stake.

A season in which faith in our national game has been restored by the countless thrills of a championship won by Everton and the honest strivings of a Littlewoods Cup lifted by Arsenal came to its climax

Have a Nice Day – Pleat Appeals for a Friendly Final

Tottenham manager David Pleat believes today's Wembley showdown will be a friendly Final – and possibly a classic.

'I think it will be played in a good atmosphere,' said Pleat. 'Bear in mind that all our supporters will be members or season ticket-holders and Coventry don't have any fans who use football as a theatre for violence.

'Yes, I think it will be a friendly Final. I hope so because there has definitely been an upswing in the game this season. And not just because attendances are up. The standard of play has improved, there has been less abuse of the offside law and, despite what some people say, refereeing standards have improved.

Pleat cites pace as one reason why it might be one of Wembley's better Finals. 'They have some very quick players – Cyrille Regis, Dave Bennett and Micky Gynn – and so do we,' he said. 'If you have players with pace who can play controlled football, you often get a very exciting game.'

in one of the finest of Wembley Finals.

Spectacle

Coventry, in their two hours of triumph, and Spurs, in their moment of dejection, performed a service which will be remembered even longer than the kind of match which is most often described as unforgettable.

Coventry's Houchen makes it 2–2, in spectacular style

The magic moment shows in three Coventry faces as the ball goes into the net

The Sky Blues celebrate the team's first ever FA Cup win

Coventry proved it is possible to overcome superior skill by intelligent strategy and positive use of their own ability rather than the application of the boot.

Spurs made the whole spectacle possible by allowing their season-long dedication to a romantic vision of the game to reach its natural conclusion ... win or lose.

Coventry's first major honour inscribed their place in the record books as well as in the hearts of those who relish the underdog having his day. This Tottenham team's fate, at least for this season, is to be remembered as one of the finest footballing sides not to win a trophy.

It would be crinimal if a solitary supporter abandoned either of these teams after all they contributed to this historic occasion.

When, in one minute and 52 seconds, Clive Allen scored his 49th goal of a personally rewarding season, it seemed that our expectations of a collective Spurs success would be fulfilled. Instead, the stage was set for unpredictable drama.

While Spurs had come to play their lovely game of flowing movement, subtle skills, and cunning angles from midfield – and for that the highest praise to manager David Pleat – Coventry's John Sillett and George Curtis had prepared their team on

how to hit Tottenham on the break, along the flanks and in the air.

Brilliant

By the end of their superlative first hour, Spurs were 2–1 up, having lost and regained the lead. But, like a brilliant boxer who has failed to finish off a brave fighter, they had punched themselves out.

Keith Houchen's diving equaliser was a blow to the heart. Allen did go close twice to his half-century before the end of 90 minutes upon which the only blemish was referee Neil Midgley's failure to caution Brian Kilcline for the solitary physical excess of the afternoon.

Shirt Bungle – Angry Spurs Order Blank Kit Inquest

The directors of losing FA Cup Finalists Tottenham Hotspur held an emergency board meeting yesterday to find out why six players appeared at Wembley in shirts which didn't contain the name of the club's sponsors Holsten.

The beer company pay Tottenham £1 million for a three-year contract which stipulates that the players must use shirts bearing the company's name.

But to the indignation of Holsten executives, Gary Mabbutt, Richard Gough, Glenn Hoddle, Ossie Ardiles, Paul Allen and substitute Gary Stevens wore plain shirts.

Secretary Peter Day said: 'No one quite knows what happened. Holsten have registered a vigorous protest and you can't blame them.'

There were 17 people other than the players in the dressing-room and not one spotted that half the team were wearing the wrong shirts. The players said there was no ulterior motive.

In the past, some players have refused to co-operate with sponsorship deals but it was being stressed yesterday that this was not the case at Tottenham.

Natural justice prevailed. Kilcline hurt himself more than Gary Mabbutt when committing that foul and had to be substituted before limping up to collect the Cup.

Of greater significance by the end was the replacement of a tired Osvaldo Ardiles for extra time. Although both teams were wearied by an open game, Spurs had poured more running into the Wembley turf and their organisation went with the departure of the little Argentinian.

It was no consolation to Mabbutt that his own-goal deflection saved the England squad to face Brazil tomorrow from being decimated by a replay on Thursday. Richard Gough, as the first Spurs captain to lose at Wembley, was plainly inconsolable also.

Contention

Never mind. For there was no doubt that with wealth available to replace, or maybe reinforce, Hoddle and Ardiles, Spurs will be back in contention for all the honours next season.

And with a West Midlands revival given lasting hope by Coventry's winning of the Youth Cup as well as the FA Cup, Saturday was a good day for all concerned.

Victory – and Coventry show their delight

1988

WIMBLEDON 1
LIVERPOOL 0

ATTENDANCE
98 203

REFEREE
B. Hill (Kettering)

GOALSCORER
Sanchez

TEAMS

Wimbledon	Liverpool
Beasant	Grobbelaar
Goodyear	Gillespie
Phelan	Ablett
Jones	Nicol
Young	Spackman
Thorn	Hansen
Gibson	Beardsley
Cork	Aldridge
Fashanu	Houghton
Sanchez	Barnes
Wise	McMahon

THE ROAD TO THE FINAL

Wimbledon
4th round
v Mansfield Town 2–1 (a)
5th round
v Newcastle United 3–1 (a)
6th round
v Watford 2–1 (a)
Semi-Final
v Luton Town 2–1

Liverpool
4th round
v Aston Villa 2–0 (a)
5th round
v Everton 1–0 (a)
6th round
v Manchester City 4–0 (a)
Semi-Final
v Nottingham Forest 2–1

Gould to Glory

An assortment of expressions as Sanchez scores with a header

TO WIMBLEDON, THE triumph of the ordinary man. To Liverpool, a humbling reminder that the wealthy can't buy everything.

If they did nothing else at Wembley – and mercifully they neither savaged their illustrious opponents nor blackened the national reputation – the unlikely lads proved it is possible still to breach this elitist society. All ye of slender means, take heart.

Wimbledon confounded the rest of us. Not so much by winning the FA Cup – enough underdogs have come through lately to fill the traps at one of Wembley's greyhound meetings – but by the manner of their achievement.

They were negative, all right, but not nasty; cunning instead of crude; honest rather than 'orrible. And since our exalted champions could not find a way past them, not even from the penalty spot, Wimbledon deserved to fill that famous silver pot with tears of happiness as they took it home to SW 19.

Bobby Gould, the manager made good,

35th, to the orthodox header which Lawrie Sanchez applied to a straightforward free kick.

But for Beardsley's defiant saves, Liverpool could have been heading for their expected landslide by half-time, instead of berating the referee for his Beardsley blunder and for failing to penalise Eric Young's kamikaze flattening of John Aldridge.

But they weren't, and it became confirmed as Wimbledon's day in the 61st minute when Mr Hill's ruling that Clive Goodyear had fouled Aldridge looked to have made dubious amends to Liverpool, only for Beasant to inflict on Aldridge his first penalty miss under Dalglish's management, at the least welcome moment.

We were left to wonder whether the entire season had been an illusion.

Of course not. Dalglish was right to issue a reminder of the brilliance with which Liverpool had sprinted away with the League championship.

And the question left over Wimbledon is why they found it necessary to play so brutally for so many excruciating months when they could come to Wembley for their biggest day of all, control themselves, and still score a 1–0 win over the best team in the country.

Coaching

The answer may be found in Howe's coaching. Instead of blatant assault, Wimbledon employed the nudge and the partial obstruction to supplement firm tackling and solid organisation.

With the ugly exception of the eighth-minute hack for which Vinny Jones should have been booked – and for which Steve MacMahon spent too much of his Final seeking retribution – Wimbledon sailed close enough to the legal limits of the game.

Not that anyone could begrudge Bobby Gould his moment of glory. At the final whistle Gould hurried to embrace his father, his wife and his chairman. Later he told me: 'I'd even have kissed you if I could have found you at that moment.'

Wimbledon supporters, offended by my evaluation of their exploits hitherto, might suggest that there is sometimes no accounting for taste. But as we keep telling each other, football is a game of opinions ... with which we will be ready again when we see in which of their guises Wimbledon approach the challenges awaiting them next season.

wept as he dedicated this Saturday to his family. In such memories is the legend of the Cup awash.

The Final was not a pretty sight. But it was hardly Wimbledon's fault that not one of Liverpool's celebrities could fathom the basic strategic puzzle posed by Howe's redeployment of Dennis Wise, a winger hardly bigger than the average mascot, to cut off the supply to John Barnes.

Tangle

No wonder Kenny Dalglish was as dis-

appointed with his own players as by the referee.

Not that Wimbledon could be blamed, either, because Brian Hill failed to give Peter Beardsley the advantage of a legitimate goal, then got in such a tangle over his penalty decisions that he is unlikely to be entrusted with a match of such importance ever again.

But for the referee's premature whistling for an idiotic foul on Beardsley, Liverpool would have been one up in the 34th minute instead of one down in the

Liverpool's John Barnes misjudges a vital shot in the early stages of the match

Unlikely Story

Liverpool has done great things for soccer. But Wimbledon's victory in the FA Cup was more than soccer.

It was a tale of the unexpected. It was suburban graft denying the prize to the greatest stylists in the game. It was the pundits proved spectacularly wrong. A custard pie in the face of predictability.

No-hopers of the world unite. You have nothing to lose but your inferiority complex.

Ugly ducklings can become swans. And, just once in a blue-and-yellow moon, Wombles can turn into Champions.

Wimbledon's Beasant making history – the first goalkeeper ever to save a penalty in a Wembley FA Cup Final

1989

LIVERPOOL 3
EVERTON 2

ATTENDANCE
82 800

REFEREE
J. Worrall (Warrington)

GOALSCORERS
Aldridge, Rush (2)
McCall (2)

TEAMS

Liverpool	Everton
Grobbelaar	Southall
Ablett	McDonald
Staunton	Van den Hauwe
Nicol	Ratcliffe
Whelan	Watson
Hansen	Bracewell
Beardsley	Nevin
Aldridge	Steven
Houghton	Sharp
Barnes	Cottee
McMahon	Sheedy

THE ROAD TO THE FINAL

Liverpool
4th round
v Millwall 2–0 (a)
5th round
v Hull City 3–2 (a)
6th round
v Brentford 4–0 (h)
Semi-Final
v Nottingham Forest 0–0*
Replay 3–1
(*match abandoned)

Everton
4th round
v Plymouth Argyle 1–1 (h)
Replay 4–0 (a)
5th round
v Barnsley 1–0 (a)
6th round
v Wimbledon 1–0 (h)
Semi-Final
v Norwich City 1–0

Liverpool's Masterpiece

Confusion in the goalmouth as McCall's goal forces extra time

THE GREAT BRITISH footballer stood alone among the administrative chaos that was Wembley on Saturday, the last figure of dignity and hope left in the English game.

Liverpool and Everton had put together an FA Cup Final to satisfy thinking fan and thrill-seeker alike.

Everton had found in the last 15 seconds their gallant response to Liverpool's opening 89 minutes of fabulous authority. Between them they had gone on to produce a crescendo in extra time, with Liverpool prevailing by the genuine virtues of somewhat superior class and more poignant motivation.

Then came their reward.

The last minutes of action were cluttered by encroaching fans who proceeded to impede their collecting of medals hard won, obstruct their parade of the trophy and engage them in unseemly scuffles.

Close

Liverpool's Alan Hansen, the most impeccable of all the day's contestants, said: 'Ninety-nine per cent of fans behaved brilliantly, and one per cent have to come on the pitch and spoil it for the rest.'

No two teams could have lent more to an extraordinary occasion. It had been said that it did not matter who won this year. Liverpool and Everton gave the lie to that excuse for continuing with the Cup, yet did so with a style which offered no affront to sensitivity.

Liverpool went out to play some of the finest football ever seen in this country. John Aldridge's goal after four minutes was a living evocation of the intelligent running and precision passing which is the hallmark of England's outstanding team.

On another day, perhaps one less scorched by the sun or under such intense scrutiny, Aldridge might have completed at least a hat-trick by half-time and John Barnes stepped in with supplementary efforts to put the Final beyond the interest of all except the record-keepers.

Grobbelaar was arrogant, Nicol remarkable, Hansen elegant, Ablett resourceful and McMahon and Whelan were in absolutely rampant command of midfield.

It was tempting to believe they could take on any club team on earth.

Best

Everton were down to Southall and the

Ian Rush in spectacular form for Liverpool as he scores the first of his two goals

best goalkeeper in the country, maybe the world, did not disappoint them. Welsh Neville worked his miracles, encouraged Everton to stave off the inevitable, cajoled them back into contention.

For a long time, Southall was a one-man phenomenon. Then Colin Harvey sent on reinforcement in the shape of Stuart McCall and the substitute plundered the equaliser even as they were tying red ribbons round the old trophy.

Kenny Dalglish is no manager's fool. At his permanent standing position on the touchline he knew the risk entailed in failing to turn superiority into goals.

At a small cost of £2.8 million last summer, he had availed himself of a luxurious remedy for just such an emergency.

Ian Rush had replaced Aldridge late enough in normal time to be fresh and full of sprinting in extra time. First he turned a pass rich in Nicol's versatility into a goal as brilliant and vital as any in his prolific career.

Then, after McCall had launched his spectacular second equaliser en route to becoming one of the unluckiest losers in Wembley history, Rush met a Barnes cross with a header as deft as it was decisive.

Southall, although confounded by a trio of classical goals, retained the spirit to stop some more before the Cup was lost.

Everton had done their duty by the living and the dead, while justice had been served by the result. What remains to be assessed is how much they have drained from Liverpool's pursuit of Dalglish's second double by prolonging the struggle through a supplementary 30 minutes of glaring heat.

Wanted

For West Ham, who need to win at Anfield tomorrow to avoid relegation from the First Division, and Arsenal, who go there on Friday still in hope of the championship, extra time for Liverpool was just what they wanted.

Last Orders at Noon

Publicans have been asked to stop serving drink to football fans at noon today in an attempt to prevent drunkenness at Wembley.

The plea was made by police to more than 500 pubs and wine bars and follows a visit from home beat officers to outline the special measures being taken after the Hillsborough disaster.

It is an attempt to get the 82 000 fans to the Stadium earlier and in a more sober state than in previous years.

It calls for a two-pronged attack to stop serving drink to fans at 12 noon and to be extra strict about refusing to serve anyone who has already had one over the odds.

A message of solidarity from the fans

MANCHESTER UNITED 1

CRYSTAL PALACE 0

(replay, following a 3–3 draw)

ATTENDANCE

80 000

(Replay) 80 000

REFEREE

A. Gunn (South Chailey)

GOALSCORERS

Robson, Hughes (2)

O'Reilly, Wright (2)

Replay: Martin

TEAMS

Manchester United	Crystal Palace
Leighton	Martyn
Ince	Pemberton
Martin	Shaw
Bruce	Gray
Phelan	O'Reilly
Pallister	Thorn
Robson	Barber
Webb	Thomas
McClair	Bright
Hughes	Salako
Wallace	Pardew

(Sealey replaced Leighton in the replay)

THE ROAD TO THE FINAL

Manchester United

4th round

v Hereford United 1–0 (a)

5th round

v Newcastle United 3–2 (a)

6th round

v Sheffield United 1–0 (a)

Semi-Final

v Oldham Athletic 3–3

Replay 2–1

Crystal Palace

4th round

v Huddersfield Town 4–0 (h)

5th round

v Rochdale 1–0 (h)

6th round

v Cambridge United 1–0 (a)

Semi-Final

v Liverpool 4–3

Two-Goal Wright Stays in Reserve

A vain bid to keep out O'Reilly's header

WHEN A PLAYER scores twice in an FA Cup Final you expect him to be picked for the replay.

But Steve Coppell, at 34 the youngest manager of a Wembley Finalist team and a Bachelor of Economics, doesn't work that way.

Ian Wright will almost certainly start on the bench again on Thursday. That information surfaced when Coppell was asked whether Crystal Palace's two-goal hero would be fit.

'I don't think so,' he said. 'He has only played one full game since 27 January and he is an explosive player. When you take that explosiveness away from him, he's average.

'The balance of the side isn't the same when he is in it.'

Wright took the news with commendable sportsmanship. 'That's up to the manager to decide and I accept whatever he says. I know I can do the business for him,' he said.

'I'm fit, but I am not match fit. People got it wrong about my leg. I didn't break it twice in the same place. It was in two different places.'

Fifty-one minutes was just about the limit for Wright. Had he played the whole 120 minutes, he might have had less left for the second game.

Tiring

As Manchester United skipper Robson said: 'I've never been in such a tiring game at Wembley. That was the first time I've ever had cramp there.'

Coppell's successful tactical plan demanded that nine of his outfield players were man-to-man markers. That can never have happened before in a Cup Final.

Nigel Martyn saves for Crystal Palace

John Salako, normally a winger, picked up Brian McClair, failing in his duty only once when the United player was allowed to squander an easy heading chance four yards out. Alan Pardew took Bryan Robson. Richard Shaw, normally the left back, moved into the middle to make life even more difficult for a labouring Neil Webb.

United only began to play more open football after Wright came on in the 69th minute and Shaw reverted to left back, leaving Webb free. Coppell's clamp on Alex Ferguson's stars was partially removed and United came back to earn a replay.

Coppell, scribbling furiously away, will have noted that. By asking lone striker Mark Bright to occupy the attentions of Steve Bruce and the injured Gary Pallister, he had enough men available to cancel out United's superiority in sheer football talent. United had more chances but Palace goalkeeper Nigel Martyn did better with most of them than the hapless Jim Leighton did with Palace's more limited opportunities.

Coppell kept the dressing-room door locked before the kick-off, emerging at the statutory 2.30 p.m. to announce his line-up. Afterwards few would argue when he concluded: 'We had 13 belters out there.'

Famed

The only possible exception was Andy Gray, who was far less influential, even with his famed set-plays, than anyone could have expected. Gray's substitution four minutes from the end caused the sporting day's only tiff.

As he lay suffering from cramp off the field, Coppell ordered substitute Dave Madden to the edge of the pitch and, when the ball went out of play, asked for him to be allowed on.

Official Roger Milford asked: 'What's the number of the player going off?' Coppell replied: 'I can't remember.'

Milford insisted: 'I can't make the change until I know. That's the rule.' Coppell fumed. 'He's over there, lying on the ground,' he said.

Milford relented and Madden came on at a time when Palace's discipline was in danger of collapsing. They survived. But it will take another stifling performance on Thursday if they are not to go the way of Brighton, who lost their replay to United 4–0 in 1983.

Ron Atkinson's side then was not as tense as Ferguson's side which lives on a knife edge with the tension of the managerial team communicating itself to the players.

That's the main reason why Palace are hanging in there thinking they can win.

Bryan Robson agonises over the extra-time miss

Ince and Bright, happy with a draw – for now

REPLAY
Lee Ends the Deadlock

The plague on Scottish goalkeepers, more humorously known now as mad custodian disease, spread to the green pastures of Wembley last night.

Jim Leighton, Scotland's first World Cup 'keeper, surrendered his Cup Final place to an Englishman borrowed by Manchester United.

Les Sealey had to seek an extension of his loan period from Luton before making his extraordinary appearance in this replay.

Sealey arrived on the famous turf to a mixture of cheers and sighs of relief as United faithful remembered the three goals their team had conceded in Saturday's elongated draw.

The way Crystal Palace attempted to take improper advantage of this bizarre situation changed the atmosphere of a balmy evening in London from festive to angry.

Reputation

Palace's supporters had filled the air with thousands of balloons and been applauded by United's fans for so doing. The mood of their team, however, was more one of aggravation than celebration. Conscious that Sealey was playing only his third game for United and aware of his reputation for volatility, Palace sought to unsettle him.

The applause for Sealey's first catch, a

reassuring jump to intercept a cross from Phil Barber, turned to accusations as the man playing a Cup Final on borrowed time was flattened by Mark Bright.

It was a calculated lunge and Bright was duly booked by referee Alan Gunn. He was not to be alone in being shown the yellow card of caution.

If Palace had suffocated United tactically on Saturday they were more physical in their attempts at spoiling the replay. Geoff Thomas was spared a booking for throwing the ball in Brian McClair's face only when the United forward interceded with the referee on his behalf.

Two smart interventions by Sealey suggested they might have failed in their attempts at unsettling United's unexpected 'keeper. Sealey warmed to his task when turning a shot from John Salako around his near post. He positively rose to the occasion in the 26th minute after Steve Bruce handled perilously close to the penalty area.

Palace's free kick specialist Andy Gray punctured United's defensive wall with a thunderous shot but Sealey was ready, spreadeagling his body in classic style and beating the ball away to safety with his legs.

Lucky

Ince was lucky to escape a caution in the melee which ensued – Palace claiming a penalty for McClair's foul on Thomas – but his manhandling was of the referee, not the opposition.

Otherwise, United kept trying to impose their smoother football with captain Bryan Robson making some forcible points in midfield and his England side-kick, Neil Webb, curling a free kick into the side-netting. For the second time, it was anything but a classic, despite all the incidents, and Palace still had their potential match-winner, Saturday's two-goal substitute Ian Wright, poised on the bench and ready for action.

Palace were dressed like a swarm of wasps in their yellow and black stripes and playing like it. It was becoming an unpleasant affair but when United's goal came it was in splendid contrast to the surrounding nastiness.

Webb launched a glorious pass over the Palace defence and at the ideal angle for full back Lee Martin to gallop forward into space, control the ball economically

and plant his shot high into the roof of the net above Nigel Martyn's right hand.

Relieved

There was no more relieved or delighted individual in the Stadium than Alex Ferguson as United took that lead. Job salvation at the end of a traumatic season was just 30 minutes away.

With Wright on at last for Barber, Palace manager Steve Coppell was to be seen urging Palace out of ambush and into a cavalry charge.

Robson headed against the bar. He should have seen United make it safe ten minutes from time but his header bounced down and out off the crossbar.

At the finish it was Coppell, not Ferguson, who was in a state of neurotic agitation. That's football. That's the FA Cup.

Lee Martin scores the winning goal for United

1991

TOTTENHAM HOTSPUR 2
NOTTINGHAM FOREST 1
(after extra time)

ATTENDANCE
80 000

REFEREE
R. G. Milford (Bristol)

GOALSCORERS
Stewart, Walker (own goal)
Pearce

TEAMS

Tottenham Hotspur	Nottingham Forest
Thorstvedt	Crossley
Edinburgh	Charles
Van den Hauwe	Pearce
Sedgeley	Walker
Howells	Chettle
Mabbutt	Keane
Stewart	Crosby
Gascoigne	Parker
Samways	Clough
Lineker	Glover
Allen	Woan

THE ROAD TO THE FINAL

Tottenham Hotspur
4th round
v Oxford United 4–2 (h)
5th round
v Portsmouth 2–1 (a)
6th round
v Notts County 2–1 (h)
Semi-Final
v Arsenal 3–1

Nottingham Forest
4th round
v Newcastle United 4–4 (h)
Replay 2–0 (a)
5th round
v Southampton 1–1 (h)
Replay 3–1 (a)
6th round
v Norwich City 1–0 (a)
Semi-Final
v West Ham United 4–0

Despair Turns to Pride and Joy

Brian Clough and Terry Venables show the true spirit of the game

GRABBING AND KISSING two royal hands, attempting to knock guardsmen's hats off as they marched into centre-field, leaving the imprint of his studs on the first Forest chest he met. It was as though Paul Gascoigne was playing under a death-wish. After 15 minutes of his first Final, Wembley had become Gazza's resting place. Then Tottenham rose from theirs, the pauper's grave in which they have spent their entire season, to win the famous Cup for the eighth time.

Gascoigne was in the back of an ambulance when Gary Mabbutt walked up the steps to collect the booty. Rarely, if ever, can it have gone into more deserving hands.

Oceans of Energy

Behind their captain trailed the Tottenham heroes, those who had played through 106 minutes free of the handicap of the bloated genius whose James Deanesque contribution to proceedings might have done irreparable damage to his career. Paul Stewart, a mighty presence in midfield, David Howells, who so mastered Nigel Clough that the Forest manager's son was a picture of mounting aggravation, Paul Allen, unselfish, possessed of oceans of energy and, finally, the captain of England.

It must have been a while since Gary Lineker had a goal disallowed – television proving that the FA's choice of officials for its showpieces was hardly faultless – missed a penalty and still gave his markers such a relentless chasing. Even Des Walker, the steadfast rock of Forest and England, became so undone by the compelling drive of Tottenham's football that he dived to head the goal in the fourth minute of extra time which lost his side the Cup. Lineker, of course, was the first to put a consoling hand on his international colleague's head.

Too Late

Brian Clough tried to get a word through to Walker as his players walked up first for the consolation prize which does not console. It was too late by then. When his players really needed to hear his words of realism and inspiration – in the crucial seconds before extra time – he had walked behind the rows of benches underneath the Royal Box with his assistant Ronnie Fenton and was chatting to a couple of bemused Metropolitan policemen.

Quite what they could do, I'm not sure. Instead, he might have been giving his bunch of young, largely inexperienced, but totally genuine players, a snippet of the knowledge that has brought Clough success in European Cup Finals. They were left to fend for themselves.

Within a few minutes, the manager's desire to put the FA Cup on the mantelpiece of his Derbyshire home had evaporated. Though his lads tried to get it back for him, they couldn't and Clough

Jump for it!

sat motionless on his seat in the moments of delirium at the end of the Final. The emotions that were passing through him, we can only imagine.

Terry Venables, on the other hand, felt free to release his emotions with his players, those he had been left to work with through the crippling confines of the

club's finances and those who responded with magnificence when it mattered.

'I feel I've earned my spurs today,' Venables said. 'We didn't just win the game, we played really well. That's the way I'd always hoped we would win it.

'Once Gascoigne had gone off, it was up to the players to make the decision.

Glory Day – Spurs' Thorstvedt with the cup

Lineker is brought down by Chettle

They either gave up hope and said "Well, people will understand if we lose," or they just rolled up their sleeves and did it for them and for him. Paul Gascoigne is a well-admired player among the other players here.'

It is a tribute to the ones he left behind that they *did* roll up their sleeves. For Gascoigne had betrayed them with two culpably reckless tackles in the first quarter of an hour, the second of which shattered his right leg against the right thigh of Forest's Gary Charles.

What was Gascoigne doing just outside his own penalty area, almost the last defender, in the first place? Perhaps Venables had told him, unlike his wondrous performance in the semi-final, not to exhaust himself. Thus, his opening contributions were mainly peripheral, tantalising us. Soon, surely, he would burst into life.

Referee Roger Milford should have cautioned him for laying his boot into Gary Parker's chest in the second minute. His lunge at Charles was equally manic. The savage irony of its consequences will not be lost on Tottenham's brokers. It might well have lost them the Final.

Stuart Pearce drove his left-footed free kick into the top corner, though Milford,

Stretcher Case Earns No Tears

When the sound and fury of a memorable Cup Final had subsided, Terry Venables was left clutching the old silver pot.

Nobody could grudge him his triumph. And nobody could deny his pragmatic and tenacious team their right to a vibrant victory.

If this really is to be Venables' last major match in Tottenham's service, then he can reflect that at last his glowing reputation has been reinforced by solid achievement.

For this was the first significant trophy that English football has granted the Tottenham manager. And on a threadbare Wembley pitch, beneath sagging, sombre clouds, his team seized their prize in the most dramatic fashion.

There must be sympathy for a splendid Forest side who fell marginally short of their real potential. There will be unqualified sympathy for Des Walker, one of the world's finest defenders, whose wretched own-goal ultimately decided the contest.

But there can be not a scrap of pity for Paul Gascoigne, who entered the game with the mindless fury of a demented child and left, damaged and discredited, upon a stretcher.

That he departed without benefit of a red card said everything about the ludicrous tolerance of referee Roger Milford, who greeted two appalling Gascoigne tackles with nothing more punitive than a fatuous smile.

The last time the young man left an arena in tears, the entire nation cried with him. This time we were glad to see the back of him.

Gascoigne on his way out of the match

perfectly positioned beside the post, did not spot the lunging shoulder charge from Lee Glover which dislodged Mabbutt from the Spurs wall.

Cultured

Tottenham's reorganisation did not do permanent damage to their composure. Indeed, Nayim came on to relish the surroundings. Vinny Samways began to use his left foot to the simple, cultured effect which Clough has tried to purchase for Forest.

An irrepressible Tottenham bandwagon had begun to roll.

Six minutes into the second half a treasured pass from Nayim was collected by Allen, who switched it to Stewart and he finished with the aplomb of a future England midfield man. Pearce, the captain and England left back, was disastrously out of position. It was a distinction quite a few Forest players shared on Saturday.

The glory, glory day was rightly Tottenham's. Gascoigne had to share it down a telephone line next to his hospital bed where the doctors were working on his damaged right knee.

Perhaps, for everyone's sake, that will be the most important lesson he ever learns.

1992

LIVERPOOL 2
SUNDERLAND 0

ATTENDANCE
79 544

REFEREE
P. Don (Middlesex)

GOALSCORERS
Thomas, I. Rush

TEAMS

Liverpool	Sunderland
Grobbelaar	Norman
Jones	Owers
Burrows	Ball
Nicol	Bennett
Molby	Rogan
Wright	D. Rush
Saunders	Bracewell
Houghton	Davenport
I. Rush	Armstrong
McManaman	Byrne
Thomas	Atkinson

THE ROAD TO THE FINAL

Liverpool
4th round
v Bristol Rovers 1–1 (a)
Replay 2–1 (h)
5th round
v Ipswich Town 0–0 (h)
Replay 3–2 (a)
6th round
v Aston Villa 1–0 (h)
Semi-Final
v Portsmouth 1–1
Replay 0–0
(won on penalties)

Sunderland
4th round
v Oxford United 3–2 (a)
5th round
v West Ham United 1–1 (a)
Replay 3–2 (h)
6th round
v Chelsea 1–1 (h)
Replay 2–1 (a)
Semi-Final
v Norwich 1–0

202

Just What the Doctor Ordered

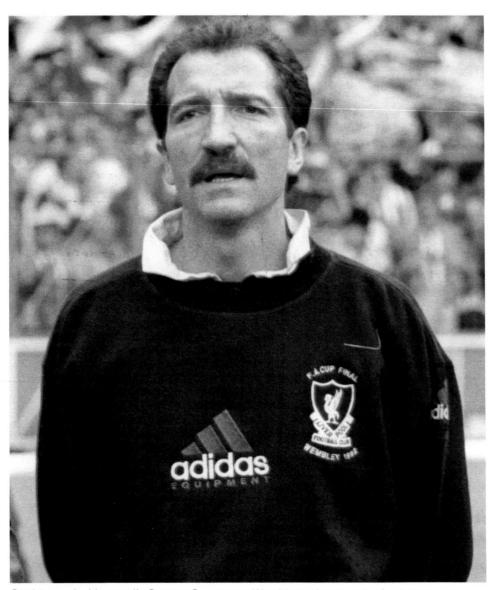

On the mend – Liverpool's Graeme Souness at Wembley only a month after heart surgery

GRAEME SOUNESS LEFT his hospital bed to clutch the FA Cup which eluded him as a player.

It could yet prove to be his first and last triumphant act as the manager of Liverpool.

But for the man who, just 32 days earlier, had undergone a triple heart bypass operation it was clearly a precious moment in a career studded with success.

Souness looked pale and thin and slightly infirm following his surgery. He chose not to lead out the team he had attempted to reconstruct in just one season at Anfield.

Instead he sat on the bench and, after a brief chat with the Duchess of Kent before the start, he did his best to withstand the peril of over-excitement.

But there were only a few anxious moments before second-half goals from Michael Thomas and the dependable Ian Rush secured an expected victory.

At the end Souness walked slowly on to the pitch to embrace every one of his players in thanks for the way they had accomplished their task in the same hard, professional manner which characterised his own career as a player.

The passionate army of Sunderland supporters converged on Wembley insisting that the last damp start to an FA Cup Final day was way back in 1973.

A significant omen, of course. For on that glorious afternoon 19 years ago the Second Division club had triumphed over mighty Leeds.

A torrential downpour throughout yesterday morning had been absorbed satisfactorily by the Wembley pitch.

Anxious

But any suspicion that the Second Division side might be swamped by the renowned class of Liverpool in the opening stages were soon to be swept away.

With the experienced Gary Bennett mopping up at the back, Sunderland ripped into their illustrious opponents.

But they soon had one anxious moment when Jan Molby swept a glorious pass across Wembley's broad acres directly in front of the feet of Ray Houghton.

The Republic of Ireland midfield player matched the accuracy of Molby's delivery with a beautifully-timed forward prod into the path of Thomas.

But the former Arsenal midfield player, famed for his ice-cool finish under pressure which snatched a League Championship away from Anfield, lifted his shot

Liverpool's Saunders and Sunderland's Atkinson tussle for control of the ball

over goalkeeper Tony Norman and the gaping target. Sunderland celebrated the great escape with a torrid spell of attacking movements and there was precious little time for some of the customary clowning from Bruce Grobbelaar.

Indeed, the Liverpool goalkeeper might have sustained serious physical damage when he cracked his head against the foot

in from the right, had already rounded Bracewell when the Sunderland skipper recovered sufficient ground to get in another challenge.

The tackle was a fraction late and clearly away from the ball. McManaman tumbled and a penalty looked inevitable. But the London official resisted the vehement demands of Liverpool players.

Ian Rush powers home Liverpool's winning goal

of a post in his scramble to squeeze out a snap-shot from Anton Rogan.

Grobbelaar recovered after treatment, but it was clearly going to take much more than a damp sponge to cool the Sunderland fervour.

From the inswinging corner by captain Paul Bracewell, top striker John Byrne inexplicably snatched at his shot in front of goal after Kevin Ball had headed the ball into his path.

Liverpool continued to feature in defence and only the outstretched foot of Mark Wright denied Bracewell an opening goal. It was fast and frenetic with the ball slipping around like an electric eel.

Sunderland could not possibly maintain such a pace and when the tempo slowed Liverpool brought their greater powers of creativity into play.

Dean Saunders had a shot saved by Norman and Steve McManaman headed narrowly over the angle following a fine cross by Rob Jones.

Right on half-time Sunderland owed much to the outrageous clemency of referee Philip Don. McManaman, coming

The influence of McManaman, replacing the injured John Barnes, had begun to take its full effect, and within two minutes of the restart Liverpool were ahead.

Glorious

The 20-year-old, who had not played a first-team game since his cartilage operation following the semi-final against Portsmouth, swept in from the right to deliver an accurate pass in the direction of Thomas.

The midfield player atoned fully for that third minute aberration with a glorious shot on the volley from just inside the Sunderland penalty area, the ball soaring well beyond the outstretched hand of Norman.

It was mostly Liverpool from then on and, despite gallant interventions by Norman, they confirmed a fifth FA Cup triumph with a second goal after 68 minutes.

Rush had all the time and space necessary to pass the ball into the net beyond the helpless Norman after Thomas had set up the opening.

To the victors the spoils

ARSENAL 2

SHEFFIELD WEDNESDAY 1

(replay, following a 1–1 draw)

ATTENDANCE

79 347

(Replay) 62 267

REFEREE

K. Barratt (Birmingham)

GOALSCORERS

Wright

Hirst

Replay: Wright, Linighan

Waddle

TEAMS

Arsenal	Sheffield Wednesday
Seaman	Woods
Dixon	Nilsson
Winterburn	Worthington
Parlour	Palmer
Linighan	Warhurst
Adams	Anderson
Jensen	Harkes
Davis	Waddle
Merson	Hirst
Wright	Bright
Campbell	Sheridan

THE ROAD TO THE FINAL

Arsenal

4th round

v Leeds United 2–2 (h)

Replay 3–2 (a)

5th round

v Nottingham Forest 2–0 (h)

6th round

v Ipswich Town 4–2 (a)

Semi-Final

v Tottenham Hotspur 1–0

Sheffield Wednesday

4th round

v Sunderland 1–0 (h)

5th round

v Southend United 2–0 (h)

6th round

v Derby County 3–3 (a)

Replay 1–0 (h)

Semi-Final

v Sheffield United 2–1

It's A Wrong Ending

Arsenal's Paul Davies curls a free-kick over the penalty area

THE GRAND SLAM dream of George Graham has been put on hold for a further five days.

The elegant Arsenal supremo was looking relaxed and assured as his record investment Ian Wright put him on course to become the first man to capture the three top trophies as both a player and a manager.

But an unscripted response from David Hirst means he must wait for his unique moment of history.

Two League Championships and two League Cup victories have already been achieved in Graham's seven years in charge, but the FA Cup continues to elude him.

That mission may well be accomplished in the Wembley replay on Thursday.

But if the second meeting between these teams fails to provide any greater entertainment then we will all be grateful for the first-ever Cup Final penalty shoot-out.

It all began brightly enough after a downpour shortly before the start ensured a surface sheen which demanded exemplary ball control.

Wednesday would have scored twice within the opening dozen minutes had Arsenal goalkeeper David Seaman not produced acrobatics to deny first Carlton Palmer and then Chris Waddle. But when it comes to eluding goalkeepers, there is surely none better than the confident Ian

Wright. He showed exactly how it should be done in 21 minutes by sneaking away from his marker before steering an emphatic downward header away from the right hand of England No. 1 Chris Woods.

Delight

Arsenal, drilled almost to perfection in the art of function without frills, looked programmed to grind out another performance of relentless efficiency.

But with Waddle at last beginning to provide an element of credence to his Footballer of the Year accolade, there was a renewed surge of inspiration and impetus in Wednesday's approach to the second half.

Sporadic glimpses of the delightful play which has characterised Wednesday's season began to dazzle Arsenal, and the hint of an equaliser was confirmed in the 62nd minute.

Ian Wright scores for Arsenal – but the game ended 1–1

After scoring in the first match, Ian Wright starts the Gunners' goal celebrations on his own

Hirst, whose season has been ruined by a sequence of debilitating injuries, was the Yorkshire hero with a poke past Seaman following sterling contributions from Sheridan, Bright and Harkes. But, despite further frenetic flurries of activity, Wednesday were unable to conjure a winner.

In fact, Arsenal finished the normal period of 90 minutes much the stronger, and had Woods not demonstrated his England class with a sensational back-breaking save from Wright in the final minute, extra-time might not have been necessary.

It was in that further period that the

rigours of an English season exacted their toll on tortured limbs.

Surprise

Wright, who had taken a knock earlier, did not reappear for the final half-hour and, with Waddle almost reduced to walking pace, the Wednesday manager

Wednesday's John Sheridan tangles with Paul Davis of Arsenal

Steve Morrow, the tragi-hero of Arsenal's Coca-Cola Cup victory over Sheffield Wednesday last month, is to have his own medal presentation before Saturday's FA Cup Final.

Morrow was wheeled off with an oxygen mask covering his face after breaking his upper arm and was on his way to hospital when the presentation ceremony was held.

But the Football Association have decided the man who scored Arsenal's match-winner should have a ceremony of his own on Saturday and League president Gordon McKeag will hand over the medal before the kick-off of the re-match with Wednesday to the acclaim of the Wembley crowd.

'It's a nice gesture,' said Belfast-born Morrow, 22, who has just returned from a short holiday in Cyprus. 'I'll have mixed emotions on the day. I'd desperately like to be out there but I'm just happy to be there and part of the squad.

'I still get pain and I've got to keep the plaster on for another six weeks. I suppose looking back we did go over the top in the way we celebrated but these things happen. Tony Adams was inconsolable. He felt so bad the players had to persuade him to go up and accept the Cup.'

introduced the young Chris Bart-Williams.

There was not the slightest hint of a final surprise and only a snap shot from Roland Nilsson that was fumbled over the target by Seaman interrupted the monotony.

Perhaps we should have expected the deadlock. The last time Arsenal won the FA Cup back in 1979 they had to play Wednesday five times in a marathon third round.

Thankfully, Arsenal and Graham will know on Thursday whether they can become the first team to win the two major Cup competitions in the same season.

REPLAY

Broken Hearts at Wembley

ANDY LINIGHAN BROKE his nose, a finger and Sheffield Wednesday hearts at Wembley last night.

His face bloodied, Linighan headed the 121st-minute goal to give Arsenal a 2–1 victory in an FA Cup Final replay that will go down as one of the most bruising matches played at the Stadium.

Linighan, 30, the oldest of four footballing brothers from Hartlepool, suffered his injuries in the 18th minute when Mark Bright caught him with an elbow. But he played on after treatment and gained his reward just when the Final seemed certain to go to penalties for the first time in the history of the competition.

He headed the winner through the hands of England goalkeeper Chris Woods and said later: 'I chose just the right time. Wednesday probably deserved to go to penalties. They made it really hard for us.'

Manager George Graham, who becomes the first manager to win all three domestic competitions as both a player and a manager, said: 'Both heroes in our Cup Finals are unrecognised players, Linighan and Steve Morrow and both of them suffered broken bones.'

Ian Wright, who scored Arsenal's first goal in the 33rd minute – the 200th in an FA Cup Final at Wembley – also ended

the match in pain. He injured an ankle in the first half and looks certain to pull out of the England squad.

Wednesday's unquenchable spirit put them back into it in the second half and they deserved their equaliser in the 70th minute though it owed a lot to luck. Chris Waddle's left-foot shot looked to be covered by David Seaman, but struck Lee Dixon's foot and changed direction.

Trevor Francis, Wednesday's manager, refused to point the finger at Woods over the winning goal. 'The shot that earned the corner was going yards wide but it was a well-taken corner and Linighan had a free header,' he said. 'I thought Woods

2–1 in the replay, and Arsenal's Ian Wright gets his hands on the FA Cup at last.

had it but the pace of the header took the ball over the line. I don't blame anyone.

'Arsenal were by far the better team in the first half but I knew as long as we kept it to 1–0 we had a chance because they couldn't keep up that tempo for 90 minutes. At 1–1 there was a marvellous opportunity for Bright to put us in front.

'We've entertained the fans up and down the country this season with our football, but we've ended up with nothing.'

Graham: We Have a Winner in the Skipper

To win battles you need a strong leader and Arsenal manager George Graham is convinced he has English football's outstanding example in Tony Adams.

It's the reason why Graham stood by him when he went to jail – and why the boss believes Adams will tomorrow lead Arsenal to a second Wembley triumph this season.

Graham won't go as far as to say it himself – he is unwilling to do Sheffield Wednesday manager Trevor Francis's motivating for him – but the opposition do not have such an inspirational figure.

The Arsenal boss ranks 26-year-old Adams right up alongside the previous all-time great captains of the club including Herbie Roberts, Tom Parker and Frank McLintock. 'And Tony's picked up more silver than any of them at an earlier age,' he said.

'He's got a great attitude. In the dressing-room he's tremendous. He bullies the others along. Talented players need that. At the highest level it's about the mental side.

'The best is yet to come from him. He's an old-fashioned stopper. Arsenal have always had a player in this tradition. Frank McLintock was a great captain, one of the all-time greats. Tony is a similar type. Great teams need good stoppers.'

MANCHESTER UNITED 4

CHELSEA 0

ATTENDANCE

79 634

REFEREE

D. Elleray (Harrow)

GOALSCORERS

Cantona (2), Hughes, McClair

TEAMS

Manchester United	Chelsea
Schmeichel	Kharine
Parker	Clarke
Bruce	Kjeldberg
Pallister	Johnson
Irwin (Sharpe)	Sinclair
Kanchelskis	Burley (Hoddle)
(McClair)	Newton
Keane	Peacock
Ince	Wise
Giggs	Stein (Cascarino)
Cantona	Spencer
Hughes	

THE ROAD TO THE FINAL

Manchester United

4th round
v Norwich City 2–0 (a)
5th round
v Wimbledon 3–0 (a)
6th round
v Charlton Athletic 3–1 (h)
Semi-Final
v Oldham Athletic 1–1 (h)
Replay 4–1 (h)

Chelsea

4th round
v Sheffield Wednesday 1–1 (h)
Replay 3–1 (a)
5th round
v Oxford United 2–1 (a)
6th round
v Wolverhampton Wanderers 1–0 (h)
Semi-Final
Luton Town 2–0 (h)

Cantona Seals United's Double Triumph

Paul Ince makes his escape from Gavin Peacock and John Spencer

IT COULD hardly have been more appropriate that the most celebrated performer of their modern generation should set up Manchester United's first League and FA Cup Double.

Even the greats of their illustrious past such as George Best, Bobby Charlton and Denis Law never matched the moment afforded to Eric Cantona as he fulfilled his date with destiny.

A rousing 113th FA Cup Final was balanced on a knife-edge until the dashing Frenchman was required to guide United along the path to glory.

Tumbling

There was no doubting the validity of the penalty awarded on the hour without protest from Chelsea after Eddie Newton had sent Denis Irwin tumbling with a mistimed challenge.

Chelsea captain Dennis Wise and full-back Frank Sinclair attempted in vain to intimidate Cantona as he prepared to take the spot-kick. The Frenchman appealed for silence to referee David Elleray, but it was academic. Cantona was not about to be deflected from his mission.

Just six minutes later Elleray decided on a second penalty which was not nearly so clear-cut. Andrei Kanchelskis had fallen, perhaps theatrically, as Frank Sinclair held him off, and with a typical flourish Cantona produced a replica of his first kick with a shot to the left side of Russian goalkeeper Dmitri Kharine.

Mark Stein was booked for protesting too much and Chelsea player-manager Glenn Hoddle promptly removed his

Edwards salutes 'greatest'

MANCHESTER UNITED chairman Martin Edwards last night hailed his Double winning United side 'the greatest ever'.

He declared: 'There have been tremendous sides at the club and tragic circumstances such as the Munich air disaster prevented some from reaching their full potential. But this one has done the Double and that makes them the most successful in the club's history.

Now Edwards intends to make sure the club stays at the top.

'We want to keep the ball rolling,' he said. 'Money will be made available but we are not going to go silly. We will demonstrate the same commitment to get players the manager wants as we have in the past.'

Manager Alex Ferguson admitted his decision to leave out Bryan Robson was 'my hardest in management'.

Robson is expected to take over as player-manager of Middlesbrough next week and Ferguson said: 'There were injury doubts concerning Eric Cantona and Andrei Kanchelskis and I needed the versatility of Brian McClair on the bench.

'I took Robbo to one side and explained the situation. He accepted it as one that had to be made for the good of the club. One day he will be a top manager and will be called on to make similar decisions. I am sure he understood.

'I would have loved to have picked him. He is without doubt the greatest player I have ever had.'

Ferguson is now aiming to lift the European Cup and said: 'We didn't do ourselves justice last season and I'm desperate to put that right.'

charged down by some frantic United defending, but his effort was straight at Schmeichel.

The thought was always there, though, that Chelsea's ambitions of a first FA Cup win since 1970 would be undermined by their failure to take their chances, and so it proved. But even when they were three goals up and cantering towards the Double, United were grateful for the agility and expertise of Schmeichel.

He saved brilliantly from Peacock, Wise and Spencer before United substitute Brian McClair capitalised on his seven minutes on the pitch by scoring the fourth goal in the third minute of time added on for stoppages after Paul Ince had done all the work.

Elated United manager Alex Ferguson, who embraced Hoddle at the finish, would have been particularly pleased that he had become the first manager to win the Double in both Scotland and England, having achieved the feat with Aberdeen in 1984.

It is fitting that after 12 rounds, 37 weeks, 668 matches involving 539 entrants, the best team and the best player in the land should do so.

tracksuit in the hope of inspiring a revival as a substitute.

Such ambition was dashed within seconds as Sinclair boobed in attempting to control the ball near the corner of his penalty area, allowing Mark Hughes to run on and dispatch United's third goal.

Chelsea's response was every bit as courageous as the attacking intent they had demonstrated throughout the first half. United were rattled then and so, too, was their crossbar as Gary Pallister made a hash of an attempted clearance.

Gavin Peacock, who had provided winning goals for Chelsea at Stamford Bridge and Old Trafford in Premiership matches, delivered a full-blooded volley from the edge of the area that beat Peter Schmeichel all the way but rebounded off the woodwork.

The weather forecasters had predicted a stormy afternoon for soccer's showpiece occasion and although we were spared the thunder and lightning they had in mind, the atmosphere crackled with excitement and confrontation.

Chelsea centre back Erland Johnson might be considered fortunate to have been allowed to go the distance. In only the second minute he applied tactics more

akin to kick-boxing to disrupt the progress of the darting Ryan Giggs.

Harrow School housemaster Elleray brandished the first of three yellow cards which was probably sufficient considering that many referees allow such offences to go unpunished so early in the proceedings.

Chelsea proceeded to banish that sinister undertone from their game and provided delightful examples of the skilled football advocated by their manager.

Enchanted

Crosses flung high inevitably foundered on the twin peaks of Steve Bruce and Pallister at the heart of United's defence, but passes kept low and delivered with pace and accuracy opened up channels of opportunity for the London team.

Bruce was booked for a late and nasty challenge on John Spencer as United found it difficult to cope with the fact that they were not being allowed to have things their own way.

Hoddle's men were clearly enjoying themselves at the sight of the finest team in England wilting under their challenge. Johnsen strayed forward far enough to try his luck after two shots had been

Ryan Giggs challenges for a header

Fergie's fears for his Double heroes

IT SEEMED STRANGE after an FA Cup Final won by such a handsome margin to be talking of his fears, but Alex Ferguson appreciates that time stands still for no football club, especially Manchester United.

Tucked away in one of Wembley's few hushed corners – offering commiseration to the depressed Chelsea staff passing by every few minutes – the manager of United's Double team wondered how hungry they will be next season after one which has produced almost total satisfaction.

With the Premiership and the Cup in their grasp, the nation almost as one as to the margin of their pre-eminence, and motivation for the future provided by another bid to conquer Europe, Ferguson asked himself out loud whether the players could cope.

'How much will they want it again, that's the question I'm asking,' he said. 'How many times do they want to do the business? It will take a lot of handling but we'll handle it. We have to keep progressing and I think the players feel they need someone to come into the club to make them aware of what playing for Manchester United means.

'I don't have any names off the top of my head but obviously, given the foreign player ruling, I'm definitely going to be buying one Englishman at least. Given that we have to play in the Coca-Cola Cup next season, it's time the youth in our club was given their chance. Any decisions I make, the club must come first.'

They are well used to that at the moment. The more United are first in everything they do, the more their ambassadorial status in football is enhanced and examined. They earned nothing but praise in front of English royalty on Saturday for the manner and magnificence of their historic achievement.

The 4–0 scoreline in their victory over Chelsea might have been a travesty of the true nature of the final but it was somehow an expression of the peerless position they enjoy in the game. The only shame of Saturday was that Chelsea's fans, so splendid in the support of their own, could not bring themselves to acknowledge that the better side won and, in the end, won handsomely.

The blue hordes saved their worst excesses for referee David Elleray and his linesmen, who had to endure a stream of spittle as they made their way back down the steps from the crowning glory of their careers, the presentation of their FA Cup Final medals. Even the contentious nature of the second penalty, which killed off Chelsea's challenge, should not make human beings act so despicably.

Glenn Hoddle, true to the vanquished manager, made dispirited noises about his own side but held United in the esteem they deserve. 'They are a great side,' he said, 'which is why I'm as proud as I am of the way we played. Over the season, they have proved they are the best team in Britain.

Chelsea made United work for the Double. At half-time, the discussion revolved around the possibility that such overwhelming favourites would fall again as they had in the Coca-Cola Cup Final to Aston Villa, or keep on stumbling, as they stumbled in the semi-final of the FA Cup to Oldham.

The answers were to come within five minutes which broke, irreparably, Chelsea's heart. When Eddie Newton came slithering across the area to try and prevent Denis Irwin breaking on to a touch from Ryan Giggs, there may not have been intent in his mind but the contact was so cataclysmic the Irishman

Andrei Kanchelskis tangles with Frank Sinclair

Manchester United Triumphant after the Sixth Double in history

was sent hurtling through the air. A penalty, no doubt.

The duel between Andrei Kanchelskis and Frank Sinclair was always going to be one on which the final might turn and so it proved in the 66th minute when a crossfield pass from Mark Hughes landed between the pair of them, Kanchelskis fractionally to the fore. There was some nudging, brief contact which began outside the penalty area and over went the Ukrainian.

This time, the referee was 35 yards back – never the best position from which to give any penalty, let alone one so decisive in its impact. Elleray's response later on Match of the Day, that he had given one so should have no fear of giving a second, was not satisfactory. He had to have been absolutely convinced of intent

in the challenge and from where he was he could not have been.

On such fine distinctions are winners separated from losers. From Eric Cantona's second spot-kick the final and the Double was secured by United. Hughes, who led the line with emphatic authority, stepped in when Sinclair fell and Brian McClair was given, in the third minute of injury-time, a squared ball from Paul Ince to rub salt into the Chelsea wounds.

'I don't think they deserved to lose 4–0,' said Ferguson, 'especially after their efforts in the first half. They'll be gutted, but in football the team that makes less mistakes wins the game and we made less mistakes.

'Eric Cantona was so confident and calm about the penalties. He passed them into the net. He has such a marvellous

awe and presence about him. Eric is truly a hero.'

There were many at Wembley on Saturday, because that is what the FA Cup Final is for. We should remember, for instance, that Gavin Peacock, twice a match-winner against United this season, hit the crossbar when the final was 25 minutes old.

He then witnessed two penalties given at the same end, was eventually on the wrong end of a sound thrashing and still found it in himself to be the only Chelsea player I saw make a point of walking ten yards to shake the referee's hand when he was suffering as much as anyone.

That is the true spirit of the game. That is the essence of the day. That is why we genuinely feel there are better times ahead and why Alex Ferguson should not fear the future too much.